A Flame of God Himself

Reflections on the Song of Songs

Joshua Elzner

To learn more about the author, or for more materials for prayer and reflection (in text or audio), you may visit his website:
atthewellspring.com

The translations of the verses of the Song of Songs are my own, based on the literal meaning of the original text or the tradition of interpretation (which is usually explained in the reflections). The bases of this translation, however, are the *Revised Standard Version-Second Catholic Edition*, and *The Jerusalem Bible*, and certain sections are taken entirely from the RSV-2CE.

Other Scripture passages, unless otherwise noted, are taken from the RSV-2CE.

Revised Standard Version of the Bible—Second Catholic Edition (Ignatius Edition), copyright © 2006 National Council of the Churches of Christ in the United States of America. Used by permission. All rights reserved.

If there is a "cf." before the verses, then I have altered the text to accord more with the original language, or at times simply changed it to follow the flow of the narrative.

Copyright for The Jerusalem Bible is:
The Jerusalem Bible, © 1966 by Darton, Longman, and Todd, Ltd., and Doubleday, a division of Bantam, Dell Publishing Group, Inc.

Copyright © 2019 Joshua Elzner

All rights reserved.

ISBN: 9781099174209

DEDICATION

This book is dedicated
to those persons who,
through their willingness
to let me look upon them in love
and to shelter them humbly
within the tenderness of my own heart,
have granted me the inestimable gift
of seeing in them the mystery of one
who is so precious, so uniquely beautiful,
that no one can adequately love them
except the divine Bridegroom, Jesus Christ.

I pray that you may ever more deeply experience
the perfect loving gaze of this Bridegroom,
the only true Spouse of your yearning heart,
and, knowing yourself to be totally loved by him,
may surrender yourself without reserve
into his welcoming embrace.

Then I can truly exclaim with John the Baptist
those words which express my own heart's desire,
when I look upon you and love you in his name:
"The One who has the bride
is the Bridegroom;
the friend of the Bridegroom,
who stands and hears him,
rejoices greatly at his voice.
Therefore, this joy of mine
is now complete."
(cf. Jn 3:29)

CONTENTS

The Text of the Song	11
Introduction: The Five Meanings of the Song of Songs	23

THE TITLE

The Song of Songs which is Solomon's	33
The Song Surpassing All Other Songs	36
My Name is Peace	38

INTRODUCTORY STANZA

The Sober Inebriation of the Spirit	43
A Kiss Ever Ancient, Ever New	46
The Kiss of Incarnation	50
The Kiss of Consummation	53
Thirst for His Unmediated Kiss	55
In Him We Are One: The Kiss of Friendship	57
A Love Unique and Incomparable	61
Your Name is Oil Poured Out	64
Encountering the Bridegroom's Gaze	66
Draw Me; Let Us Make Haste!	68
The King Has Brought Me into His Chambers	70
Drawn into the Dimension of His Love	74
To Savor His Sweetness: Exercising the Spiritual Senses	78
Three Ways of Sensing What Cannot Be Sensed	82
Arise, My Beautiful One	86

FIRST POEM

In the Very Place of My Darkness, He Unites Me to	91

Himself

The Most Intimate Embrace	95
Even As I Look Upon You, You Are Within Me	99
The Bed of Virginal Creation	102
In the Shadow of His Love	107
I am Wounded by Love	110
The Wound of Love that Heals All Wounds	114

SECOND POEM

Arise, and Come to Me	121
A Heart Filled with Life Anew	123
Sheltered in the Wound of His Heart	125
The Absence which is a Deeper Presence	128
Catch Us the Foxes	132
Encircle Me, My Beloved	135
I Sought Him Whom My Heart Loves	139
Even in the Shadows of this Life, I Rest in Your Embrace	144

THIRD POEM

What is This?	151
The Ark of His Presence	155
I Pledged Myself to You	159
The Coronation which is a Marriage	163
You Have Ravished My Heart	166
In His Affirming Love	171
Authentic Tenderness	175
The "Word" of the Heart	178

The Ways in which the Heart Speaks	181
A Garden Enclosed	184
Under the Tree of Life	188
In the Paradise of God	191
One Within His Heart	194
Faith, Hope, and Love	199
The Paradise of the Resurrection	202
Love as a Response to the Beauty of the Beloved	205
Transformed in the Place of Greatest Need	210
A Well of Living Water	213
I Come to My Garden	215
The Ontology of Gift, The Metaphysics of Love	217
Beauty Encounters Beauty	222
The Paradise of Creation Renewed	226

FOURTH POEM

The Healing of Memories	233
Weakness Transformed into Strength	236
A Homeless Culture	240
Holy Unselfconsciousness	244
To Say "Forever": The Meaning of Vocation	246
My Heart was Thrilled within Me	249
They Wounded Me	253
Where is He?	254
Cradling You in Silence	257

Transformed and United in His Love   259

FIFTH POEM

Beautiful as Tirzah and Jerusalem   265

The Victorious Bride   269

A Dance between Two Camps   271

The Universal Dance   274

Held Captive in the Tresses   276

May Your Breasts be like Clusters   279

The Beauty and Meaning of the Body   282

Sheltered in Your Bosom   287

The Final Breath   289

EPILOGUE

Love is Stronger than Death   295

שִׁיר הַשִּׁירִים, אֲשֶׁר לִשְׁלֹמֹה .

THE SONG OF SONGS
WHICH IS SOLOMON'S

ישוע

FIRST POEM

BRIDE

> Let him kiss me with the kiss of his mouth!
> For your love surpasses wine,
> and your anointing oils are fragrant;
> yes, your Name is oil poured out,
> therefore do the virgins love you.
> Ah, draw me after you; let us make haste!
> The King has brought me into his chambers.
> We will exult and rejoice in you;
> we will extol your love beyond wine;
> how rightly do they love you!

> I am dark but lovely,
> O daughters of Jerusalem,
> like the tents of Kedar,
> like the curtains of Solomon.
> Do not gaze at me because I am swarthy,
> because the sun has burned me.
> My mother's sons were angry with me,
> and they made me keeper of their vineyards;
> if only I had kept my own!

> Tell me, you whom my heart loves,
> where you pasture your flock,

where you make it lie down at noon;
for why should I be like one who wanders
beside the flocks of your companions?

CHORUS
If you do not know, loveliest of women,
follow in the tracks of the flock,
and take your kids to graze
close by the shepherd's tents.

BRIDEGROOM
I compare you, my love,
to my mare, harnessed to Pharaoh's chariots.
Your cheeks are lovely with ornaments,
your neck with strings of jewels.
We will make you ornaments of gold,
studded with silver.

DIALOGUE BETWEEN BRIDE AND BRIDEGROOM
While the king was on his couch,
my nard gave forth its fragrance.
My Beloved is to me a sachet of myrrh
that lies between my breasts.
My Beloved is to me a cluster of henna blossoms
in the vineyards of Engedi.

Behold, you are beautiful, my love,
behold, you are beautiful!
Your eyes are doves.

Behold, you are beautiful, my Beloved,
and delightful!
All green is our bed.

The beams of our house are of cedar,
the paneling of cypress.

I am the rose of Sharon,
the lily of the valleys.

As a lily among thorns,
so is my love among maidens.

As an apple tree among the trees of the orchard,
so is my Beloved among young men.
In his longed-for shade I am seated
and his fruit is sweet to my taste.
He has taken me to his banqueting house,
and the host that overwhelms me is his love!
Sustain me with raisins,
restore me with apples;
for I am wounded by love!
His left hand is under my head,
and his right arm embraces me.

I adjure you, daughters of Jerusalem,
by the gazelles, by the hinds of the field,
not to stir my love, nor rouse her,
until she is pleased to awake.

ישוע

SECOND POEM

BRIDE
The voice of my Beloved!
Behold, he comes,
leaping upon the mountains,
bounding over the hills.
My Beloved is like a gazelle, or a young stag.
Behold, he stands behind our wall.
He is looking through the windows,
gazing through the lattice.
My Beloved speaks and says to me:

BRIDEGROOM
Arise, my love, my beautiful one, and come to me,
for behold, the winter is past,
the rain is over and gone.
The flowers appear on the earth,
the time of singing has come,
and the cooing of the turtledove
is heard in our land.

The fig tree puts forth her first figs,
and the vines, with their blossoms,
give forth fragrance.
Arise, my love, my beautiful one, and come to me.
O my dove, in the clefts of the rock,
in the hidden places of the cliff,
let me see your face,
let me hear your voice,
for your voice is sweet,
and your face is lovely.

Catch us the foxes,
the little foxes,
that bind the vines,
for our vines are in blossom.

BRIDE
My Beloved is mine, and I am his;
he pastures his flock among the lilies.
Until the day breathes
and the shadows flee,
encircle me, my Beloved,
like a gazelle or a young stag,
upon the mountains of the covenant.

Upon my bed, at night,
I sought him whom my heart loves;
I sought him, but found him not.
So I will arise now and go about the city;
in the streets and in the squares
I will seek him whom my heart loves.
I sought him, but found him not.

The watchmen found me,
as they went about in the city.
"Have you seen him whom my heart loves?"
Scarcely had I passed them,
when I found him whom my heart loves.
I held him fast, and would not let him go,
until I had brought him into my mother's house,
into the chamber of her who conceived me.

BRIDEGROOM
I adjure you, daughters of Jerusalem,
by the gazelles, by the hinds of the field,
not to stir my love, nor rouse her,
until she is pleased to awake.

ישוע

THIRD POEM

CHORUS
What is this coming up from the desert,
like a column of smoke,
breathing of myrrh and frankincense,
with all the fragrant powders of the merchant?
Behold, it is the throne of Solomon!
About it are sixty champions
of the champions of Israel,
all belted with swords
and expert in war,
each with his sword at his side,
against alarms by night.

King Solomon made himself a throne
from the wood of Lebanon.
He made its posts of silver,
its back of gold, its seat of purple;
it was lovingly wrought within
by the daughters of Jerusalem.
Go forth, O daughters of Zion,
and behold King Solomon,
with the crown with which his mother crowned him
on the day of his wedding,
on the day of the gladness of his heart.

BRIDEGROOM
Behold, you are beautiful, my love,
behold, you are beautiful!
Your eyes are doves behind your veil.
Your hair is like a flock of goats,
moving down the slopes of Gilead.

Your teeth are like a flock of shorn ewes
that have come up from the washing,
all of which bear twins,
and not one among them is bereaved.
Your lips are like a scarlet thread,
and your mouth is lovely.
Your cheeks are like halves of a pomegranate
behind your veil.
Your neck is like the tower of David,
built for an arsenal,
whereon hang a thousand bucklers,
all of them shields of warriors.
Your two breasts are like two fawns,
twins of a gazelle,
that feed among the lilies.
Until the day breathes and the shadows flee,
I will hasten to the mountain of myrrh
and the hill of frankincense.
You are all fair, my love;
there is no flaw in you.

Come with me from Lebanon, my bride;
come with me from Lebanon.
Turn your gaze from the peak of Amana,
from the peak of Senir and Hermon,
from the dens of lions,
from the mountains of leopards.

You have ravished my heart, my sister, my bride,
you have ravished my heart with a glance of your eyes,
with one jewel on your neck.
How sweet is your love, my sister, my bride!
How far your love surpasses wine,
and the fragrance of your oils any spice!

Your lips distil nectar, my bride;
honey and milk are under your tongue;
the scent of your garments
is like the scent of Lebanon.
A garden enclosed is my sister, my bride,
a garden enclosed, a fountain sealed.
Your shoots are an orchard of pomegranates

with all choicest fruits, henna with nard,
nard and saffron, calamus and cinnamon,
with all trees of frankincense,
myrrh and aloes, with all chief spices—
a garden fountain, a well of living water,
and flowing streams from Lebanon.

BRIDE

Awake, O north wind,
and come, O south wind!
Breathe upon my garden,
let its fragrance be wafted abroad.
Let my Beloved come to his garden,
and eat its choicest fruits.

BRIDEGROOM

I come to my garden,
my sister, my bride,
I gather my myrrh with my spice,
I eat my honeycomb with my honey,
I drink my wine with my milk.

Eat, O friends, and drink:
drink deeply, O friends!

ישוע

FOURTH POEM

BRIDE

I sleep, but my heart is awake.
Hark! my Beloved is knocking.

"Open to me, my sister,
my love, my dove, my perfect one;
for my head is wet with dew,
my locks with the drops of the night."

I had put off my garment,
how could I put it on?
I had bathed my feet,

how could I soil them?

*My Beloved put his hand to the latch,
and my heart was thrilled within me.
I arose to open to my Beloved,
and my hands dripped with myrrh,
my fingers with liquid myrrh,
upon the handles of the bolt.
I opened to my Beloved,
but my Beloved had turned and gone.*

*My soul failed me when he spoke.
I sought him, but found him not;
I called him, but he gave no answer.
The watchmen found me,
as they went about in the city;
they beat me, they wounded me,
they took away my mantle,
those watchmen of the walls.*

*I adjure you, daughters of Jerusalem,
if you find my Beloved,
that you tell him
I am wounded by love.*

CHORUS

*What is your Beloved more than another beloved,
O loveliest among women?
What is your Beloved more than another beloved,
that you thus adjure us?*

BRIDE

*My Beloved is all radiant and ruddy,
distinguished among ten thousand.
His head is the finest gold;
his locks are wavy,
black as a raven.
His eyes are like doves
beside springs of water,
bathed in milk, fitly set.
His cheeks are like beds of spices,
yielding fragrance.*

His lips are lilies,
distilling liquid myrrh.
His arms are rounded gold,
set with jewels.
His body is ivory work,
encrusted with sapphires.
His legs are alabaster columns,
set upon bases of gold.
His appearance is like Lebanon,
choice as the cedars.
His speech is most sweet,
and he is altogether desirable.
This is my Beloved and this is my Friend,
O daughters of Jerusalem.

CHORUS
Where has your Beloved gone,
O loveliest among women?
Where has your Beloved turned,
that we may seek him with you?

BRIDE
My Beloved has gone down to his garden,
to the beds of spices,
to pasture his flock in the gardens,
and to gather lilies.
I am my Beloved's and my Beloved is mine;
he pastures his flock among the lilies.

ישוע

FIFTH POEM

BRIDEGROOM
You are beautiful as Tirzah, my love,
lovely as Jerusalem,
terrible as an army with banners.
Turn away your eyes from me,
for they assault me—
Your hair is like a flock of goats,
moving down the slopes of Gilead.

Your teeth are like a flock of ewes,
that have come up from the washing,
all of them bear twins,
not one among them is bereaved.
Your cheeks are like halves of a pomegranate
behind your veil.
There are sixty queens and eighty concubines,
and maidens without number.
My dove, my perfect one, is only one,
the darling of her mother,
flawless to her that bore her.
The maidens saw her and called her happy;
the queens and concubines also,
and they praised her:

CHORUS
Who is this that looks forth like the dawn,
fair as the moon, bright as the sun,
terrible as an army with banners?

BRIDEGROOM
I went down to the nut orchard,
to look at the blossoms in the valley,
to see whether the vines had budded,
whether the pomegranates were in bloom.
Before I knew it, my desire had hurled me
on the chariot of my people, as their prince.

CHORUS
Return, return, O Shulammite,
return, return, that we may look upon you.
Why should you look upon the Shulammite,
as upon a dance between two camps?

BRIDEGROOM
How graceful are your feet in sandals,
O queenly maiden!
Your rounded thighs are like jewels,
the work of a master hand.
Your navel is a rounded bowl
that never lacks mixed wine.
Your belly is a heap of wheat,

encircled with lilies.
Your two breasts are like two fawns,
twins of a gazelle.
Your neck is like an ivory tower.
Your eyes are pools in Heshbon,
by the gate of Bath-rabbim.
Your nose is like a tower of Lebanon,
overlooking Damascus.
Your head crowns you like Carmel,
and your flowing locks are like purple;
a King is held captive in the tresses.

How fair and pleasant you are,
O loved one, delectable maiden!
You are stately as a palm tree,
and your breasts are like its clusters.
I say I will climb the palm tree
and lay hold of its branches.
Oh, may your breasts be like clusters of the vine,
and the scent of your breath like apples,
and your kiss like the best wine
that goes down smoothly,
gliding over the lips of those who sleep.

BRIDE
I am my Beloved's,
and his desire is for me.

Come, my Beloved,
let us go forth into the fields,
and lodge in the villages;
let us go out early to the vineyards,
and see whether the vines have budded,
whether the grape blossoms have opened
and the pomegranates are in bloom.
There I will give you my love.

The mandrakes give forth fragrance,
and over our doors are all choice fruits,
new as well as old,
which I have laid up for you, O my Beloved.

ישוע

EPILOGUE

BRIDE
> O that you were a brother to me,
> that nursed at my mother's breast!
> If I met you outside, I would kiss you,
> and none would despise me.
> I would lead you and bring you
> into the house of my mother,
> and into the chamber of her that conceived me.
> I would give you spiced wine to drink,
> the juice of my pomegranates.
>
> His left hand is under my head,
> and his right arm embraces me!

BRIDEGROOM
> I adjure you, daughters of Jerusalem,
> not to stir my love, nor rouse her,
> until she is pleased to awake.

CHORUS
> Who is that coming up from the wilderness,
> leaning upon her Beloved?

BRIDEGROOM
> Under the apple tree I awakened you,
> there where your mother was in travail with you,
> there where she who bore you was in travail.

THE TWO LOVERS IN UNISON
> Set me as a seal upon your heart,
> as a seal upon your arm;
> for love is stronger than death,
> jealousy is relentless as the grave.
> Its flashes are flashes of fire,
> a flame of God himself.
> Many waters cannot quench love,
> neither can floods drown it.

INTRODUCTION:
THE FIVE MEANINGS OF THE SONG OF SONGS

I invite you to join me on an in depth journey through the greatest love poem of the Bible, and indeed of the whole of world history: the Song of Songs. This is a breathtakingly beautiful drama that occurs, not merely between two human hearts, but between every single human heart and the God who is passionately in love with us. In this drama, we will encounter the pain of longing for a Beloved who seems to be absent, and we will encounter the ecstatic joy of discovering that he is never far away. We will rest in the joy of his indestructible love, which cradles us without ceasing even in our darkest place, delighting in us and cherishing us in our own unique and unrepeatable beauty. And our hearts will hopefully be inflamed with an ardent longing to love the One who has so passionately loved us, drawing us to surrender ourselves to him and to enter into ever deeper intimacy with he who is "the fairest of the sons of men" (Ps 45:2), who is indeed the Beautiful One himself.

I want to ask a question before we begin, however. It is this: Who is the "bride" and who is the "bridegroom" in this sacred Song? The answer is so rich that it will take me a little while to unfold. Let me first say that there is a current tendency to read this book as if it were written primarily about the erotic love between a man and a woman, which was later (and perhaps arbitrarily) interpreted in the light of the love between God and his people, and between Christ and each individual soul. My conviction is that the intention of God, and indeed almost certainly of the author of the Song himself, goes in exactly the opposite direction. In other words, the Song of Songs was written primarily as an exposition of the nuptial love between God and his people, and yet, in this light, it also most certainly casts light upon the intimate love of man and woman, and can be understood accordingly as expressing their union with one another as well.

Here both themes—the divine and the human, the mystical and the sexual—come together and flow into one another continually, enriching one another and interpreting one another. But the divine meaning, the mystical meaning of nuptial intimacy with God, has priority. And it alone can make full sense of the imagery and narrative of the text, even as, simultaneously, it casts light upon (and in turn draws upon) the intimate experience of man and woman approaching one another for the consummation of marital union.

We should not be afraid, as John Paul II noted, to interpret the Song of Songs as speaking of the sexual and marital union of man and woman, husband and wife. As he said, "He who does not believe in the human love of the spouses, he who must ask forgiveness for the body, does not have the right to rise higher... With the affirmation of human love, by contrast, it is possible to discover God in it" (TOB 108.96). One cannot enter into intimacy with God (at least not in the fullness of one's incarnate humanity) if one neglects or denies the full richness of one's human nature and bodiliness, if one's own living of sexuality is dwarfed and crippled. After all, human love and divine love are not opposed to one another, but are meant to be inseparably united together as two living dimensions of the life of love and intimacy in the likeness of the Trinity! Therefore, the holy living of marital and sexual intimacy—as well as chaste intimacy in all of our relationships—prepares our hearts and impels them towards the ultimate "super-fulfillment" found in intimacy with God himself. And intimacy with God himself, in turn, distills down into all the contours of our human relationships and allows them to be what God intends them to be: sacred incarnations of the very life of God.

Human love and divine love, in a word, are not opposed to one another, but flow into one another and enrich each other. Thus, "the content of the Song of Songs is at the same time sexual and sacred" (D. Lys), and it is "only by putting these two aspects together that one can read the book in the right way" (TOB 108.97). Nonetheless, it is only in the light of God that human love can manifest and preserve its true nobility and dignity. And it is intimacy with God himself, a nuptial intimacy of total mutual self-giving and intimate belonging in gratuitous embrace, that alone fulfills all that the longing human heart desires in its thirst for intimacy. In the light of this intimacy between God and humanity, an intimacy that sweeps us up into the very innermost life of the Father, Son, and Holy Spirit, we come to the throbbing heartbeat of all reality. We come to the mystery that runs as a thread throughout the whole Bible as its central truth, the truth that gives meaning to all else. It is the revelation of the inner life of the Trinity as a life of sheer love and intimacy, as an embrace of mutual belonging in the gratuity of sheer happiness, and a revelation of God's desire to incorporate us into this same intimacy. From the heart of the Trinity—from the innermost love of the Father, Son, and Holy Spirit—therefore, this love extends into the relationship between Christ and the Church, and then distills further into the love between human persons, in particular between man and woman. In this commentary, therefore, while recognizing the rightful place of the humanly marital dimension in interpreting the Song of Songs, my desire has been to express *primarily the mystical dimension, the dimension of the virginal* *communion of Christ with the Church, and, in the Church, with each human heart.* In my opinion, this is in fact the primary dimension as intended by God, God's own super-affirmation of the nuptial dimension of love, which is incarnated in the love of man and woman, but finds its full perfection, and indeed has its ultimate origin, in his own relationship with creation, and in the inner life of the Trinity itself.*

So who are the bridegroom and the bride? They are each bridegroom and bride who has ever lived or ever will live; they are each man and woman created in the image of God and called to communion. And yet they are, first of all and before all, the Bridegroom God and his Bride, the people whom he has created and redeemed for himself. This is the almost unanimous witness of the entire history of the Church, and of her mystics, saints, and theologians, as well as indeed of the Jewish people themselves, in whose womb this Song was first conceived and born. Actually, there seems to be only one ancient Christian writer who claimed that the Song of Songs celebrated a merely human love. Therefore, as we stand at the threshold of the sacred space of this Song, we realize that we are invited to remove our shoes, for the place where we stand is holy ground. We are entering

---

*If you are interested in a beautiful exposition of this mystical origin of the Song of Songs, which truly unseals the meaning of the verses in the light of their original context, and on the basis of the whole of Scripture, I would recommend the book *The Cantata of Love: A Verse-by-Verse Reading of the Song of Songs*, by Blaise Arminjon. If you read this book, I think you will see, by the harmonious radiance of his own interpretation, that this spiritual, mystical understanding of the Song of Songs as a celebration of the virginal union between God and Israel, between Christ and the Church, and between God and each one of his beloved children, is incontrovertible. As Cardinal Henri de Lubac said in a letter to Arminjon: "You won me over. I started to read your book in a somewhat sceptical vein. But the more I read, the more it seemed to me that the principle of interpretation was plausible—highly plausible; indeed, it was almost forcing itself upon me. Moreover, it was strengthened by a proof a contrario: a sustained 'naturalistic' reading of the text would obviously be very difficult."

Again, as I said, a merely naturalistic reading—as if the poem was merely or *primarily* about natural spousal love and sexual union—cannot fully express the meaning of the text. But if the divine dimension is given priority, then the human also finds its place freely, and quite beautifully. In this way we can affirm all that Saint John Paul II says in his own reflections on the Song of Songs (interpreting it as referring to man and woman) while also situating it within the wider context of the "great mystery" of spousal love between Christ and the Church (Eph 5).

into the sphere of the sacred, into the sphere of intimate love uniting God and his people, and the sacred space in which human love manifests and incarnates the love of God, even and in particular in the body and in sexuality. Here the sacred divine Mystery flows into the sacredness of the human mystery, and the human mystery impels our hearts back to the Mystery of God. Therefore, on every level and in every shade of meaning that can be found in the Song, we are entering into the atmosphere of the sacred love of the eternal God. We are encountering his love for the creation which has been born from the abyss of his divine generosity, calling them into an everlasting nuptial intimacy with himself; and we are entering into the rich beauty with which this same intimacy is made present in the love of human persons for one another, bathed in the radiance of the everlasting intimacy of the Father, Son, and Holy Spirit.

Let me quote two examples, both from the Jewish tradition, which show that from the very beginning this Song has been understood as a sacred book treating of sacred mysteries. The first quote, more general, comes from Rabbi Aqiba, who said: "If all the Scriptures are indeed holy, the Song, for its part, is very holy to the extent that the whole world is not worth the day when the Song was given to Israel." There is a theme unveiled here that will recur throughout these reflections, and which I will speak much more about later. Namely, we will see that the Song of Songs is indeed in a way *at the very heart of the Bible*. Centered as it is in the middle of the canonical text, it ties together in a single thread—or rather in the beauty and harmony of a single melody of love—all the strands of divine revelation. It brings together into a unity the two book-ends of Scripture, the beginning and the end, in *the reality of a marriage effected in a garden*: the first is that of Adam and Eve, which however also prepared for, and was a symbol of, the definitive marriage of the Lamb, who espouses humanity to himself at the heart of his Bride, the Church, as we see in the closing chapters of the book of Revelation. Standing as it does at the center of Scripture, therefore, the Song of necessity *expresses* the center of Scripture, which can be *nothing else than Jesus Christ and his redeeming love, who, through his Incarnation, Passion, and Resurrection espouses the world to himself and draws us back into the intimacy of the House of his Father*. This is what I hope to show throughout these reflections, what, indeed, I hope to open the way for you to experience and to feel, in the intimate and ineffable joy of the love of the divine Bridegroom.

Let me now quote the words of a more contemporary Jewish author, André Chouraqui. I think his words will help to open up before us the sacred atmosphere of prayer, adoration, and reverence in which we should approach this most sacred Song, this "Holy of Holies" of the divine Scripture:

> I was born in a Jewish family faithful to the traditions of Israel. Since early childhood, I heard the Song of Songs chanted on the ancient rhythms that inspired the Gregorian. While I was a child, I was imbued, every Friday night, with the fervor that filled our beautiful synagogue of Ain-Temounchent during the evening office as it started with the recitation of the Poem introducing the liturgies of the Sabbath. Men, women, children were singing this text or listening to it as if in ecstasy. It was indeed a sacred text, a transcendent song. Nobody ever imagined that there could be in it anything obscene, trivial or even carnal. ... All sang lovingly this Poem of love, and it never occurred to anybody to censure or expurgate it. ... In all my life, I have never heard from the mouth of those who live in the intimacy of the Poem a single complaisant innuendo about its content. Being transparent, it was welcomed in the transparency of pure hearts. It was understood in reference to the Bible, to the love of *Adonai* for creation, for his people, for each one of his creatures. We were too carried away by the great and powerful current of Hebrew thought to see in the poem anything but the song of absolute love, on the heights of the loftiest revelations. Strange as it is, it remains true that for over two thousand years, the Jews never saw in the Shulamite anything but a symbol, that of Israel; in the King, anything but a reference to God; in the love uniting them, anything but the revelation of the mystery of divine love.[1]

ישוע

I hope that you see in my previous words that the Song of Songs exists in a fruitful tension between the divine and the human dimension, between divine love and human love. Indeed, is this not part of the very essence of human life—the bringing together of grace and nature, love for God and for our brothers and sisters, the lifting up of the whole creation into the presence of God and the incarnation of God's love into the whole creation and into every moment of our lives? And this tension plays out precisely in that a statement made about one dimension of the reality also has implications for the other dimension; the fruitful interrelationship between the two is unavoidable. I would like, therefore, to begin this journey by noting the *five levels of interpretation* that have flowered throughout the history of the Church in her reading of the Song of Songs. When this is established, we can dive into the text itself.

1) The original, most basic meaning of the text of the Song of Songs is that it is an allegory, using the image of marital love, to explain and "dramatize" the covenant love *between God and the people of Israel*, whom he has chosen for himself and made his own. There are many other places in the Old Testament where this same image is used, and we will soon look at them in following reflections. But first let's look at the other three meanings.

2) The second meaning of the text, flowering from the first, is brought about when the covenant of love between God and Israel reaches its full and everlasting consummation in the marriage effected between God and humanity in Jesus Christ. The Song of Songs itself, we will see, is a beautiful prophecy of the Incarnation, Passion, and Resurrection of Jesus, understood as the consummation of this marriage between God and humanity. Thus, the second meaning is that which understands *the Bridegroom of the Song as Christ, and the Bride as the Church* whom he has ransomed for himself by his Blood, and has purified to united her to himself. Saint Paul says the same: "Christ loved the Church and gave himself up for her, that he might sanctify her, having cleansed her by the washing of water with the word, that he might present the Church to himself in splendor, without spot or wrinkle or any such thing, that she might be holy and without blemish... 'For this reason a man shall leave his father and mother and be joined to his wife, and the two shall become one flesh.' This is a great mystery, and I mean in reference to Christ and the Church" (Eph 5:25-27, 31-32). These two meanings of the text, as you may have noticed, are both "general" or communal. They do not speak so much of individual persons as of the community as a whole. But God does not love humanity in the abstract, as if each one of us was just an anonymous part of the whole, lost, nameless and faceless, in the crowd. Rather, his love is always unique and unrepeatable, indeed exclusive, such that he can say to each of us what he said in the Song of Songs: "My dove, my perfect one, is only one" (Sg 6:9).

3 and 4) Thus we are led to the third and fourth meanings of the text. The third is the intimate, passionate, and "virginally-spousal" love that God has for *each one of us individually*. And the fourth is the way that this love has first been revealed in its full glory in *the Virgin Mary*.

5) The fifth meaning, which is admittedly more recent in being treated of explicitly as its own "theme," is *the natural human love between man and woman, husband and wife*. This, clearly, proves to be a kind of "substratum" of the other four meanings, in that it is employed as the analogy that provides the imagery to explain the other dimensions. But it is not merely a tool of interpretation, as if the love of man and woman has no substance, no purpose, no beauty in itself. Therefore, it also should be recognized as having meaning and beauty (indeed sacredness!) in its own right—and therefore as having a rightful place in the interpretation of Scripture and the life of the Church. In the light of the radiance of the other four dimensions, therefore, we can wholeheartedly rejoice also to discover anew the breathtaking beauty of the love of man and woman, redeeming and made new in the light of Christ, who reveals the vocation of man and woman to love and intimacy in the likeness of the Trinity.

To conclude, therefore, we can say that the Song of Songs operates on five different levels, and yet each of these levels is inseparably intertwined with the others, such that they interpenetrate in a harmonious unity. The covenant God established with Israel passes over into the Church and is consummated in her. And yet Mary realizes the mystery of the Church in her fullness as an individual person, even before the communal, structural elements of the Church come into existence. And both Mary and the Church become focused, in a particular way, in God's ardent desire to reach out to touch the unique, individual human heart, and to make him or her a "bride of God." We are, each one of us, cradled in the world-embracing love of Mary, in the universal womb of the Church, and in the all-enfolding yet utterly unique love of God, Father, Son, and Holy Spirit. Our loving God seeks us out as the Bridegroom beyond all bridegrooms, with a love so deep, so pure, that it surpasses any created images of human love, even while filling them with meaning and unsealing their true sacredness and beauty in the light of the eternal and undying Love of the Trinity.

To conclude, let me quote one of the deepest and most influential writings on the deep interconnection between the realities of Mary, the Church (Israel), and the individual person. It was written in a different context, in which the author is explaining a verse from one of the Psalms, but we see the same theme. It is from a sermon of Blessed Isaac of Stella, read by the Church for the Office of Readings on Saturday of the Second Week of Advent:

> The Son of God is the first-born of many brothers. Although by nature he is the only-begotten, by grace he has joined many to himself and made them one with him. For to those who receive him he has given the power to become the sons of God.
>
> He became the Son of man and made many men sons of God, uniting them to himself by his love and power, so that

they became as one. In themselves they are many by reason of their human descent, but in him they are one by divine rebirth.

The whole Christ and the unique Christ – the body and the head – are one: one because born of the same God in heaven, and of the same mother on earth. They are many sons, yet one son. Head and members are one son, yet, many sons; in the same way, Mary and the Church are one mother, yet more than one mother; one virgin, yet more than one virgin.

Both are mothers, both are virgins. Each conceives of the same Spirit, without concupiscence. Each gives birth to a child of God the Father, without sin. Without any sin, Mary gave birth to Christ the head for the sake of his body. By the forgiveness of every sin, the Church gave birth to the body, for the sake of its head. Each is Christ's mother, but neither gives birth to the whole Christ without the cooperation of the other.

In the inspired Scriptures, what is said in a universal sense of the virgin mother, the Church, is understood in an individual sense of the Virgin Mary, and what is said in a particular sense of the virgin mother Mary is rightly understood in a general sense of the virgin mother, the Church. When either is spoken of, the meaning can be understood of both, almost without qualification.

In a way, every Christian is also believed to be a bride of God's Word, a mother of Christ, his daughter and sister, at once virginal and fruitful. These words are used in a universal sense of the Church, in a special sense of Mary, in a particular sense of the individual Christian. They are used by God's Wisdom in person, the Word of the Father.

This is why Scripture says: *I will dwell in the inheritance of the Lord*. The Lord's inheritance is, in a general sense, the Church; in a special sense, Mary; in an individual sense, the Christian.

Christ dwelt for nine months in the tabernacle of Mary's womb. He dwells until the end of the ages in the tabernacle of the Church's faith. He will dwell for ever in the knowledge and love of each faithful soul.

THE TITLE

THE SONG OF SONGS WHICH IS SOLOMON'S

Note:

The symbol that occurs between each of the following reflections is the Name of Jesus in Hebrew—ישוע—Yeshua. This is therefore much more than a "space filler." Rather, the holy Name of Jesus is intended to be the very life-breath of this book. These markings, therefore, exist in order to stop you in your tracks, to slow your mind and heart from proceeding too quickly from one reflection to another. Rather, you are being invited to dwell, to abide in the presence of Christ, breathing forth repeatedly the Name of Jesus with tenderness and love, as he, first, has so lovingly spoken your name, calling you gently to himself so that he may press you intimately to his Heart.

THE SONG OF SONGS
WHICH IS SOLOMON'S

'Shir Hashirim asher Lishlomo.'
The Song of Songs which is Solomon's.
(Sg 1:1)

The first verse of this book of the Bible is its title—or rather, it's "title page," as it were, giving us both the name of this song and its author. It is the "Song of Songs," and its author is Solomon. But did Solomon, the son of King David and the heir of his kingdom, really write this book? And what does it mean to call a song "the song of songs?" Are not all songs songs of songs, since any song is a song like any other song?

Let's take a look at the second question first. What does it mean to call this book the Song of Songs? In Hebrew there is no such thing as a *superlative*, or even, for that matter, a *comparative*—or at least so I've learned. In other words, in Hebrew one cannot say "better" or "best," "beautifuller" or "beautifullest" (I could probably use better examples, but you get the picture!). Instead, what one would do to indicate something being "better" or a fuller expression of a certain quality is to *repeat the word*. Thus, as a way of hailing our Almighty God as the Holiest, we cry out: "Holy, Holy, Holy!" He is not just holy…and he is not just holy, holy…but he is holy, holy, holy! Another way of saying that something or someone is the highest of all, the fullest expression of a particular reality (or indeed surpasses all other incarnations of this reality) is to call it the "blank" of "blank" (insert word in the blank). This seems to be why the inner sanctuary of the temple, for the Jews, was called *the Holy of Holies,* that is, the holiest place. We also see why Jesus is called the King of kings and the Lord of lords. In other words, all the partial expressions of kingship, all the frail and imperfect men who have called themselves king, point towards and are also infinitely surpassed by the one who is the true King.

And here we immediately come to the answer to our first question: why is this book said to belong to Solomon? It was a common practice (or at least not unheard-of) in those times to write under the pseudonym of a famous personage. This might be why the Psalms claim to be written by King David, even if perhaps they were not actually penned by him, but are rather interpretations of his spirit and his life. What matters for us is not if King Solomon actually wrote the Song of Songs—that is, the greatest of all songs, the Song that surpasses all others—but what it means to say that this Song belongs to Solomon. Here we need only look at who Solomon is in the plan of

God, at who and what he represents. He is *the son of David, and the heir of his kingdom*.

Let's take a glance back at the promise that God made to the one who would be David's son. This is what he said to David through the mouth of Nathan the prophet:

> I will appoint a place for my people Israel, and will plant them, that they may dwell in their own place, and be disturbed no more; and violent men shall afflict them no more, as formerly, from the time that I appointed judges over my people Israel; and I will give you rest from all your enemies. Moreover the LORD declares to you that the LORD will make you a house. When your days are fulfilled and you lie down with your fathers, I will raise up your offspring after you, who shall come forth from your body, and I will establish his kingdom. He shall build a house for my name, and I will establish the throne of his kingdom for ever. I will be his father, and he shall be my son. And your house and your kingdom shall be made sure for ever before me; your throne shall be established for ever. (2 Sam 7:10-14a, 16)

So we see that David's true son would be the one who would inherit a kingdom that is everlasting, and for whom God would build a true and enduring house, and who, in turn would "build God a house." However, this prophecy was not perfectly fulfilled in Solomon himself, since, even though Solomon built the earthly temple, the kingdom of David already began to fall apart within his own lifetime. Therefore, we can begin to see the deeper meaning of this prophecy revealed in the words that hint that *David's son would also be God's own Son*. Let's immediately jump to the point: *the true Son of David is Jesus Christ, and therefore he is the true Solomon*. Did not Jesus himself say, "Something greater than Solomon is here" (Mt 12:42)? We could translate, "Is not the Solomon of Solomon here?"

We also see this, for example, in the words of the man born blind, who on hearing that Jesus of Nazareth is passing by, cries out: "Jesus, son of David, have pity of me!" This is also apparent in the genealogy provided by Matthew, who presents the ancestry of Jesus in three sets of fourteen generations: "So all the generations from Abraham to David were fourteen generations, and from David to the deportation to Babylon fourteen generation, and from the deportation to Babylon to the Christ fourteen generations" (Mt 1:17). What is the significance of the number fourteen? Again, in Hebrew, numbers were signified by letters, and the name David—*Dawed*—signifies the number fourteen. Finally, what this reveals to us is that Jesus is both the *true David* and the *true Solomon*. Indeed, he will be presented as such throughout the Song of Songs. This is because he is the true "son of David," the true King of Peace (*Shlomo*), and indeed, the original King himself, foreshadowed by David (whose name is derived from *Dod*, which means "Beloved"). This word, "Beloved," appears throughout the Song of Songs to refer to the Bridegroom, who is Solomon/David/Christ, or rather who is Christ present under the veiled symbolism of David and Solomon: *the Bridegroom who alone brings true and lasting peace.*

Thus we have at the very beginning of the Song of Songs an indication of *the depth of the reality* with which we are dealing. This is not just any love song, not just any dramatic tale, not just any epic poem. This is the Song of Songs, the greatest Song of all songs ever written, and it is the greatest because it is a Song that belongs to the true Solomon, to the true son of David and heir of the promised kingdom: *Jesus Christ.* He is our Solomon, whose reign lasts forever. He is our true David, our true Beloved. He is our King of kings and Lord of lords. But what kind of kingdom is his, and what kind of reign? As we will repeatedly see, his is a kingdom of love, a kingdom that is best understood not in terms of master-servant, or ruler-subject, but *of Bridegroom and Bride!*

His is a kingdom of love…and it is a kingdom of peace. For the name Solomon, *Shlomo*, means Peace (from the word *shalom*, from which we also derive the name Jerusalem). Yes, Jesus is the Prince of Peace, who comes into our world to espouse us to himself as a Bridegroom does his Bride, and in doing so he takes us "to be with him" in the House of his Father, which is "the new Jerusalem," the City of Peace (cf. Jn 14; Rev 21-22). Here there will be everlasting wholeness and harmony, and the full blossoming of the intimacy for which every human heart longs. God himself has placed this longing in our hearts, and we will not experience perfect rest until we rest finally in the eternal and everlasting Jerusalem, enfolded and irradiated with the perfect peace of God—Father, Son, and Holy Spirit.

ישוע

THE SONG SURPASSING ALL OTHER SONGS

I want to speak more about the first verse of the Song of Songs in this reflection, since there is still a great wealth to be unpacked from these few words: "The Song of Songs which is Solomon's." We have seen how, in a beautiful and perhaps unexpected way, the very attribution of this Song to Solomon is a prophecy of the "true Solomon," the true son of David: Jesus Christ. Indeed, it is a revelation that this greatest of all songs truly belongs to Jesus; it is *his* Song, and this is precisely why it is the greatest, since he is the divine Beloved whom we glimpse in all love, and in whom alone the human heart finds perfect and enduring rest.

There are two things that I want especially to reflect more upon before moving on. The first is the theme of the *song*. The second is the name of Solomon (and of Christ) as *peace*. Let's dive into the first one first. What does it mean to call the Song of Songs a song? Was it first put to music and sung? Perhaps, but I think a deeper meaning is revealed by looking for a moment at what a song is, at its unique beauty. We can get a first insight into this simply by calling to mind the adage: "Only the lover sings." There is something about music, something about song, which pushes against the boundaries of human expression, which reaches out beyond the mundane ordinariness of daily life and tries to pull back the veil, if only for a moment, to glimpse the unspeakable beauty of the eternal Reality.

Song therefore reveals the limitations of human language, while also stretching this language to its utmost capabilities, as it strains to express something eternal, as it seeks to mediate something that words alone cannot convey. And this unspeakable mystery, this awesome reality that we reach out for through song, and which through song reaches out to us, *is Love*. This unique gift of music is revealed, for example, in how different an experience it is to merely *read* the parts of the Mass on a page, than to *experience* them being chanted, and to chant them oneself. If you have ever joined a monastic community (one that still uses Gregorian chant) for Mass or the Divine Office, you understand what I mean. In the dancing voices of the monks, rising and falling, soaring and descending, one feels the words of Scripture come alive. Indeed, it is almost as if the unspeakable Mystery itself allows its radiance to show through, however dimly, mediated as it is by the beauty that touches the heart through the harmony of word and melody, meaning and harmony, intellect and emotion.

The Song of Songs is a song, therefore, not necessarily because it can be put to music, but because it seeks to evoke an experience that is similar to that of music: *it seeks to express and to make palpable a Reality—the Reality of Eternal Love—that transcends expression in mere words.* We will spend the rest of these reflections trying to open ourselves to this Reality, to allow it to express itself and make itself felt and known by us. If we experience it in this way, I am confident that it can radically transform us.

This also explains why a recurring theme in the commentaries of the fathers and saints of the Church on the Song of Songs is that, before approaching this sacred Song, *a degree of spiritual purity must exist within the reader.* If this does not exist, then the images (sometimes apparently erotic and sometimes bizarre) will remain opaque, and the mind and heart of the one who contemplates will remain stuck on the level of nature and the flesh. On the other hand, it can be affirmed that a true reading and contemplation of the Song of Songs can have the inverse effect as well: *it can reorient our mind and heart, our affectivity and will, by drawing us up from the fragmentation and multiplicity that bind us, and by giving us a glimpse of the sacred Love that surpasses all love, the eternal Love that is the true thirst of the human heart.*

Let me quote the beautiful words of Saint Bernard of Clairvaux on this point:

> We must conclude then [that] it was a special divine impulse that inspired these songs of [Solomon] that now celebrate the praises of Christ and his Church, the gift of holy love, the sacrament of endless union with God. Here too are expressed the mounting desires of the soul poured forth in figurative language pregnant with delight. It is no wonder that like Moses he put a veil on his face, equally resplendent as it must have been in this encounter… [This is the song] which, by its unique dignity and sweetness, excels all those I have mentioned and any others there might be; hence by every right do I acclaim it as the Song of Songs. It stands at a point where all the others culminate. Only the touch of the Spirit can inspire a song like this, and only personal experience can unfold its meaning. Let those who are versed in the mystery revel in it; let all others burn with desire rather to attain to this experience than merely to learn about it. For it is not a melody that resounds abroad but the very music of the heart, not a trilling on the lips but an inward pulsing of delight, a harmony not of voices but of wills. It is a tune you will not hear in the streets, these notes do not sound where crowds assemble; only the singer hears it and the one to

whom he sings—the lover and the beloved. It is preeminently a marriage song telling of the chaste souls in loving embrace, of their wills in sweet concord, of their mutual exchange of the heart's affection.[2]

ישוע
MY NAME IS PEACE

First of all, take note of the appropriateness of the name "Peaceful," that is, Solomon, at the head of a book which opens with the token of peace, with a kiss. Take note too that by this kind of opening only men of peaceful minds, men who can achieve mastery over the turmoil of the passions and the distracting burden of daily chores, are invited to the study of this book.[3]

So speaks Bernard of Clairvaux. This is a Song, therefore, that we must approach with peaceful hearts, with hearts recollected in the presence of God and docile to the touch of his Spirit. But how can we attain to such peace, to this "mastery over the turmoil of the passions"—passions which submerge us on the periphery of our being, out of touch with the sacred space of our inner heart where the Bridegroom speaks? The answer, truly, is clear, though it takes a lifetime for us to understand it and to make our own: *the Bridegroom's presence alone can bring peace.*

Did I not say that the name of Christ is peace, that he is the true Prince of Peace, the true Solomon? Therefore, if we were to try to attain a state of perfect peace *before* approaching him, if we were to try to somehow "achieve" a state of harmony, serenity, and wholeness in order to, at last, enter into his presence, *we would forever be fighting ourselves and never casting ourselves into the arms of his Mercy.* The movement, rather, should go in the opposite direction: we look upon him, our Beloved, first, and only then can we cast a side glance back upon ourselves. Or rather, precisely in looking upon him we can truly begin to see ourselves authentically, bathed in the light of his Love and Mercy, reflected in the tenderness of his gaze.

In saying this, indeed, I have touched directly on the heart of authentic peace. In Hebrew, the word *shalom* means more than just an absence of conflict, or even more than a sense of restful quiet; rather, peace in its fullest sense implies an experience of wholeness, completeness, and harmony. It signifies the satisfaction of our desires, the quelling of our fears, the sheltering of our vulnerability, the cradling of our lives and our hearts in a security that does not depend on ourselves or our own efforts, but rather comes as a gift that unceasingly sustains us and that can never be taken away.

How can we possibly experience such a total sense of well-being, a true harmony and shelteredness even in the midst of painful and dark times—indeed, even in times of great personal suffering and anguish? I will seek to answer this question throughout our journey through the Song of Songs, and, particularly, I will take it up in the reflections that immediately follow on the words of the second verse of the Song: "Let him kiss me with the kiss of his mouth!" But from all that we have said, we can already approach the answer: our peace lies in being sheltered within the peaceful reign of the King of kings, within the ceaseless care of the Good Shepherd, within the loving embrace of the divine Bridegroom, who has taken us as his own in an eternal and unbreakable covenant. As Saint Paul says, HE IS OUR PEACE (Eph 2:14).

Our peace lies not in our ability to be in control of our lives, to make sure everything turns out okay, or even to correspond completely with all the demands and tasks placed upon us. Rather, our most fundamental peace, the peace which nothing can take away and which enfolds all things, is *the peace of being totally and unconditionally loved*. When I glimpse this love in the eyes of Christ, when I sense it coming to me at the heart of my own deepest need, then I begin to taste authentic peace. It comes, not as something I have attained, but as a pure gift of grace. Yes, I come to understand that the whole of my life, from my conception to my last breath, is cradled in the arms of perfect Love, and therefore is cradled in the arms of Peace. Thus my whole life can unfold—it can flower freely like a blossom opening its petals to the sun and sky, revealing its beauty and its perfume—within the sheltering arms of the One who is perfect Peace, and who is holding me and will never let go.

This reality is indeed present in the very word *shalom*. Not only does this word mean peace, but it also bears in it the root of the word *surrender*. But isn't surrender a scary reality? Doesn't it mean letting go of control and foresight, even "admitting defeat" before the superior strength or understanding of another? It does indeed mean letting go into the hands of One who is greater…but this One is not a Taskmaster or Judge who wants to rule over us with his superior might, who wants to impose upon us a yoke which keeps us subject to an arbitrary will, who wants to preserve his prerogatives over us. Rather, *the One to whom we surrender is the most loving and tender Father, the gentlest Bridegroom, and the cradling womb of perfect Love itself: Father, Son, and Holy Spirit!*

Our surrender then is not really a matter of "gathering up" all our fears and desires, our anxieties and joys, our hopes and wishes, and somehow "giving" them to God, in the process losing them ourselves. Rather, it is more a matter of being like a little child who, feeling afraid and insecure, and clinging tightly to a little toy for comfort in the middle of the night, cries out for peace and safety. But then the mother comes and reaches out to the little child, saying, "Come here, my love, you don't need to cry any more…" Immediately the child drops the toy and reaches out her arms to her mother, who sweeps her up in her embrace and gives her what she truly needs, cradling and caring for her in the arms of her own tender and enduring love.

"Even should a mother forget her child, I will not abandon you," God says to us (cf. Is 49:15). Do we believe this? Do we believe that we can come to him in our vulnerability, poverty, and need, letting him take us in his arms and offer us the complete shelter for which our hearts thirst? This is his one desire: to cradle and care for us with the perfect wisdom and tenderness that are possible only to him, and in this way to unite our hearts intimately to his own, woven together in a seamless fabric of enduring and unbreakable peace.

INTRODUCTORY STANZA

THE OVERTURE

THE SOBER INEBRIATION
OF THE SPIRIT

Let him kiss me with the kiss of his mouth!
For your love surpasses wine.
(Sg 1:2)

> Tell us, I beg you, by whom, about whom and to whom it is said: "Let him kiss me with the kiss of his mouth." How shall I explain so abrupt a beginning, this sudden irruption as from a speech in mid-course? For the words spring upon us as if indicating one speaker to whom another is replying as she demands a kiss—whoever she may be. But if she asks for or demands a kiss from somebody, why does she distinctly and expressly say with the mouth, and even with his own mouth, as if lovers should kiss by means other than the mouth, or with mouths other than their own? But yet she does not say: "Let him kiss me with his mouth;" what she says is still more intimate: "with the kiss of his mouth."[4]

I couldn't improve upon these words of Saint Bernard, and the delightful way in which he expresses the sense of wonder and intrigue created by the beginning of this Song. We are indeed immediately immersed into the heart of a dialogue, into the passionate request of this woman that "he would kiss me with the kiss of his mouth." But who is *he*, and indeed who is *she*, and why does she phrase her request in such an abnormal way?

What is also intriguing is how this woman immediately alters the object of her address—in mid-sentence. She cries out, "Let *him* kiss me with the kiss of his mouth; for *your* love surpasses wine." It is as if, at the mere remembrance of her Beloved, at the mere vocalization of her longing for him, she immediately enters into a dialogue with him and addresses him directly. "Let *him*...for *your*..." Perhaps in this we also find our doorway into understanding who is being addressed, and also who is addressing. Is this not at the heart of prayer: getting in touch with our innate longing for God and opening it to him, precisely in this way experiencing that he is intimately present?

My mind goes immediately to a scene from the Gospel of John that is deeply rooted in the Song of Songs, as is indeed the whole of John's Gospel. Mary approaches Jesus during a wedding at Cana and says, "They have no wine." A marriage banquet, and there is no wine! "What is that to me and to you?" Christ replies to his Mother, "My hour has not yet come" (cf. Jn 2:3-4). The hour to give the true wine of the new and everlasting covenant has not yet come, and yet Mary knows that the Love of her Son far surpasses wine. She knows the joy of his kiss, and wants all to experience it, and so she invites him to respond to the need of an earthly couple, thus symbolizing the gift of the divine Love which effects a heavenly marriage. The gift of the wine of his Love brings a lasting joy that is greater, purer, and truer than any wine, or even any merely human love, can provide.

It is in your kiss alone, my Jesus, that I will find the satisfaction of my desires. No other kiss can satisfy me, no other joy, no other inebriation—except that which is given by your own Love. As the beautiful hymn of Saint Ambrose so touchingly celebrates:

> *Christusque nobis sit cibus,*
> *potusque noster sit fides;*
> *laeti bibamus sobriam*
> *ebrietatem Spiritus.*
> Let Christ so be our food,
> and faith so be our drink,
> that we may joyfully receive
> the sober inebriation of the Spirit.

Your Love alone, Jesus, can bring me the sober inebriation for which I thirst, breaking beyond the boundaries of fear, beyond the constricting confines of my woundedness and pain, not with a substance that obscures mind and heart and submerges the spirit in the flesh, but by filling me with the very Spirit's presence and lifting me up to be made one spirit and one flesh with the Bridegroom who is Incarnate Love himself. Yes this is an inebriation which is wholly sober, not a dulling of the faculties but an awakening to greater lucidity, not an alteration of the body which effects the mind but an illumination of the mind which irradiates even the body. It is the permeation of my entire being by the outpouring of the Spirit's presence, who pervades me with the joyful and life-giving vibrations of his eternal breath.

But here I am getting ahead of myself... Let me step back and pose the question again: why does the loving heart, made a bride of Christ, cry out in this way, "Let him kiss me with the kiss of his mouth"? Why not just ask him to kiss me? Or, at least, why not ask him to kiss me with his mouth? Why ask him to kiss me with the kiss of his mouth? What does it mean, anyway, to kiss someone with a kiss, as if we could kiss them with something else than a kiss? Well, there...I've asked the same question in four different ways, but let me see if I can give a single answer. *The answer is the Trinity.*

There is an inherent Trinitarian structure to the request of the bride: there is *the one who kisses*, there is *his mouth*, and there is *his kiss*. The One who kisses is the Father, and he kisses us with his mouth, his eternal Word, who is his beloved Son, and the kiss that the Son bestows on us in the Father's name is the very kiss of the Holy Spirit. It is therefore a sign of humility and reverent awe that the bride does not ask directly, "Let him kiss me," for she knows that "no one can see God and live." But she is urged on by the confidence that, even though "no one has ever seen God, yet the only-begotten Son, who is in the bosom of the Father, has made him known" (Jn 1:18). It is the Son himself who receives the direct and unmediated kiss of the Father, in the radiant light of eternal glory. And the kiss that the Father and the Son share is the Holy Spirit. The kiss of the Spirit seals the union of Father and Son in a movement of ceaseless exchange and self-communication, as both are made one in a single life of love, as lip presses upon lip and breath is exchanged between two in a single breathing of eternal bliss.

And yet, and yet this kiss is then turned toward us and seeks to communicate itself to us! The mouth of the Father comes to us, and he sends us the Spirit, so that by pressing upon us, he may breathe into us the fullness of his own divine life. "Let him kiss me with the kiss of his mouth." Yes, let the Father unite himself to me in the Son through the Holy Spirit; and let the Spirit draw me in himself, through the Son, to the Father. I dare not ask for the direct kiss of the Father, but I know that "whoever has seen" the Son "has seen the Father" (Jn 14:9), and that this same Son has breathed upon us the fullness of the Spirit's presence, in this way kissing us most intimately. Therefore I can ask for this kiss, and in bold confidence I can even expect it, for he himself said that he would send the Spirit, that he would kiss me in this way.

Breathe into me, Holy Spirit, from the mouth of the Incarnate Son. Be for me the tender kiss of his love, and by your very presence, irradiating my whole being, grant me to experience the sober inebriation of true joy. Yes, bring to maturity in me this chaste union of my heart with God, which fills and transforms even my very flesh with the purity and gentleness of the Trinity. Come to me and kiss me in such a way that I may open my mouth and God may fill it, that the One who was made man for my sake may also make me one flesh and one spirit with him, in the mystery of the Holy Eucharist and in the resurrection of the body at the end of time.

ישוע

A KISS EVER ANCIENT, EVER NEW

To begin this reflection, let me again quote Saint Bernard and his beautiful words on "the kiss of the mouth," which summarize well what I said in my own words in the previous reflection:

> I think I should begin by considering the higher truths, and it seems to me that a kiss past comprehension, beyond the experience of any mere creature, was designated by him who said: "No one knows the Son except the Father, just as no one knows the Father except the Son and those to whom the Son chooses to reveal him" (Mt 11:27). For the Father loves the Son whom he embraces with a love that is unique; he who is infinite embraces his equal, who is eternal, his co-eternal, the sole God, his only-begotten. But the Son's bond with him is not less affectionate... Now, that mutual knowledge and love between him who begets and him who is begotten—what can it comprise if not a kiss that is utterly sweet, but utterly a mystery as well? ... If, as if properly understood, the Father is he who kisses, the Son he who is kissed, then it cannot be wrong to see in the kiss the Holy Spirit, for he is the imperturbable peace of the Father and the Son, their unshakable bond, their undivided love, their indivisible unity.
>
> Thus the Father, when he kisses the Son, pours into him the plenitude of the mysteries of his divine being, breathing forth love's deep delight, as symbolized in the words of the psalm: "Day to day pours forth speech" (Ps 19:2). As has already been stated, no creature whatsoever has been privileged to comprehend the secret of this eternal, blessed and unique embrace; the Holy Spirit alone is the sole witness and confidant of their mutual knowledge and love. ... [Yet the Spirit] it is then who inspires the daring spirit of the bride, he it is whom she trustingly petitions to come to her under the guise of a kiss. ... Therefore, she dares to ask for this kiss, actually for that Spirit in whom both the Father and the Son will reveal themselves to her. For it is not possible that one of these could be known without the other.[5]

How healing it is to our understanding of God to realize that *the inner life of the Trinity is an eternal kiss between the Father and the Son, a kiss who is the Holy Spirit himself!* And as I said in the previous reflection, this kiss is turned out toward each one of us, in that God ardently desires to "kiss us with the kiss of his mouth." In other words, the Father yearns to unite us to himself in the bond of the Holy Spirit's love, sheltering and cradling us in the Heart of Christ, in this way drawing us back into his own paternal embrace.

These words of the Song of Songs, therefore, seek to unseal deep within us our innermost longing for love and intimacy. We already bear this longing within us, since it has been impressed upon us from the moment we were first created by God, knitted together by his love within our mother's womb. But it is often buried over by fear, or shame, or the disordered desires of sin, seeking to find its expression and fulfillment in unhealthy ways, or simply buried in the ground like an unused talent. These words of the bride that burst in upon us at the start of the Song, therefore, seek to get beyond the barriers we build up around our hearts and to touch something deep within us, awakening it to life. What is it that they awaken? *The realization that I thirst, more than anything else, for the kiss of God's mouth…*

Perhaps I've never formulated it to myself in this way; perhaps I have never even explicitly acknowledged my thirst for intimacy with God. But the words resonate with something in the innermost sanctuary of my heart, pulling back the veil to the "holy of holies" of my own personal being where the Holiness of God's own presence dwells. And yet I myself cannot fulfill this thirst! I myself am hardly even aware of it! It is rather Jesus Christ, coming to me as the Bridegroom seeking out his wayward bride, who unveils to me the innermost longings of my own heart. And not only does he awaken these longings—not only does he ask me, "What do you desire?"—but he also enfolds these desires in the tenderness of his love and says to me, "Come and see" (Jn 1:38-39). If I allow myself to be wrapped in the bands of his love, to be bound with the sweet yoke of his gentle calling, I will find myself drawn in his footsteps into the innermost chambers of his own Sacred Heart. And there I will drink of the inebriating wine of his love, the outpouring of his Spirit, and will rejoice in him exceedingly in the fulfillment of my desires, in the life-giving intimacy of his own embrace.

But again, I am getting ahead of myself, for that is what follows in the text:

Let him kiss me with the kiss of his mouth!
For your love surpasses wine,
and your anointing oils are fragrant;
yes, your Name is oil poured out,
therefore do the virgins love you.
Ah, draw me after you; let us make haste!
The King has brought me into his chambers.

We will exult and rejoice in you;
we will extol your love beyond wine;
how rightly do they love you!
(Sg 1:2-4)

How rich each line of these verses is, how full of meaning and beauty! We see in these very words a beautiful foundation for two of the most touching expressions of devotion to Jesus Christ—namely, devotion to *his Holy Name* and devotion to *his Sacred Heart*! I will treat each of these in a separate reflection, but first I want to dwell a little longer on the theme of the kiss. Really, I would like to quote Saint Bernard again, in one of the passages of his commentary that has touched me the most. (Don't worry, I won't be quoting Bernard in every reflection! It is more or less only in these early ones where I feel myself most indebted to him.) Here are Bernard's words:

> But I feel that one of you may now want to say: "What voice thundered forth to you a secret that, you insist, was made known to no creature?" Unhesitatingly I answer: "It is the only Son, who is in the Father's bosom who has made it known" (cf. Jn 1:18). But he has made it known, I will say, not to the sorry and unworthy creature that I am, but to John [the Baptist], the Bridegroom's friend, whose words these are; and not only to him but to John the Evangelist also, the disciple Jesus loved. For his soul was pleasing to the Lord, entirely worthy both of the name and the dowry of a bride, worthy of the Bridegroom's embraces, worthy that is, of leaning back on Jesus' breast. John imbibed from the heart of the only-begotten Son what he in turn had imbibed from the Father. Nor is John the only one, it is true also of all to whom the Angel of the Great Counsel said: "I call you friends, because I have made known to you everything I have learned from my Father" (Jn 15:15). Paul drank of it, because the Good News he preaches is not a human message nor did he receive it through men, it is something he learned only through a revelation of Jesus Christ.
>
> All of these indeed could say with felicity and truth: "It is the only Son who is in the Father's bosom who has made it known to us." And this revelation—what can you call it but a kiss? But it was the kiss of the kiss, not of the mouth. Listen if you will know what the kiss of the mouth is: "The Father and I are one;" and again: "I am in the Father and the Father is in me" (Jn 10:30; 14:10). This is a kiss from mouth to mouth, beyond the claim of any creature. It is a kiss of love and of peace, but of the love which is beyond all knowledge and that peace which

is so much greater than we can understand. ... He who received the fullness is given the kiss of the mouth [namely, Christ], but he who received from the fullness is given the kiss of the kiss.

Felicitous, however, is this kiss of participation that enables us not only to know God but to love the Father, who is never fully known until he is perfectly loved. Are there not surely some among you who at certain times perceive deep within their hearts the Spirit of the Son exclaiming: "Abba, Father" (Rom 8:15)? Let that man who feels that he is moved by the same Spirit as the Son, let him know that he too is loved by the Father. Whoever he be let him be of good heart, let his confidence never waver. Living in the Spirit of the Son, let such a soul recognize herself as a daughter of the Father, a bride or even a sister of the Son, for you will find that the soul who enjoys this privilege is called by either of these names. Nor will it cost me much to prove it, the proof it ready to hand. They are the names by which the Bridegroom addresses her: "I come into my garden, my sister, my bride" (Sg 5:1). She is his sister because they have the one Father; his bride because joined in the one Spirit. For if marriage according to the flesh constitutes two in one body, why should not a spiritual union be even more efficacious in joining two in one spirit? And hence anyone who is joined to the Lord is one spirit with him. But we have witness too from the Father, how lovingly and how courteously he gives her the name of daughter, and nevertheless invites her as his daughter-in-law to the sweet caresses of his Son: "Listen, daughter, pay careful attention: forget your nation and your ancestral home, then the king will fall in love with your beauty" (Ps 45:10-11).[6]

I feel like it would be difficult to improve upon what he says about the "revelation" of the kiss of the Trinity given through Christ and the Spirit. And indeed I wanted to quote his words precisely because, at a distance of nine-hundred years, they express things that I myself would deeply want to say. It is a beautiful witness, therefore, to the living truth of the Gospel and to the continuity of the life of the Church, who is "ever ancient, ever new." Yes, her communion with Christ stretches from John the Baptist, through John the Evangelist, Paul the Apostle, and Bernard of Clairvaux unto our own day. After two thousand years the kiss of Christ still reaches us in and through his Church, touching our own hearts intimately and uniquely—inviting us also to be for Christ a friend, sibling, and spouse.

Yes, Bernard's words are a beautiful exposition—I would say a profuse overflowing—of the heart of the Gospel, especially as it is so deeply concentrated in the account of the Last Supper given by John the Evangelist. Here Jesus unveils his Sacred Heart before his apostles and speaks to them so intimately, so vulnerably, that he is able to say to them, "I have called you friends, for everything that I have heard from my Father I have made known to you" (Jn 15:15). And we—we too are invited into this intimate space, where we may rest against the bosom of Christ, feeling the throbbing of his Heart as it beats in unison with the Father, and listening to him speak tenderly of the intimacy that he always shares with his Father in the single kiss of their Holy Spirit.

ישוע

THE KISS OF INCARNATION

Before I begin to speak about verses 3 and 4, and how they unveil for us the beauty of Jesus' Holy Name and his Sacred Heart, I want to dwell a little longer on verse 2: "Let him kiss me with the kiss of his mouth! For your love surpasses wine." While I was in prayer, a number of other beautiful meanings of this holy kiss were impressed upon my mind, and I would like to try to express them. I have said that this kiss is the very Person of the Holy Spirit himself, who is the unbreakable bond of love between the Father and the Son—a kiss that we have each been created to receive and participate in, already in this life and perfectly for all eternity in heaven.

The first thing I want to speak about is how this kiss, besides signifying the Holy Spirit himself, can also signify *the union of humanity and divinity*. Just as a human kiss is an expression and a sign of the union of two persons in love, an external manifestation of the mutual gift of their hearts, so when God unites himself to humanity we can describe this union as a kiss. In this light, we can see that God has kissed humanity in many ways throughout history. Every covenant he has made with us has been a kind of kiss—whether it is the covenant with Adam and Eve, the covenant with Noah, the covenant with Abraham, the covenant with Moses and all of Israel on Mount Sinai, or the covenant with David. And yet none of these kisses has really brought together God and humanity in a true unity, a true binding together of hearts that is unbreakable and everlasting.

Therefore, the writings and ministry of the prophets of the Old Covenant was a matter of continually reminding the people of their longing for this definitive kiss, and of God's ardent desire to bestow it. Yes, their task was to prepare the people to hope for this kiss, to long for it, to open themselves to receive and to welcome it when it came. "Let him kiss me with the kiss of his mouth!" This is the cry of the people of Israel throughout their history, and indeed it is the cry of all humanity.

All are crying out unceasingly for the fulfillment of the mystery expressed in the words of Psalm 85: "Mercy and faithfulness will meet; righteousness and peace will kiss each other" (v. 10). In other words, until now God has made covenants with us continually, but even though the Lord is "faithful to his covenant forever," our hearts are unfaithful, and we continually falter. How can a true and everlasting covenant be established at last, if we are not faithful to the law that is given to us, if our faithfulness does not correspond to, and cannot measure up to, the undying faithfulness of God? It is only possible for "faithfulness" to "spring up from the earth" when "righteousness looks down from heaven" (v. 11), when God's own mercy drops down like dew from above to saturate our hearts and renew them from within.

Yes, the mercy of God will descend from heaven to irradiate our hearts, to grasp, purify, and possess us—and it will make our faithfulness spring up, not through our own efforts alone, but through the gift of the Spirit who will "write the law upon our hearts," and who will, indeed, "take from our bodies our stony hearts, giving us natural hearts" (Jer 31:33; Ez 36:26). Then we will truly be able to cry out, "Abba! Father!" allowing ourselves to "be led by the Spirit of God," in this way experiencing the freedom of the "children of God" (Rom 8:14-15). This divine kiss alone can effect such a union. This divine kiss alone can bring together mercy and faithfulness in a bond of everlasting union, in which our faithfulness is but an expression of his own mercy at work within us. This divine kiss alone, the gift of his own righteousness bestowed freely upon us, can bring us the enduring peace for which our hearts so deeply thirst.

But when...when was this definitive kiss first bestowed, this kiss of the new and everlasting covenant? When were humanity and divinity truly and forever united for the first time? *In the womb of the Virgin Mary.* Yes, Mary was the first person to be kissed by God in this way. All of the hopes and aspirations of humanity burdened by the yoke of sin and death, all of the longing of the chosen people crying out for the fulfillment of the promises made to them, indeed, all of the groaning labor pains of the whole creation—*all of this converged in the heart and in the body of a young woman in Nazareth.*

An angel came to her and spoke to her in the name of the Lord God Almighty. And what was his message? *He revealed this threefold kiss of the Trinity!* He responded to that heartfelt cry of the bride, a cry arising in every thirsting heart, and in a special way in the heart of the Virgin Mary: "Let him kiss me with the kiss of his mouth!" Yes, the Father sends the Holy Spirit to overshadow Mary with his presence, and to bring the eternal Son to birth within her womb. The Father sends the *Uncreated Kiss* to this woman, and by impressing himself tenderly upon her, he makes her the *created kiss* of divinity and humanity—or rather he brings this kiss to consummation within her.

This kiss that unites humanity and divinity is Jesus Christ himself, the "mediator between God and men" (1 Tim 2:5); this kiss is the inseparable union of humanity and divinity effected in the single Person of the Son. When humanity and divinity meet and are united in the Son, in the unity of his Person, drawn together through the power of the Holy Spirit, we can truly speak of the definitive kiss. And Mary offers her own humanity to be the soil from which the humanity of Christ is fashioned; she offers the faithfulness and peace that spring up from the earth, through which the humanity of Christ is knitted together in her womb. Yes, here is the fulfillment of what God anticipated in the creation of the first Adam from the dust of the earth, and yet also in the creation of the first woman from the side of the man.

Now it is not a man who comes from dust and is filled with the breath of life to "become a living soul;" nor is it a woman who is fashioned from the side of a man. Rather, it is now the New Adam who is fashioned from the very flesh of the New Eve, in order to become "a life-giving spirit," so that all of us, "who have borne the likeness of the man of earth" may also come, in the New Adam, Jesus Christ, "to bear the likeness of the man of heaven" (1 Cor 15:45-49). Yes, "it is he who is our peace, who has broken down the dividing wall of separation that has kept us apart" (Eph 2:14). He has joined together God and humanity, God and every human heart, through the kiss that is effected within the depths of his own Sacred Heart.

ישוע

THE KISS OF CONSUMMATION

In the light of what I said in the previous reflection, I think we can confidently say that this first exclamation of the Song of Songs, "Let him kiss me with the kiss of his mouth!" sets the theme for the entire song. It is, as it were, the motif that gives harmony and meaning to all the rest. Throughout the unfolding of the drama the bride will continually be searching for her Beloved, calling out for him, and seeking to draw near in order to receive this kiss of his love. The whole movement of the Song of Songs is the ardent pressing forward of the longing heart for the consummation of intimacy, for the kiss that consummates the marriage between God and humanity.

And we find ourselves, each of us uniquely and unrepeatably, caught up into this drama. We too yearn for this kiss. We too long for this consummation. Therefore, we can let ourselves be swept up into the words and the melody of this sacred song, allowing it to bring to the surface within us our deepest desires. Indeed, it can help us to allow these desires to begin to be "knitted together" into an ever-deepening intimacy with our God and our Bridegroom, who, having kissed humanity in the womb of the Virgin Mary, seeks to kiss us too by effecting this union also within us.

Indeed, as we will see more deeply later, as the Song begins with this passionate cry for a kiss, so it concludes with the mysterious fulfillment of this desire, as the bride cries out anew: "O that you were a brother to me, that nursed at my mother's breast! If I met you outside, I would kiss you, and none would despise me" (8:1). And the Bridegroom responds to this request by truly becoming her Brother, bearing a flesh like her own and born of the same mother. In other words, he becomes "kissable" in the Incarnation!

But not only this; he goes even further, for he knows that his bride still sleeps the slumber of sin, and he must awaken her fully to life in order to bestow upon her that consummating kiss. Perhaps better said, it is this kiss of consummation itself that fully awakens her to life, as he says: "Under the apple tree I awakened you. There your mother was in travail with you, there she who bore you was in travail" (8:5). Under which tree does he awaken her? Where is the tree under which her mother is in travail? Is he referring to the tree of the Garden of Eden under which Eve was corrupted by the tempter? No... there were two trees in the Garden: the tree of the knowledge of good and evil and the tree of life. And this second tree, the Tree of Life, from which our first parents were banished, is implanted anew in the earth once again with our new parents, the New Adam and the

New Eve. This is the Cross of Christ, the tree under which our true Mother was in travail. This is the tree of the definitive kiss that Christ the Bridegroom bestows upon his bride, offering the very gift of his Body and Blood to her and for her. This is the kiss of union after which he can truly exclaim: "It is consummated!" (Jn 19:30). And then he can breathe forth his Spirit in his last dying breath, in order to fill the suffocating lungs of his bride, awakening her finally to the fullness of life.

And then he rises from the dead, borne by the very breath of the Spirit whom he exhaled so lovingly in the gift of himself! Yes, his gift of himself is not a loss, but rather the welcoming of his bride into the innermost space of his own Sacred Heart, where he bears her back to the Father. Yes, our life is already "hidden with Christ in God" (Col 3:3), but we await the definitive, eternal consummation—glimpsed already now in faith and sacrament—but which will reach full flowering only when Christ comes again from heaven. As he himself said: "I am going away, but I will come to you. ... In my Father's house there are many rooms; if it were not so, would I have told you that I go to prepare a place for you? And when I go and prepare a place for you, I will come again and will take you to myself, that where I am you may be also" (Jn 14:2-4, 28). Jesus here unveils himself as the Bridegroom who, having betrothed his spouse to himself through the Sacrament of the Eucharist and pledged himself to her forever, goes to prepare the home in which they are both to live, for all eternity, in the joy of their union in the House of the Father.

How beautiful all of this is! In the radiant light cast from the Incarnation, Passion, and Resurrection of Christ, I discover myself to truly be the bride spoken of in the Song of Songs. I see myself in her, and her in me. Or rather she reveals to me who I truly am as God's beloved, as "his dove, his perfect one" (Sg 6:9), created for an everlasting intimacy with the Father, Son, and Holy Spirit. Thus I can step into the drama, I can let myself be swept up into its movement, as I passionately seek my Beloved, as I earnestly inquire after his kiss... only to discover that, in the end, he is not far away, but has always been seeking me even more passionately, and comes to me unceasingly to kiss me in love, until he is at last able to bestow that final kiss of consummation at the end of time.

ישוע

THIRST FOR HIS UNMEDIATED KISS

Before I proceed to speak about the Name and the Heart of Christ, I want to offer one more interpretation of the bride's request, "Let him kiss me with the kiss of his mouth." The first, and most profound, meaning of this kiss is that it is that eternal, ineffable kiss shared by the Father and the Son in the heart of the Trinity's life: the kiss who is the Holy Spirit himself. This is the bond of enduring and unbreakable intimacy, the union of perfect peace and gladness, and the breath of mutual sharing in which each Person breathes forth into the others, and receives from the others, the unique beauty of each Person and yet also the single substance of the divine life, which is the Love that all three share together as One.

The second meaning of this kiss, I said, is the union of humanity and divinity in the hypostatic union of two natures in the one Person of the Incarnate Son, Jesus Christ. This kiss is first bestowed within the sanctuary of the womb of the Virgin Mary—and consummated as she stands at the foot of the Cross, united intimately to the divine Bridegroom as he gives his life. And therefore she is the bride *par excellence* of the Song of Songs, who receives the Bridegroom's kiss in both incarnation and consummation. And yet in her we are each invited into the same sacred space of intimacy, into the same nuptial kiss. This kiss, further, allows the "incarnation" of Christ to continue in our flesh and our life, as he perpetuates his saving mystery in the Church and in every human heart until the end of time. In other words, within the sinews of our own hearts—united to the Heart of Christ and to the heart of the Virgin Mary—God can continue to twitch the threads of love and intimacy uniting God and humanity together as one.

The third meaning of this kiss, or rather of the bride's request for this kiss, refers to her desire to get beyond all the partial, imperfect experiences of God that she glimpses in created realities, and to enter into a direct, unmediated union with the Beloved himself. This is the passionate thirst for the kiss of God that lies at the heart, for example, of the teaching and experience of Saint John of the Cross. As he writes in his own poem, *The Spiritual Canticle*, which is a kind of commentary on the Song of Songs:

> Where have you hidden,
> Beloved, and left me moaning?
> You fled like the stag
> after wounding me;
> I went out calling you, but you were gone.

> O woods and thickets,
> planted by the hand of my Beloved!
> O green meadow,
> coated, bright, with flowers,
> tell me, has he passed by you?
> Pouring out a thousand graces,
> he passed these groves in haste;
> and having looked at them,
> with his image alone,
> clothed them in beauty.
> Ah, who has the power to heal me?
> now wholly surrender yourself!
> Do not send me
> any more messengers,
> they cannot tell me what I must hear.
> All who are free
> tell me a thousand graceful things of you;
> all wound me more
> and leave me dying
> of, ah, I-don't-know-what behind their stammering.
> (Stanzas 1, 4-7)

The bride complains, from the depths of her love-wounded heart, that all of the beauty of created realities only reflects imperfectly the image of her Beloved, as if he just passed by them in haste. Her heart is touched by their beauty and goodness, but she thirsts to encounter him—the Beloved himself—in the full radiance of his glory and his ineffable Beauty. Indeed, she asks that he not send her any more messengers, any more imperfect ideas and experiences, through which divine light glimmers, but only as if with dim rays filtered through crevices of rock or through the thick fabric of a veil separating this life from the next. Even all those who are free—that is, humans and angels—while they tell her graceful things of the beauty of God, only wound her heart the more and leave her dying of longing for the Beloved himself.

In her encounter with other persons, in other words, she glimpses the "I-don't-know-what" that is both revealed and concealed by their presence and their words. It is this I-don't-know-what, this unspeakable Beauty, that her heart thirsts for, and in which alone she can find definitive and enduring rest. This is "the kiss of his mouth," offered not through the mediation of another creature, nor filtered through created realities, good but imperfect as they are, but the direct touch of lip upon lip, the very substance of God touching the inner substance of the soul in an unmediated union of unspeakable delight and eternal consummation.

This is the cry of the love-wounded heart for heaven, the cry expressed by Saint Paul "to depart and be with Christ" (Ph 1:23), the cry of any heart which has glimpsed the beauty of the divine Beloved and has come to realize that only in direct, unmediated communion with him will the deepest longings of the heart be fulfilled. Yes, this is the cry of a heart madly in love with God, the cry of a heart which, touched by the vision of his beauty, ravished by his rays of his countenance "shining on the face of Christ," draws near "with unveiled face to gaze upon the beauty of the Lord," in this way "being transformed into his likeness from glory unto glory" (2 Cor 4:6; 3:18), until this transformation is consummated in the perfect face-to-face vision of eternity.

Here alone will the full beauty of God, Father, Son, and Holy Spirit, be unveiled before our eyes, communicating itself to us directly and fully—so fully that it will totally permeate our entire consciousness, even unto our very body, so that we are utterly saturated with God. Then it will no longer be the case that we glimpse God obscurely through the beauty of his creatures, but rather that all creatures are seen, reverenced, and loved in their authentic truth and deepest beauty from within the fullness of God's own light and love, from within the cradling arms of the divine Beloved.

ישוע

IN HIM WE ARE ONE: THE KISS OF FRIENDSHIP

I spoke in the previous reflection about the transformation that occurs through a direct union with God—a union that flowers secretly in this life, in the obscure light and radiant darkness of faith, hope, and love—and that will flower fully in endless Day, in the face to face vision of God in the consummation of eternity. The bride thirsts ardently for this, and asks for it, that she not be kissed indirectly, through the mouth of created reality, but with the very "kiss of the mouth" of her divine Beloved. Every heart which has felt this thirst, which has been touched by God's beauty, understands to some degree this thirst, and cries out with the same longing for the direct, unmediated consummation of union with God. Indeed, the more deeply the heart has been touched by him, the more deeply does it thirst for the fullness of this union.

Yet this very ardent thirst, drawing the heart of the bride out of itself in longing for the Beloved, is enfolded in a mysterious restfulness, in the certainty that the kiss of the Beloved already envelops and upholds her. She does not feel it, she does not make direct, palpable contact with it as she will in heaven, and yet in faith, hope, and love she is already in unmediated communion with this kiss, the substance of her being united to the very substance of the Trinity. And therefore, even in the pilgrimage of this life, she can rest in confident hope and filial trust, letting herself be cradled in the arms of perfect Love. She can thirst, ardently and passionately, within the repose that already holds and sustains her. And her thirst for ever-deeper immersion in love only intensifies her experience of this repose, as it plunges her whole being ever more into the burning Furnace of the Trinity, into the enfolding embrace of the Father, Son, and Holy Spirit.

Indeed, her yearning to pass beyond the partial glimpses of God's Beauty in created reality does not empty created things of their goodness, their beauty, their truth, but rather unveils for her their deepest and authentic meaning. For already in this life she begins to see them more through God than to see God through them. Her heart, affixed in the heart of God through faith, is dilated, expanded, stretched…to see, welcome, and reverence all of creation in a tender generosity that reflects the very generosity of God's own heart. And this tender generosity, this opening of her being to be a receptive and sheltering space, is manifested most especially in her relationships with other human persons. Aflame as she is with the thirst for God, and touched already with his mysterious touch, she can open herself to gaze upon others as she has first been gazed upon by God; she can open herself to welcome others as she has first been welcomed; she can open herself to see and love in them the unique reflection of divine Beauty that they are…each person utterly unique and unrepeatable.

Thus her heart becomes a meeting-place between God and humanity. Her own heart becomes a "kiss" that God bestows upon others to help them experience his love and tenderness, and to awaken in their hearts a longing for his own direct, unmediated touch. This is the gift of friendship, a friendship not based merely on a natural affinity, or camaraderie, but a true sharing and union of hearts on the model of the Trinity. It is a reflection of that "divine friendship" that is the complete openness in mutual self-giving of the Father, Son, and Holy Spirit, a friendship that has been opened up to each one of us as our true Home: "As the Father has loved me, so have I loved you; abide in my love… I have called you friends, for all that I have heard from my Father I have made known to you" (Jn 15:9, 15).

This experience of the blessedness of friendship was expressed beautifully by Aelred of Rievaulx, a twelfth century Cistercian monk. He explains tenderly how the intimacy between human persons not only manifests the love of the Trinity—allowing it to become, in a way, incarnate in the love of those who are joined together in Christ —but also how this very "kiss of friendship" enkindles anew in the human heart the longing for the fullness of the Bridegroom's kiss itself…for the direct and unmediated kiss of him who alone is the ultimate and everlasting Spouse of every person. Here are his words:

> In friendship are joined honor and charm, truth and joy, sweetness and good-will, affection and action. And all these take their beginning from Christ, advance through Christ, and are perfected in Christ. Therefore, not too steep or unnatural does the ascent appear from Christ, as the inspiration of the love by which we love our friend, to Christ giving himself to us as our Friend for us to love. … And thus, friend cleaving to friend in the spirit of Christ, is made with Christ but one heart and one soul, and so mounting aloft through degrees of love to friendship with Christ, he is made one spirit with him in one kiss. …
>
> The spiritual kiss is characteristically the kiss of friends who are bound by one law of friendship; for it is not made by contact of the mouth but by the affection of the heart; not by a meeting of lips but by a mingling of spirits, by the purification of all things in the Spirit of God, and through his own participation, emits a celestial savor. I would call this the kiss of Christ, yet he himself does not offer it from his own mouth, but from the mouth of another, breathing upon his lovers that most sacred affection so that there seems to them to be, as it were, one spirit in many bodies. And they may say with the Prophet: "Behold how good and how pleasant it is for brethren to dwell together in unity" (Ps 132:1-Vulgate). The soul, therefore, accustomed to this kiss and not doubting that all this sweetness comes from Christ, as if reflecting within itself and saying, "Oh, if only he himself had come!" sighs for the kiss of grace and with the greatest desire exclaims: "Let him kiss me with the kiss of his mouth" (Sg 1:2). So that now, after all earthly affections have been tempered, and all thoughts and desires which savor of the world have been quieted, the soul takes delight in the kiss of Christ alone and rests in his embrace, exulting and exclaiming: "His left hand is under my head and his right hand shall embrace me" (Sg 2:6).(*Spiritual Friendship*, 2.20-21, 26-27)

Here we encounter the beautiful union between human friendship and divine friendship. From the heart of my own intimacy with God, from the depths of my own ardent thirst for his unmediated kiss, I can also open myself to love all those whom God entrusts to me. I can be for them a true friend, as Christ has first made me his friend, drawing me so close that I can lean against his breast as he says, "I have called you my friend, for all that I have heard from my Father I have made known to you." Having received the kiss of the divine friendship, I find myself opened to recognize in others the beauty of one uniquely seen, chosen, and desired by the divine Bridegroom. Indeed, I find in myself the love of the Bridegroom himself burning, and thus I receive and reverence in others the mystery of the bride, being myself in this way a true "friend of the Bridegroom" (Jn 3:29). Yes, from myself being cradled in the Heart of Christ, from myself receiving the kiss of Christ, I am able to bestow this kiss upon others in the name of Christ, and to welcome them in his name in such a way that they may trace their way, more freely, more vulnerably, more ardently, back into the consummate embrace of his own love.

On the other hand, a true and pure friendship can impel my heart more deeply towards Christ, as I encounter another person who is for me, in a way, a manifestation of the "kiss" of Jesus, and in whom I glimpse his own beauty. Indeed, Aelred goes so far as to say that *"I would call this the kiss of Christ, yet he himself does not offer it from his own mouth, but from the mouth of another*, breathing upon his lovers that most sacred affection so that there seems to them to be, as it were, one spirit in many bodies." How beautiful a union is this! How beautiful a sharing, how pure a love, in which each person reverences the other as one who is unspeakably beautiful in being loved by God, and, further, as one in whom the very beauty of the divine Beloved is manifested! How blessed an intimacy, as hearts are joined together by grace through the very love of Christ that draws them together and makes them one! Yes, they are made one precisely by the Uncreated Kiss of God, who is breathed forth into their relationship through the mouth of Christ—"the love of God that has been poured into our hearts through the Holy Spirit who has been given to us" (Rom 5:5).

Just as in a natural kiss the breath of two mingles together as one, an expression of the gift of the inner heart, so in the kiss of friendship the breath of the Holy Spirit is exhaled from the heart of the Trinity and fills the spirits of those who believe. His tender presence vibrates within the hearts of those who love one another, and who are made one, in the intimacy that the presence of God alone makes possible.

ישוע

A LOVE UNIQUE AND INCOMPARABLE

Let him kiss me with the kiss of his mouth!
For your love surpasses wine,
and your anointing oils are fragrant;
yes, your Name is oil poured out,
therefore do the virgins love you.
Ah, draw me after you; let us make haste!
The King has brought me into his chambers.
We will exult and rejoice in you;
we will extol your love beyond wine;
how rightly do they love you!
(Sg 1:2-4)

In these beginning verses of the Song of Songs, we encounter a dynamic movement of love, springing from the first burst of enthusiasm in which the bride cries out for the kiss of her Beloved. I have already spent a good deal of time dwelling with the first verse of this movement, the exclamation of the bride: "Let him kiss me with the kiss of his mouth!" These words are the first part of a stanza which is composed of two parallel sections. The first, begun with the outburst of the bride's request for a kiss, leads immediately into her praise of her Bridegroom and her exclamation of his lovableness. The second begins with another exclamation—the bride's request to be "drawn" by her Beloved in haste—which leads immediately into her joy in having been brought into the chambers of the King (her Beloved), and the exultation and joy that spring from this great gift, climaxing again in her exclamation about his lovableness. In other words, each section begins with an ardent request of the bride and concludes with her affirmation that her Bridegroom is worthy of being passionately loved.

Let me note outright something that may appear rather puzzling. In the intimacy of the bride's praise of her Bridegroom, there is a surprising recurrence of *the plural*; and even in her request to be drawn this plural is present: "Draw *me*, let *us* make haste." She extols the love of her Beloved as far beyond wine and says that his very Name is an oil poured out. And the conclusion she draws? "Therefore do the virgins (or young women) love you." Now what kind of bride would say this to her bridegroom? "You are so good and beautiful, my love, that all the young women love you!" Does this bride not feel insecure that other women love her one Beloved? Does she not feel a sense of competition? There must, therefore, be something special about this Bridegroom that makes him unlike any other earthly bridegroom, something that makes his love so deep, so intimate, that *he draws each heart uniquely to himself, and yet draws all hearts together as one.*

Indeed, we see the same thing in the bride's joy in being brought into the chambers of the King. Experiencing this deep intimacy, she cries out: "We will exult and rejoice in you; we will extol your love beyond wine; how rightly do they love you!" The bride's words "how rightly do they love you" correspond directly with the earlier "therefore do the virgins love you." This parallelism shows us very clearly the two sections of this introductory stanza of the Song. It begins with the outburst of the bride's longing for a kiss, and passes by way of her praise of the Bridegroom to her request to be drawn by him. And then, immediately after her request, she finds herself sheltered in the chambers of her King; and this moves her anew to praise, a praise that sweeps up others into the same movement of her happiness and delight in the Beloved.

But this doesn't answer our question. How is it that the bride is not jealous that other women love her one Beloved? Is it that, no matter how much other women may love the Bridegroom, he truly has only one love: his one and only bride? Does she know his special love so deeply that she feels no insecurity about him loving another? Does she experience the shelter of his tenderness so profoundly that she experiences no fear of his ever turning away to other women? The affirmative answer to these questions is itself shown very clearly in a number of the Bridegroom's statements in the text: "As a lily among brambles, so is my love among maidens... Open to me, my sister, my love, my dove, my perfect one... My dove, my perfect one, is only one" (2:2; 5:2; 6:9). Indeed, the Bridegroom's exclusive love for his bride is a continual refrain throughout the entire Song, and the bride expresses a number of times her security in this love. For example, she says: "My Beloved is mine, and I am his... I am my Beloved's, and his desire is for me" (2:16; 7:10). And yet, on the other hand, there is another refrain present in the Song as well. It is the desire of all—and not only of the bride—for the beauty of the Bridegroom, such that they are continually being drawn into the orbit of the bride's desire, and, as it were, fall in love with him just as she has.

I think in saying this we can at last find some reconciliation between these two contrasting themes. And it also reveals to us how clear it is that the Bridegroom of the Song of Songs *cannot possibly be anyone else than God himself, incarnate in Jesus Christ.* How so? If I look at my own experience of God's love, my own encounter with the tenderness of his loving gaze and with his invitation to nuptial intimacy with himself, what do I see? I realize that the way that God loves me is so pure, so total, so unique that it simply cannot compare with the way that he loves anyone else. *For him, I truly am the only one.*

Therefore, I have no reason to fear that he may love another, since his love is, in all truth, completely and totally for me as his one and only bride. But at the same time, as I fall ever more in love with him, my spontaneous response is not to lock him up and keep him all to myself. Rather, I desire for all to fall in love with him as I have! I yearn for them to know the tenderness of his gaze, the sweetness of his embrace, the inebriation of his love!

Yes, this spousal relationship that Christ establishes with me—and with me uniquely and unrepeatably—is, in a mysterious way, both *utterly exclusive* and *utterly open*. Unlike with a human spouse, Jesus' nuptial love for each person does not hinder him from loving any one else. Rather, Jesus' love is so intimate, so total, that it manifests *an even deeper and more absolute exclusivity than married love*. This is because it is founded, not on a natural attraction, nor even on a vowed commitment to the other, but rather on *his tender receptivity to the unique and unrepeatable beauty of the person that I am*. His love for me is therefore utterly unique and unrepeatable because it is founded on the very core of my unique identity. I am indeed "his dove, his perfect one, his only one." And his Heart spontaneously cries out as he gazes upon me: "You are precious in my eyes, and beautiful, and I love you!" (Is 43:4).

Therefore in all truth I can say that Jesus loves me as he loves no other; I can joyfully exclaim, "I am my Beloved's, and his desire is for me!" Indeed, Christ loves me with such depth, such passion, such intensity, that I am for him the only person in the entire world. There is, and can be, simply no comparison between me and any other person, for when Christ looks upon me with love (as he does at every moment) he does not, and cannot, cast a side-glance to any other. He sees me, and me alone, as he pours forth into me the abundant fullness of his love, and as he welcomes me into the depths of his own sheltering Heart, so that I may make my home forever in the tenderness of his loving embrace.

ישוע

YOUR NAME IS OIL POURED OUT

Let him kiss me with the kiss of his mouth!
For your love surpasses wine,
your anointing oils are fragrant;
yes, your Name is oil poured out.
(Sg 1:2-3)

Thus resounds the bride's praise of her heavenly Bridegroom. She praises his love as surpassing wine, and then speaks of the fragrant oil of his anointing and of his very Name as oil poured out. The second and third of these indeed refer to a single reality, to *the anointing oil of the Name of Jesus*. Indeed, is he not called *Christ*, a word that means precisely *the Anointed One*? The bride in this way makes contact with the deepest truth of her Beloved—that is, with his Name, his identity, and she praises him for who he is. And yet she is able to praise him precisely because she has experienced his love pouring forth upon her as a precious oil, covering her entire body and permeating her with its peace, its gentleness, its balm, its fragrance.

But what, we can ask, is her Bridegroom's identity? Is it truly to be the Anointed One? But was he not anointed at some point in time—whether at his conception, or his baptism, or some other point in his human life? If so, then this anointing cannot be his true identity, but rather a secondary aspect of his existence. What, then, lies at the very core of his Personhood, such that the bride can really say it is his Name, a Name which is uniquely his own and yet which is poured out tenderly and lovingly upon her? Ah…how beautiful is this! The identity of her Bridegroom is *to be the eternally beloved Son of the Father, anointed in the bosom of the Trinity with the unction of the Father's eternal delight, with the kiss of the very Spirit himself!*

For all eternity, the Son receives himself as a pure gift of the Father's outpouring generosity, and gives himself totally back to the Father in return. This mutual self-giving, this shared "outpouring" of life and love between the Father and the Son, is eternally consummated in the perfect intimacy of the Holy Spirit. The Spirit is, therefore, the anointing of the love of the Father and the Son, just as he is the kiss of their union. These are two images used to express the same awesome reality. If this is true, then indeed the identity of the Son is to be the Anointed One, yet not in the sense that he is anointed King of creation, or even anointed to be the Messiah or Christ, or even for that matter anointed for a saving mission for all humanity. No, his identity is deeper than any "mission," and his Name is more intimate, more profound than any of these secondary things. His eternal anointing is simply the very truth of the Father's incomparable love for him. This love is poured out in an eternal act of generosity which constitutes the Son in his very identity as the Beloved. And this is an anointing, further, which is eternally sealed, as the fruit of the mutual self-giving of Father and Son, in the intimate bond of the Holy Spirit.

What then is the meaning of the anointing that occurs when the Bridegroom's Name is "oil poured out" upon the bride? The eternal Son, from the heart of his own identity and out of the fullness of his love, becomes incarnate as a man by taking to himself a human nature in the womb of the Virgin Mary. And when he becomes man his identity in no way changes. In other words, *at every moment of his human life he simply continues to live the life that is his in the bosom of the Trinity!* And yet now he lives it in the context of our world, permeating all the faculties of a human soul and all the concrete experiences of a human body! And this human nature that he has taken to himself is precisely the human nature of his bride, of his deeply beloved one. Therefore, at the very first instant of his Incarnation, the Name of the eternal Son is "poured out like oil" upon the bride, penetrating and permeating her entire being and her whole existence.

This is the very meaning of the Incarnation: that the mutual self-giving of the Father, Son, and Holy Spirit turns itself "outward" in order to pour itself out into creation and into the depths of our own human hearts. And it does this in order to "anoint" us with the very unction of God's incomparable love, *revealing in each one of us our true identity, our intimate personal truth as God's beloved*. Ah, yes, for as the identity of Jesus is to be the beloved Son of the Father, so in him I realize that my identity, too, is to be a beloved child of God! He unveils this truth to me through the very outpouring of his Name upon me as a precious and fragrant oil.

There is, in this anointing, a sacred encounter between the identity of the Son and my own unique identity. There is an unspeakably profound *meeting of hearts*, in which he communicates himself totally to me in love, and in doing so awakens my response, in which I give myself back to him in return. Through experiencing his Name poured out like oil upon me, my heart spontaneously experiences the desire to pour myself out in return. Yes, I yearn to surrender myself into his sheltering embrace in an act of radical entrustment, so that he may care for me freely in the tenderness of his love, and also simply in order to praise and adore the One who has ravished my heart with his unspeakable beauty, and for whom I want my entire existence to be a single cry: "Behold, you are beautiful, my Beloved!" (Sg 2:16).

ישוע

ENCOUNTERING THE BRIDEGROOM'S GAZE

In the last reflection I spoke about the beautiful meeting of hearts that occurs when I experience Christ's Name being poured out like precious oil upon me—when his identity as beloved Son of the Father touches me in the innermost recesses of my heart and awakens my own awareness of being a beloved child of God. This is a sacred encounter in which the deepest longings of my heart truly begin to be fulfilled—or better, in which I can already taste and experience the fulfillment that, while completely real and totally present now, will only reach its consummation in the marriage of eternity. My deepest longings for love and intimacy, my longing to be loved absolutely and uniquely and to surrender my life entirely into the loving arms of another—all of this is brought to fulfillment in my encounter with Christ.

I have always had a sense, a profound and innate awareness, that I am beautiful, precious, and sacred—and yet I have also felt deeply insecure precisely about this! I feel a deep need, a deep desire to be loved for who I am, deeper than anything I do, or say, or have, or achieve. I yearn to be seen and known as beautiful and lovable in the very depths of my personhood, where I am naked with nothing to cover or hide me. But I am also terrified of encountering the gaze of another in this place, for I fear that I will be condemned, or used and abused, or simply dismissed as undesirable and uninteresting. But I cannot live without this certainty of being loved! I cannot live—and I mean truly live!—without the security of knowing that I am truly beautiful, precious, and sacred as the unique person that I am. But I cannot give this security to myself, however much I may try. Rather, it is only when I encounter the loving gaze of another, when I find myself truly sheltered and cradled in the arms of their affirming love, that this sacred mystery within me is set free. Then it can truly flower from within, opening its petals and giving forth its fragrance like a blossom spreading out in the sun.

Here is the great gift of the divine Bridegroom, who looks upon me at every moment with infinite tenderness, with a gaze that is loving, cherishing, and protecting. And through this gaze Jesus welcomes me and shelters me in the innermost chambers of his own Sacred Heart. He seeks to hide me from the eyes, actions, and words of those who would look upon me in my vulnerability and would hurt me. And when I have been hurt, he seeks to pour forth upon me the anointing of his love that will soften, ease, and ultimately heal my wounds, transforming them into places of deeper grace and intimacy with himself. Yes, he holds me tenderly in his Heart at every moment, and says to me, with his eyes, with his voice, and indeed with every throbbing of his heartbeat: "Behold, you are beautiful, my love, behold, you are beautiful" (Sg 2:15).

And what is my spontaneous response, when I experience such a cradling and cherishing love, when I encounter a gaze that pours out upon me unceasingly like a fragrant oil? I yearn to pour my life into his hands, to place myself unreservedly into his care. And yet this gift is not a matter, as I have said before, of in some way "gathering myself up" in order to place myself into the hands of Jesus. Rather, it is a matter of *allowing my heart to relax under the radiance of his loving gaze*. It is a matter of *letting myself be loved, and in being loved to be gently cradled, held, and cherished*.

And I do this not by fixing my gaze upon my own fears, my own hesitations, my own deep need, but rather simply *by looking into his loving gaze upon me*. It is the loving gaze of Jesus that becomes like a bridge, thrown in trust and walked in trust, which draws me out of my own loneliness and pain, my own fear and shame, and *into the perfect security of his welcoming embrace*. The gaze of Jesus, as it were, envelops me in my entirety, becoming like arms that sweep me up in my weakness and carry me where I myself cannot go on my own. I find my fears and anxieties eased by his touch, and then my deepest and most authentic desires spontaneously spring up within my heart. I can name them and open them to him, and he takes them and fulfills them with his own infinite love and tenderness.

For all of my desires ultimately spring from two fundamental desires. The first is *to know and live from my true identity*—but this ultimately means to know myself as beautiful and lovable in the eyes of Another, so that I may live in freedom, playfulness, and joy from within the shelter of his love. The second desire is *to experience a deep and lasting intimacy*—and indeed this intimacy is the only thing that can fulfill my first desire to experience my identity. These two desires are inseparably united, and ultimately come together as one when I realize that *my identity is precisely to be God's beloved, to be intimately united to him from the first moment of my conception*. In realizing this, I can let myself sink back into the authentic truth of who I am in the depths of my heart, because here I experience myself cradled at every moment in the sustaining and sheltering love of God.

And thus my heart spontaneously begins to sing a hymn of thanksgiving and praise to the One who has loved me so purely, and who, in turn, has touched and ravished my heart with his unspeakable Beauty. My life freely expands within this sacred space of his love and becomes as an "oil poured out" for my Beloved, filling the house of the Church with its precious fragrance. This oil of my unique beauty given to my Beloved brings him great joy and delight, for he created me simply in order to love me, and he has no other desire than to gaze upon me in my beauty and to unite me intimately to himself.

Yet the fragrance of my beauty spreading forth before Christ my Beloved also spontaneously has an effect on others, as they sense in me and through me the marvels of God's love, and indeed can begin to glimpse his own tender gaze which wants to touch them, heal them, and unveil before them their own unique and unrepeatable beauty in his eyes.

ישוע

DRAW ME; LET US MAKE HASTE!

The Name of Jesus is an oil poured out upon the bride to anoint her with the beauty of his own love, to clothe her entirely within the security of his own tender embrace—indeed, within the embrace of the heavenly Father in whose bosom he unceasingly rests, and where he wants to welcome his beloved, there to cradle her eternally in the perfect bliss of the Trinity's life. She comes to know who she is, to experience her own beauty, only because his loving gaze reveals this to her. She comes to accept herself only because she is totally accepted by him. Indeed, she comes to desire to be the person that she is, to delight in the beauty God has created in her, since Christ looks upon her and ardently desires her, since he embraces her with an embrace that surges his own Heart with profound delight. And in turn, the bride falls head-over-heels in love with the beauty of Christ, and in him with the beauty of the Father and the Spirit too. Her heart is dilated and stretches out in love to welcome ever more tenderly and sensitively the embrace of her Beloved, and to let herself be received and cradled by him in return.

Here there is a mutual communication of hearts in which Bridegroom and bride are bound together with the bond of a single love. Here he bestows upon her his own kiss, the kiss that he has first received from the Father of them both, a kiss that is the very bond of unshakable intimacy who is the Holy Spirit. In this way, already in this life and perfectly forever in heaven, the bride is swept up into the innermost dance of love ever occurring in the heart of the Trinity. She is held and cradled right at the meeting-place where the Father kisses the Son and the Son kisses the Father, and where, in the Spirit, they both kiss her, their precious daughter and dearly beloved spouse.

How beautiful all of this is! How am I possibly to proceed speaking from this point…from this sacred space where the heart is captured and stands rapt in reverent awe before the Mystery that is truly the fulfillment of all our desires? But we haven't even left the fourth verse of the Song! Loving God, infinitely beautiful and unspeakably lovable Trinity—Father, Son, and Holy Spirit—may you grasp my hands and heart, my mind and words, and pour forth for your precious children the tenderness of your love that you so deeply desire to make known to them!

"Your anointing oil is fragrant; it is your very Name poured out…" It is the Name of the beloved Son, who touches me tenderly in the most intimate place of my own belovedness, my own identity as one immeasurably precious in the eyes of God…his only one, his precious one, loved uniquely and incomparably. If only each heart within this world knew this and experienced it! When the human heart begins to learn to see, it is as if a veil is pulled back from creation—a veil that keeps us from encountering each other as we really are. And then the heart will never again be able to rest in her aloneness and superficiality; and yet, on the other hand, she already begins to rest, truly and unceasingly, within the arms of the Beauty that cradles the world. Yes, she is wounded by the beauty that has touched her, and which she continually encounters anew bursting forth through the eyes, the face, the words, the silence, the tears, the sorrow, and the joy of each one of God's uniquely precious and incomparably beloved children!

A person who has seen this, a heart that has been pierced by the rays of God's infinite Beauty—and is thus enabled to see this Beauty present uniquely in each child of God, cradling their unique beauty within itself—a heart such as this will ache with a blessed longing (and rejoice with an indescribable joy!) until she at last passes beyond the veil of mortality and into the consummation of intimacy that awaits us in the next life. The death of such a person is not an unavoidable fate, or even something merely "done to me" from the outside. Rather, it is transformed into a prayer—into an act of most profound love and trust-filled obedience, just as was the death of Jesus.

At every moment of her life, such a heart cries out with the Virgin Mary, silently but truly: "Let it be to me according to your word," which in all reality means, "Let it be in me and in all of your children according to the fullness of your unspeakable Love!" Yes, and when the time of death at last comes, then the tearing of the veil is something long desired, and something wholeheartedly accepted. It is the final prayer which brings to a consummation all the prayers uttered throughout life. It is the final "let it be." It is the final passage beyond the limitations of this earthly life and into the sphere of limitless self-communication, the sphere of pure and total relationship. Here the person, returning into the embrace of the Father, Son, and Holy Spirit, and made pure loving relationship with God, is also able to welcome, embrace, love, and accompany every person from within the radiant light of God's own vision and from within the world-cradling tenderness of his own love.

Ah…how beautifully and unexpectedly I realize that I have commented precisely on the following verses of the Song of Songs! I had no intention of doing so, but the Mystery itself is one and indivisible, and to speak of it is to speak from the place of harmony where all partial words converge together in the single Heart of Christ, in the sheltering embrace of the Trinity!

Now the heart, as the true bride, has spontaneously cried out: "Draw me after you; let us make haste!" yearning for the consummation of intimacy that awaits her in the bosom of the Trinity. She has even exulted: "The King has brought me into his chambers," as she delights already in anticipation. Indeed, she rejoices in the joy of the intimacy that already flowers in this life between her and the One she loves; she rejoices in experiencing herself cradled in the Heart of her Beloved and being carried forward toward the definitive consummation of the eternal Marriage. And touched by the beauty of such immense Love, cradled in the arms of such Tenderness, she cannot but exclaim, as she cradles in her own heart all those whom she loves within her one Beloved: "We will exult and rejoice in you; we will extol your love beyond wine; how rightly do they love you!"

ישוע

THE KING HAS BROUGHT ME INTO HIS CHAMBERS

How can I not but turn, at the conclusion of these reflections on the "oil poured out" in love, to the pages of the Gospel? There we find a woman who understood this outpoured love of Christ, who experienced the healing tenderness of his gaze, and, in her own fragrant outpouring of her life at his feet, symbolized the fragrance of his own love which would pour forth on the Cross for the salvation of all.

Six days before the Passover, Jesus came to Bethany, where Lazarus was, whom Jesus had raised from the dead. There they made him a supper; Martha served, and Lazarus was one of those at table with him. Mary took a pound of costly ointment of pure nard and anointed the feet of Jesus and wiped his feet with her hair; and the house was filled with the fragrance of the ointment. But Judas Iscariot, one of his disciples (he who was to betray him), said, "Why was this ointment not sold for three hundred denarii and given to the poor?" This he said, not that he cared for the poor but because he was a thief, and as he had the money box he used to take what was put into it. Jesus said, "Let her alone, let her keep it for the day of my burial. The poor you always have with you, but you do not always have me." (Jn 12:1-8)

What a beautiful squandering of the most precious and valuable of all things upon the body of Jesus! Judas does not like this, because he is a "calculator," because he understands charity as a primarily monetary or transactional affair rather than a romantic matter. And indeed John the Evangelist explicitly tells us more than this: that we was a thief. But clearly we are being given here a vibrant contrast between two attitudes of heart: the attitude of *the miser* and the attitude of *the squanderer*. If you don't like me using the title of squanderer, then we could replace it with *the uncalculating lover*. For it is indeed true that anything poured forth recklessly upon our beloved Jesus is never lost, never squandered. Rather, he says, in response to our every act of trusting surrender, to every sigh of our heart for his love, to our every prayer, to every desire we have for others to discover his love—he says in response to the littlest and most hidden movements of our heart: "Gather up all the fragments, that absolutely nothing may be lost" (Jn 6:12). As Jesus says in Matthew's account of this same scene of Mary's anointing: "Why do you trouble the woman? For she has done a beautiful thing to me… Truly I say to you, wherever this gospel is preached in the whole world, what she has done will be told in memory of her" (Mt 26:10, 13).

In receiving the gift of our loving surrender, Jesus takes all the threads of our existence and cradles them gently within his love; he knits them together as one with the fabric of his own Sacred Heart, until we are "of a piece" with him, a seamless fabric in the abiding intimacy of love. This is that kiss for which our hearts so deeply thirst, a kiss that will not cease, but which, in being bestowed, will seal an everlasting and unbreakable intimacy. I was first kissed this way at the moment of my conception, in which God "breathed into me the breath of life" and created me as his image and likeness. Therefore I bear, at the very core of my being, in the innermost depths of my heart—in the inner sanctuary that no human hand can touch and no wound can efface—in this place I bear the very *kiss-print* of God!

And this is precisely why I thirst for his definitive kiss, because I have already, in some way, experienced it. Even more, I have been kissed by God in Baptism, when the mouth of the Trinity was impressed directly upon my spirit, "kissing me with the kiss of his mouth" and thus making me a sharer in the very life of the Father, Son, and Holy Spirit. In Baptism the fullness of the divine life was truly implanted within me, a seed to germinate, mature, and flower throughout my life until it reaches its full blossoming in heaven. And this kiss of love, begetting the Trinity's life within me, is continually deepened and renewed through the other sacraments, especially through the Eucharist. In the act of receiving Holy Communion I am, truly, receiving the kiss of the Bridegroom's mouth in the most intimate and real way. In this sacred moment the Beloved gives his very Body and Blood to me and becomes "one flesh" with me in a way deeper than any human intercourse; and he breathes forth into my entire being the breath of his Spirit, to fill me and bring me more deeply to life, to touch me and to inundate me with his joy.

This kiss is also an anointing, as we have seen, in which the deepest identity of Christ touches me in my own deepest identity and gently cradles me in this place. The tenderness of his love is poured out upon me and washes over me, permeating my entire being and spontaneously awakening the response of my own love for him. In this way, through this mutual kiss, this anointing of love, Christ makes his home within my heart. Indeed, with him the Father and the Holy Spirit come and dwell within me, as Jesus promised: "We will come to him and will make our home within him" (Jn 14:23). And yet for God to make his home within my heart really means for him to shelter and cradle me in the home of his own perfect embrace. Therefore, when God comes to me so intimately—in the life of grace, in prayer, in the Eucharist—I can truly exclaim: "The King has brought me into his chambers!" I begin to taste, and to exult in, the experience of being seen, known, loved, and sheltered; I can begin to rest, to play, to dance for joy within the cradling arms of the Love for which my heart has always thirsted.

And when I take refuge in the chambers of the Sacred Heart of Jesus, when I let myself be unceasingly cradled in the arms of the Trinity's love, I am indeed offering the greatest gift that I possibly can—both to God and to my brothers and sisters. In letting myself be "drawn in haste" in the footsteps of my heavenly Bridegroom, I am not only allowing myself to be taken more deeply into the sacredness of Love's embrace, but I am spontaneously allowing God, through the magnetism of my own life, to draw others also. This "drawing" into the chambers of my King in a sense lies at the heart of the whole salvation history, as well as of my own personal "salvation history." I may often feel that I am the one who is always active, that I am the one who is seeking God, while he passively waits for me to come to him. Perhaps I feel that I'm the one who is ardently desiring, seeking, and begging for the Bridegroom to come, while he seems not to care. This is a most troublesome misconception, and could not be further from the truth.

The bride's very cry, "Draw me after you; let us make haste!" is but a response to the fact that the Bridegroom has already touched her, and that he already draws her unceasingly. We see this throughout the Old Testament, as God has always taken the initiative to draw his people to himself. This drawing movement is visible from the very first moment of our sin, when God sought out Adam and Eve, naked and afraid, in the Garden of Eden, crying out to them, "Where are you?" And their reply, "I was afraid, because I was naked, so I hid myself," is so often our reply. And so he continues to seek, to ask, to draw. "Cain, where is your brother?" "Abraham, I want you to go out to the land that I will show you." "Moses, I have heard the pain of my people, and I want to lead them out." And even after the sin of the chosen people led them into exile once again from the promised land, God still spoke to them: "The people who survived the sword found grace in the wilderness; when Israel sought for rest, the LORD appeared to him from afar. I have loved you with an everlasting love; and this is why I have drawn you with loving kindness" (cf. Jer 31:2-3). Yes, God wraps his beloved one in the bands of his own tenderness, yoking her with the bond of love which is true freedom, leading her into the wilderness where, alone with her Beloved, she may be espoused to him anew in marital love: "Behold, I will draw you, and bring you into the wilderness, and speak tenderly to you… And I will espouse you for ever; I will espouse you in righteousness and in justice, in steadfast love, and in mercy. I will espouse you in faithfulness; and you shall know the LORD" (cf. Hos 2:14, 19-20).

This drawing movement, finally, reaches its climax in the glorification of Jesus Christ—in his Passion, Resurrection, and Ascension. As he says: "I, when I am lifted up from the earth, will draw all of humanity to myself" (cf. Jn 12:32). And I have already quoted his words, "I am going away, but I will come to you. … In my Father's house there are many rooms; if it were not so, would I have told you that I go to prepare a place for you? And when I go and prepare a place for you, I will come again and will take you to myself, that where I am you may be also" (Jn 14:2-4, 28). Indeed, his final prayer uttered to his Father before going to his Passion is this: "Father, I desire that they also, whom you have given me, may be with me where I am, to behold my glory which you have given me in your love for me before the foundation of the world" (Jn 17:24). But this is not merely a future reality. Even if I must await the definitive coming of the Bridegroom, in which he will at last tear the veil of this mortal life and take me, fully, into the House of the Father, it is also true that "I have" already "died, and my life is hidden with Christ in God." Therefore, "when Christ who is my life appears, then I also will appear with him in glory" (cf. Col 3:3-4), but this is a glory that already dwells in me now, and which draws me unceasingly by enfolding me in the arms of divine Love, until it draws me at last into the consummation of my Beloved's embrace.

Therefore, let me not be afraid to cry, "Draw me!" in the confident security that he is already doing so, and that, from the very beginning, he has already been at work, that he has already been ardently seeking me with more passion, more intensity, and more constancy that I have ever sought him.

ישוע

DRAWN INTO
THE DIMENSION OF HIS LOVE

In the last reflection, I mentioned that, in allowing myself to be drawn by Christ into the intimate chambers of his Sacred Heart, I am indeed offering the greatest gift that I can give, both to God and to my brothers and sisters. How is this so? The most immediate and central answer is that *this is precisely the reason that God created me; it is his most intimate desire for me!* He has made me to be drawn, to be drawn in love into the intimacy of his loving embrace, and it is only here that I find my true and enduring rest and the radiant joy of authentic happiness.

And yet this joyful fulfillment that I experience in the chambers of the Heart of Christ, in the intimate embrace of the Trinity—as intimate, unique, and unrepeatable as it is—does not prove to be a "private" matter. Rather, it bursts forth with an expansive fruitfulness for the good of all the children of God throughout the world. We have seen this already in the way that the uncalculating generosity, the tender and loving surrender, of Mary of Bethany filled the entire house with its fragrance (the house which symbolizes the Church), and Jesus himself affirmed that "wherever this gospel is preached throughout the whole world, what she has done will be told in memory of her." And why would it be told? For two reasons. First, because the Bridegroom wants all to know the love of his beloved, and to see in her the truth and beauty that he himself sees. Second, because in seeing this they themselves will be drawn closer to the Bridegroom and will learn to surrender their lives to him as well!

This is something that in our current culture (even within the Church) we have too much forgotten: that the most important thing for each one of us to do is not to expend ourselves in evangelizing efforts, to minister to others generously, to fulfill all the obligations of our state of life—as important as each of these things is—but *first of all, in all, and beyond all, to let ourselves be drawn into a deep and lasting intimacy with Jesus Christ*. What this does is, not only bring to fulfillment our own hearts, whom God created precisely in order to unite us intimately to himself, but also makes us like a magnet that draws other hearts closer to the Heart of Jesus, which, lifted up in love, draws all hearts to himself. By allowing this magnetism of love to polarize us, we spontaneously become a force that exerts the same pull as does the Heart of Christ.

In my reflections until this point I have been speaking from my own heart, from my own thought, but now I want to quote some of the words of Blaise Arminjon in his book on the Song of Songs. Actually, I haven't had his book in my possession until yesterday. I may refer to and quote it at times, but above all I want to continue speaking directly from my reflection on the text of the Song. This is because I don't want to just be repeating what another person has said, or summarizing the tradition—since this has already been done beautifully (for example by Arminjon himself). Rather, I hope only to offer my unique little "note" to the great symphony of words that has been poured forth throughout history about the mysteries of divine love concealed in this most sacred Song. But let me return to what I was saying. I find that Father Arminjon's comments are very pertinent here—and especially the words of those whom he is quoting—so let me include what he says:

> The "we" of "let us run" is not only that of the Bride and the Bridegroom; it is also the "we" of the Bride and her maiden companions, the maidens she just mentioned and who are inseparable from her, the nations of the world. Saint Bernard understands this well: "We run," he writes, "i.e. the maidens join

me in the race; we run together, I following the fragrance of your perfume, and they following my example and my encouragement. The Bride is imitated just as she herself is imitating Christ. Therefore she does not use a singular form, 'I shall run,' but 'let us run.'" The same interpretation is to be found in the words of Thérèse of Lisieux, who frequently quoted this verse of the Song, in which her whole missionary spirituality seems to be condensed: "One day, after Holy Communion, Jesus let me understand this sentence of the Song: 'Draw me; we run after the fragrance of your perfumes.' O Jesus, it is therefore not necessary to say: in drawing me, also draw the souls I love. This simple phrase, 'draw me,' is enough. Yes, when a soul lets itself be captured by the intoxicating smell of your perfumes, it cannot run alone. All the souls it loves are drawn together with it; this is a natural consequence of its being drawn to you ... I feel that the greater the fire of love ignited in my heart, the more I will say, 'draw me,' and the more the souls that will come close to me will swiftly run toward the fragrance of the beloved's perfume. Yes, they will run; we will run together...for a soul that is afire with love cannot remain inactive." It is also necessary to remember here that when she saw herself buried, so to speak, in the depths of the Heart of Christ, Saint Margaret-Mary heard the sentence: "I want to make of you an instrument to draw hearts to my love." Whoever is drawn to love must draw and attract others in his turn: "Ravish those you can, ... ravish them to love" *(rapite quos potestis ... rapite ad amorem)*. These words of Augustine become the law of her heart.[7]

This quote reveals how deeply, how constantly, this truth of being drawn lovingly in the footsteps of Christ is experienced by those who believe in him. Perhaps in times of darkness or desolation we are tempted to forget this, to feel like we are the ones putting in all the effort to move forward, searching for the hidden face of our Beloved. After all, why doesn't he make himself more visible? Why isn't his presence more obvious, more palpable in our life? If he really loved us, after all, he could reveal himself to us like he did to the so-called great saints—in visions or locutions or ecstasies. Instead, he came into our world visibly only for a short span of just over thirty years, was crucified and, rising from the dead, revealed himself to relatively few persons. And then...and then he told them to tell others! He told them to "do this in remembrance of me." He has seemed to confine himself to coming to us in the most humble, subtle, and, it seems, indirect of ways. But this, too, is not exactly true. Yes, it is proper to

God "to be present within the littlest and yet not to be contained by the greatest." But the loving heart gradually begins to realize that *the ways in which he comes to us are precisely the deepest, most intimate, and most effective.*

Just as Mary Magdalene after Jesus' Resurrection, when she wanted to hold on to him, heard him reply, "Do not hold me; for I have not yet ascended to my Father," so he says to us. Do not hold on to the imperfect glimpses of my beauty and my love that you experience in this life. Yes, receive them, let them water the seed of grace within your heart, let them awaken gratitude and a deeper love for me; let them stretch thin the veil separating this life from the next, allowing you to glimpse something of the eternal, uncreated light shining through. But never cease to cry out, "Let him kiss me with the kiss of his mouth!" You will only be able to see me face to face, as I really am, and to receive the true kiss of my mouth, when you join me in the fullness of eternal life. But until then I must adapt myself to your limitation, I must communicate eternity in the midst of time, must reveal true life in a realm marked by death, must convey the immensity of love to a heart that is frail. I touch you here, in the place where you are, and only over time does your heart dilate, expanding to proportions that reflect those of my own love. And then, then beloved, you will find yourself entering into ceaseless communion with the mystery of eternity, with the Risen Life that is indestructible—and which is present fully already in this world, even if veiled by mortality, hidden like a seed buried in the earth.

Know that I come, my beloved, in the most intimate way that I can. If I were to appear visibly before you, could I still be as intimately close as the air that surrounds you, as the breath that fills your lungs? If you could touch me externally, could I still be the Body and Blood that pervade you and that surge through your veins? I you could somehow "get a grip" on me and hold me tight in your thoughts, in your imagination, in your emotions, would I still be the Reality that permeates your every thought, your every feeling, with the fullness of my self-communication and my ceaseless outpouring of love? Only in eternity, my beloved, will this be possible—as seeing, touching, and perceiving become one with, manifestations of, the deepest interpenetration of your spirit and my Spirit, your heart and my Heart, your being and my Being, as your being is sheltered and cradled in the fullness of the Being that is mine with the Father and the Holy Spirit.

But the way that I come to you in this life is the most intimate way that I can, secretly pervading and transforming your life from within by the mysterious reality of my own Risen Life. You cannot directly see, directly feel, directly taste, because I have passed into another dimension, a dimension of fullness in Love, into the realm of pure and ceaseless relationship. And only insofar as you allow me to draw you into this place as well will you also begin to see, feel, taste, smell, and hear me—in a way beyond the physical senses, but sanctifying them from within. Yes, my dear one, you will be able to perceive me, who am eternal Love, to the degree that you yourself become love. And I will do this in you; I do it already, insofar as you give your "yes" to my loving action, and never cease to cry out with your heart's longing: "Draw me after you; let us make haste!"

ישוע

TO SAVOR HIS SWEETNESS:
EXERCISING THE SPIRITUAL SENSES

The King has brought me into his chambers!
We will exult and rejoice in you;
we will extol your love beyond wine.
How rightly do they love you!
(Sg 1:4b)

Already within the limitation and mortality of this life, the King brings the bride into the most intimate chambers of his Sacred Heart. She is buried in the sacred Abyss of the Trinity's Love, immersed in the embrace of the Father, Son, and Holy Spirit. She receives the very kiss of God's mouth upon the lips of her soul, and yet this kiss is bestowed in the night, mediated by faith, hope, and love. She does not yet experience the kiss of eternal Day, in the radiant, face to face vision of God's infinite Glory. But this does not hinder her from rejoicing as she praises her King for what he has done for her, and for what he has done for all of those who have been drawn along with her.

She has learned, even in the apparent aridity of the desert of this life, to perceive and welcome the presence of her divine Beloved, to shelter him lovingly within her own heart, as she in turn is lovingly sheltered by him. Let us recall that we are still in the introductory stanza of the Song, and that this stanza summarizes in a few verses the whole trajectory of the drama, bringing together in a few words what will unfold gradually throughout the five poems that constitute the "acts" of this single Drama, of this most sacred Poem. Therefore, if the bride in these first verses seems already to rest in the perfect and enduring embrace of her Bridegroom, inebriated with the unspeakable sweetness of his love and experiencing the very kiss of his mouth, we will see that she has traveled a long journey to get here.

Or rather, she has always been here, nestled within the love of her King—and carrying him within the enclosed garden of her own heart—but only over time have her senses been purified and healed so that she can truly enter into a living and life-giving communion with the reality of his love for her. I already began to speak of this "purification of the senses" in the last reflection. Indeed, I also noted it indirectly even earlier when I spoke of the way that a certain purity of heart is encouraged by the tradition before approaching this sacred Song, so as not to misinterpret it in a carnal way—but also how the very reading of the Song can foster this purity within us. Indeed, the Song is saturated with sense imagery of all kinds. It speaks continually about seeing, tasting, touching, hearing, smelling…and in doing so it seeks to "evangelize" our heart, permeating us with the anointing of the Bridegroom's love.

Therefore, some words on this evangelization of our heart are in order. This is the awakening of our spiritual senses and also the irradiation of the deepest recesses of our being (which often remain in darkness) by the light of eternal Love. This "evangelization" is an important part of the gradual flowering of baptismal grace within us, the accommodation and transformation of our being according to the very life of the Trinity, which has grafted us into itself and operates within us through faith, hope, and love. It is also important in overcoming the division that exists in many of us between the "head-God" that we believe in and the "heart-God" that we emotionally experience. The former refers to the way that we affirm God with our mind, our acceptance of the God presented to us in Scripture and the teaching of the Church. The latter refers to the way that we spontaneously experience God in our emotions, "gutturally," as it were. And while Scripture also addresses us in this intimate sphere of our being, our heart-experience of God is usually more rooted in our own life experiences, often poorly interpreted and not adequately evangelized by the truth of God and by his presence and activity within those experiences. Sadly, what many people believe about God with the head is more positive than their experience of him with their heart. They claim that he is a loving and merciful Father, but their spontaneous emotional reaction is to flee from his face in shame or the fear of being punished in his anger; they believe that he is loving them first and pursuing them in love, but it can take a long time for this "head knowledge" to distill into the depths of the heart and to become a spontaneous, intimate, and deeply felt reality that lies at the very wellspring of one's attitude and experience of life.

In approaching the Song of Songs, therefore—or another book of Scripture—it is well to "engage" our senses in making contact with the sense-imagery offered to us. However, the senses that are here awakened are not merely natural, bodily senses, but the senses of the spirit, the activity of grace grafted onto the core of our spirit and onto the very senses of our body, elevating them to a higher level, while also surpassing them. These spiritual senses, however, are more "impalpable," less obvious to us, and therefore we can experience the outpouring of God's love into us in this way without even realizing what is going on. And the ways of experiencing God here are also more rich, more diversified, than the bodily senses. For example, we can experience the intimate presence of God, not only by a tangible feeling that he is close to us, by a sense of peace and spontaneous joy, but also by the pain of longing awakened in us which causes us to cry out with the bride: "I am wounded by love!" (Sg 2:5). Though the latter may seem to be an experience of absence, it is really not. It is, rather, an experience of the very infinite tenderness of God touching our soul in its narrowness and dilating us by this touch, making us reach out for the true experience of his love that will be consummated only in eternity.

To pray with Scripture in such a way that its words and images touch, deep within us, the wellsprings of our spiritual senses, is therefore to facilitate this "evangelization" of the heart. To let the echo of God's voice, to allow his impalpable grace, to evoke from within us the deep things that perhaps we have buried over and hidden—this is to allow them to come to the surface in order to at last be permeated by his light and his presence, and therefore made radiant with joy, gratitude, and praise. I want to speak more about this in the following reflection, but to conclude this one I want to quote Arminjon again, as he draws together (in a different place in his commentary) a number of authors from the tradition on precisely this topic:

> Origen is undoubtedly the first to have noticed that, in parallel with the body, the soul also has senses of a sort: "In man," he says quite explicitly, "besides the bodily senses, there are five other senses which need to be exercised;" to wit: sight, smell, taste, hearing and touch, which are properly spiritual and through which the soul has a certain experimental knowledge, diversified according to each sense, of divine things. "Thus," Origen writes, "the soul has a sense of sight to contemplate supernatural objects, a hearing capable of distinguishing voices that do not resound in the air, a taste to savor the living bread come down from heaven, … in the same way, a smell, leading

Paul to speak of the perfume of Jesus, and also a sense of touch, which John had since he told us that he touched with his own hands the Word of God." Following Origen, Gregory of Nyssa says just as clearly: "We have two kinds of senses, those of the body and those of the spirit."

It may seem strange to hear these writers speak of approaching God through the senses of the soul because we practice most often a prayer that is far too abstract and cerebral [isn't this true!]. But if Christ became flesh, and not only Spirit, it was in order to be reached also by all the senses of the soul, which correspond indeed to those of the body, without any possible ambiguity, because they are interiorized, purified, decanted, unified, and, so to speak, spiritualized. ... This is a point that Origen, and after him all the great mystical tradition, has stressed very strongly: "Christ," he comments, "becomes the object of each sense of the soul. He calls himself the true light, to enlighten the eyes of the soul; the Word, to be heard; the bread of life, to be tasted; he is also called oil of anointing and nard because the soul is delighted by the perfume of the Logos. He became the Word made flesh, tangible, substantial, so that the inner man would be able to grasp the Word of life." ... In a similar vein, Saint Ignatius Loyola, who is not generally blamed for giving an excessive place to senses and sensitivity, asks a retreatant, in the meditation on the Incarnation or the nativity, "to sense and taste through smell and taste the infinite sweetness and gentleness of the Divinity." And how rich is the orchestra of the senses that John of the Cross calls to magnify the obscure night of the faith! To underestimate the importance of the spiritual senses in the contemplative experience is to cause grave damage to the self, as Saint Teresa of Avila admits: "It was very bad for me," she says, "to ignore that it was possible to see something with eyes other than those of the body." The painters of icons could teach us much in this respect. Instead of using a human model, as did the painters of the Renaissance in their workshops, in order to paint, for instance, a transfigured Jesus, the icon painters first stayed long hours in inner contemplation, letting the eyes of the soul be slowly penetrated by his face. Thus the icons are at the same time so human and so transcendent.

All the senses of the soul can contribute equally to unite us to God, as Saint Augustine attests in a famous passage of the *Confessions*. This passage of Augustine has, moreover, the great merit of stressing very precisely what separates the experience of the carnal senses (of which he had a certain knowledge before his conversion) from the experience of the spiritual senses: "O God," he asks himself, "what do I love in loving you? It is not the beauty of the bodies, nor their perishable grace, nor the radiance of the light so dear to my eyes, sweet melodies with their varied sounds, sweet smells of flowers, perfumes, aromatic spices, manna, honey nor limbs made for carnal embraces. No, this is not what I love when I love my God... And yet, there is a light, a voice, a perfume, a food, an embrace that I love when I love my God. It is the light, the voice, the perfume, the embrace of the inner man in me, where there shines in my soul a light that is not limited by space, where melodies are heard that time does not drive away, where perfumes are wafting that are not scattered by the wind, where one tastes a food that cannot be devoured by any voracity and embraces that are never sated. This is what I love when I love my God."[8]

ישוע

THE THREE WAYS OF SENSING WHAT CANNOT BE SENSED

Speaking about the "senses of the soul" can perhaps be puzzling for a lot of people. What exactly is being meant by saying that one can see, taste, touch, smell, and hear realities that are impalpable to the bodily senses, but can be perceived in the spiritual realm? Is this just an analogy, by which what is really meant is simply that meditating on God's Word is *like* hearing, *like* tasting, *like* touching? Is the activity of the *mind* being compared with the senses, whereas it is really not sensible at all, but rather intellectual—not a palpable contact of the spirit in a sensible way with reality, but rather an impalpable contact that, by using comparisons drawn from the bodily senses, is made more palatable to our understanding?

Perhaps some examples can help open the way for us to grasp what is being said here. First of all, it is important to note that the spiritual senses can operate in three different ways. First of all, they can operate within the very experience of the bodily senses, the interior "resonance" awakened by our very bodily seeing, feeling, tasting, hearing, or smelling. Second, they can operate directly within themselves, and this occurs when they are touched by God or by other created spirits without the mediation of the bodily senses. Third, they can be awakened and sensitized through the "overflow" of divine grace and mystical contemplation that occurs in the inner sanctuary of our being, which is deeper and more intimate even than the spiritual senses themselves.

The first case is probably the easiest to provide examples for. We need only think, for example, of the way in which our spirit can be profoundly *touched* by listening to a breathtakingly beautiful piece of music. If there were only bodily senses, only the operation of the brain in response to sense stimuli, it would be impossible for us to experience *beauty*. It would, indeed, be impossible for us to get in touch, at all, with *the world of value*. (A value is something that is important and good in itself, simply because *it is*, because it reveals something of the grandeur of God himself, and not merely because it is "good for me," i.e. satisfies one of my desires or appetites.) Animals, who do not have spiritual senses, cannot make contact with value. They live in a mere "environment," in which they relate to all things on the basis of appetite and of the things' relation to the animal itself. In other words, for animals, all is reduced to an attitude of "for me," and is not open to the gratuitous wonder and awe of contact with being "in itself and for itself."

But for human persons, since we are spirit, our attitude bursts beyond a mere "environment" and we experience a much deeper and broader contact with reality—this contact which could be called a contact with the "world of value." In our music example, this contact with the world of value is palpable in the way that our heart dilates on the encounter with beauty, wounded as it is with an unspeakable longing and a mysterious joy. There is "something" mysterious here, something spiritual…something beyond the mere notes of the music itself that is being conveyed to us through the bodily senses. This is the *something* that was referred to by John of the Cross in the stanzas we quoted earlier: the "*I-don't-know-what behind their stammering.*" Here the spiritual hearing is operative directly within, and mediated by, the bodily hearing.

As for the second form of feeling with the spiritual senses—the direct contact of spirit-to-spirit—I can try to provide a couple examples. It is important to note that this is an essential element of what is meant by *the spiritual states of consolation and desolation*. Saint Ignatius of Loyola speaks of these two states in the following way:

> I call it consolation when some interior movement in the soul is caused, through which the soul comes to be inflamed with love of its Creator and Lord; and when it can in consequence love no created thing on the face of the earth in itself, but in the

Creator of them all. Likewise, when it sheds tears that move to love of its Lord, whether out of sorrow for one's sins, or for the Passion of Christ our Lord, or because of other things directly connected with His service and praise. Finally, I call consolation every increase of hope, faith and charity, and all interior joy which calls and attracts to heavenly things and to the salvation of one's soul, quieting it and giving it peace in its Creator and Lord.

I call desolation all the contrary of the third rule [above], such as darkness of soul, disturbance in it, movement to things low and earthly, the unquiet of different agitations and temptations, moving to want of confidence, without hope, without love, when one finds oneself all lazy, tepid, sad, and as if separated from his Creator and Lord. Because, as consolation is contrary to desolation, in the same way the thoughts which come from consolation are contrary to the thoughts which come from desolation. (*Rules 3 and 4 of the First Week*)

In other words, being in a state of consolation or desolation is not merely a mood, caused by physical exhaustion or hunger or nervous tension. Rather, it is truly something that has its origin in the spirit, even if it also overflows into the body. There is a feeling of the presence and the activity of the good spirit or the evil spirit, and this immediately causes in us either an experience of "spiritual dilation," the lifting-up of our spirit closer to God and to the things of God (the increase in faith, hope, and love), or an experience of "spiritual constriction," as our spirit spontaneously recoils in fear and anguish under the touch of the forces of evil which oppress us. The answer in both situations, however, is essentially the same (though if you would like to know in greater depth the ways of responding to and walking through the states of consolation and desolation, I would direct you to the "rules for the discernment of spirits" of Saint Ignatius, or a book that explains them, for example, those of Father Timothy Gallagher). The answer is *to plunge ourselves anew, and more deeply, into the shelter of the Heart of Christ, in which we will not only be protected, but will also be touched anew with grace and dilated into an ever more intimate contact with the Trinity*. This was the advice given by John of the Cross to the experience of temptation. It is not wise to confront the temptation head-on, but rather to simply pass beyond it by making an act of faith, hope, and love—in other words, surrendering ourselves anew into the sheltering embrace of the Trinity, in whom alone we are safe.

But let me return to what I was saying. I said that I would give a couple examples of this "direct" touch of the spiritual senses. When I go into a time of prayer, perhaps I will feel a mysterious peace and restfulness come over me, and I will desire, not to read or meditate or pray the rosary, but simply to rest in this experience. This is an experience of the spiritual senses—perhaps especially the sense of spiritual touch—in which my spirit is being touched and cradled by the Spirit of God. On the other hand, this spiritual touch can also occur, not only between the human spirit and the divine Spirit, but also between two created spirits. For example, it can happen that my heart receives and feels the "resonance" of the heart of another person. Perhaps, for example, I am praying silently in the chapel and another person comes in to pray. As we pray together in silence, I spontaneously begin to experience the "current" of their own prayer surging into my own, as if the prayer of each of us begins to intermingle in the sharing of a single "wavelength." This is the experience of a kind of "spiritual interference," analogous to the way that two radio stations can be heard trying to broadcast on a single wavelength. But, of course, the term "interference" is not really the best here, since such an experience is not a threat, but a great gift—in which I am allowed to feel and hear the beating of another person's heart in their dialogue with God, and to receive and shelter it in some way within the space of my own prayer.

Now let me use one more example of this direct touch of the spiritual senses, which also bridges immediately into speaking about the third way of experiencing these senses: the unmediated touch of God's Being in my innermost heart (the kiss of his mouth!) which then overflows into the spiritual senses. Saint John of the Cross speaks about how the evil spirits, envious of the growing intimacy that a human spirit has with God, will try to distract it and hinder in it the work of the Spirit of God. Whereas God is "drawing" the human person together into a greater unity within themselves—gathering them together from multiplicity and fragmentation into the inner sanctuary of their being—the evil spirits will try to touch the spiritual senses in order to awaken fear, confusion, or panic, and thus to keep the heart on the surface, out of the safe space at the core of their being (where the evil spirits indeed have no access, for here only God dwells in the "holy of holies" of our innermost being). However, as God draws us beyond the grasp of the evil spirits, who would seek to constrain us on the surface of fears, anxieties, and spiritual oppression, we find ourselves reposing, beyond their grasp, within the safety of the Trinity's embrace.

Here our spiritual senses themselves are stilled through the direct contact of the substance of our soul with the substance of the Trinity. John of the Cross calls this substance the "center" of the soul—which is not a spatial center, but rather, as it were, the "apex" of our being where we exist in pure loving relationship with God, where we exist as pure self-reception and self-communication in intimate love. Yet when this recollection into the substance of our soul occurs, even though such a substance-to-substance contact is itself impalpable in this life—sheltered behind the sacred and protective veil of faith, hope, and love—it often nonetheless overflows anew into the spiritual (and even bodily) senses. Thus, if before this experience I was disturbed and oppressed by the attacks of the evil spirits or even by other naturally-caused anxieties, after experiencing this direct heart-touch of God, my whole being is stilled and quieted. The light from the inner sanctuary of my being radiates out to illumine my spiritual gaze; the sound of the sacred hymn of God's love in my most intimate being resounds also in my spiritual hearing; the fragrance of his delectable perfume wafts forth from here into my spiritual smell; the hearty nourishment of the living Bread fills my sense of spiritual taste, and I find myself nourished mysterious from within; the very touch of the Bridegroom makes itself in some way felt, and I am able to exclaim: "His left hand is under my head, and his right arm embraces me!" (Sg 2:6).

ישוע

ARISE, MY BEAUTIFUL ONE

The Bridegroom desires to come and to "evangelize" the most intimate places of my being, irradiating them with the consoling light of his loving presence. The whole path of the bride in response to the loving invitation of her Beloved is, in a way, precisely this: her willingness to lay herself ever more totally and vulnerably before him, so he may gaze upon her with a gaze that is cherishing and affirming, sheltering and protecting. Indeed, she comes to deeply desire to share herself vulnerably with him, for she learns that only in his tender gaze is she truly safe. Opening her vulnerability before the One who loves her is indeed the safest thing that she can do, since with him she is totally reverenced, totally protected—for she is fully seen, known, and loved in her unique beauty, and cradled always in the embrace of his tenderness and love.

Those places in my heart which I still keep hidden in the darkness therefore yearn to come out into the open, to make contact with the light. For when they remain hidden they continually cause anxiety, fear, and lies to well up within me, even if I myself cannot trace these feelings back to their root. But when I am willing to pull the roots up and to expose them to the light—or rather to allow my Bridegroom to unveil them—I find that in these places I am not condemned for my ugliness or failure, but rather am sheltered tenderly in my nakedness and vulnerability. Indeed, I realize that what before appeared to me as sheer darkness, as pure ugliness, is not really so at all. Rather, present within it as the true and deeper reality is something ineffably sacred, something profoundly beautiful, which the gaze of my Beloved both touches and sets free. In the tenderness of his gaze, before which I lay my heart, I find my authentic truth affirmed and liberated.

Indeed, as we will see much more deeply soon, the Bridegroom himself approaches me first, and offers the tenderness of his loving gaze as the "bridge" upon which I can walk, trustingly, into the vulnerability of love. He says to me: "Arise, my love, my dove, my beautiful one…let me see your face, let me hear your voice, for your voice is sweet, and your face is beautiful" (Sg 2:10, 14). However broken, sinful, and shameful I may feel, this is truly how the Bridegroom sees me. And the very vision of my unique beauty draws his Heart spontaneously towards me. He approaches ardently yet tenderly, passionately yet gently, with immense longing yet with infinite respect. He invites, with a tender voice that does not accuse, that does not even plead, that does not chastise or make me feel guilty, and that gives not even a hint of forcing me in any way. Rather, he simply says: "Arise…come…and let me look upon you in your beauty and hear the sweetness of your voice."

And thus, as I come to him, arising from the narrowness of my shame and fear, I begin to experience ever more deeply his coming to me. This indeed is the continual dynamic that unfolds throughout the Song of Songs: the bride feels that her Beloved has gone away and so she arises to search for him, only to realize (ever anew but always the same!) that he has never departed, but rather has been seeking her first, and indeed has taken up his place of perpetual abode within the most intimate depths of her heart. Her very searching is but a response to the mysterious voice of his love within her: "Arise…let me gaze upon you…let me love you."

It is in this way that prayer progresses, ever more intimately, ever more deeply, into a mutual beholding in which Lover and beloved gaze upon each other and rejoice in one another's beauty. It is in this way that their hearts interlace so intimately, so totally, that they become inseparable from one another, woven together in a single reality of love and communion. Ah! But here I am going beyond the opening stanza of the Song and anticipating what shortly follows: this mutual beholding of Bridegroom and bride, their mutual repose in the intimacy of a single embrace, their ecstatic joy in the movement of mutual surrender.

Let me therefore bring these reflections on the introductory stanza to a close, preparing, like a diver ready to plunge into the water, to jump into the unspeakable beauty of this most holy Song, which we have already begun to glimpse, and which, hopefully, has begun to unveil before us the ravishing Beauty of our divine Beloved, who invites us unceasingly to intimacy with himself.

FIRST POEM

THE WINTER OF EXILE

IN THE VERY PLACE OF MY DARKNESS, HE UNITES ME TO HIMSELF

We have now finished looking at the opening stanza of the Song of Songs, which provides a kind of "panorama" view of everything that will follow. In this opening stanza we saw laid out before us, as it were, the whole trajectory of the bride's journey—of the unique journey of each one of us—from the first kiss of God received at conception, indeed from the redeeming kiss of Baptism that betroths us to the heavenly Bridegroom, unto the definitive consummation of this union in the endless kiss of eternity.

Immediately after this the scene shifts before our eyes, and we witness a bride in exile, longing for her Bridegroom but unsure of how to encounter him. She cries out:

I am dark but lovely,
O daughters of Jerusalem,
like the tents of Kedar,
like the curtains of Solomon.
Do not gaze at me because I am swarthy,
because the sun has burned me.
My mother's sons were angry with me,
and they made me keeper of their vineyards;
if only I had kept my own!
(Sg 1:5-6)

Here we can hear the cry of exiled Israel, mourning in the sorrow of her slavery—as she is made to keep the vineyard of "her mother's sons," that is, her Chaldean brothers who have taken her into captivity. She recalls the blessed time when she was once betrothed to the Lord God as his one spouse. She recalls the loving kindness with which he liberated her from the slavery of Egypt and drew her into the wilderness of Sinai to espouse her to himself, and indeed admitted her into the promised land of intimacy and marital union. At that time she knew and experienced her beauty, her loveliness. But now she looks upon herself and calls herself "dark," burned as she is by the hot desert sun. And yet even in her darkness she is lovely; even in her blackness she is beautiful. If she looks like the blackened tents of the tribe of Kedar, wandering as a nomad through the desert of this life, she also acknowledges (how could she forget!) that she is also lovely like the curtains of Solomon's temple.

In these words of the bride we can see very vividly the multiple layers of meaning present within the Song of Songs. This woman crying out in the darkness of her exile is simultaneously the chosen people of Israel, the Church of Christ on pilgrimage in this world, and each individual soul—drawn out of slavery, through the Red Sea, and into the desert of purification and espousal. She is now journeying with the flocks toward the definitive place where there will be endless rest and perfect delight, where the aridity of the desert will be no more, and all will be a garden of intimacy and never-ending nuptial union.

Israel experienced this movement physically, but underwent a spiritual journey that corresponded in some way with the external events of the Exodus. And yet even after entering the promised land, because the fullness of redemption was not yet accomplished, she found herself unfaithful to the covenant and taken back into exile from her land. She found herself again in the wilderness, crying out for the Bridegroom she could not see. Thus she cries out to her Beloved:

Tell me, you whom my heart loves,
where you pasture your flock,
where you make it lie down at noon;
for why should I be like one who wanders
beside the flocks of your companions?
(Sg 1:7)

Is this not true also, in a way, of the Church of Christ, who finds herself trudging through the desert of this earthly existence? Yes, she has already been united with the divine Bridegroom in the definitive betrothal of the New Covenant; she already has the pledge of everlasting union, and yet she does not yet see her Beloved face to face. She is not yet able to lie down with him "at noon," and to repose in the full experience of his tenderness and love. In other words, she still walks at night, or perhaps in the morning, but does not yet experience the full and endless light of the eternal Day.

"I am dark but lovely…" Does not every heart wish that it could say this? But perhaps it feels that it would be a lie. "I am dark; yes. My sins have blackened me; the things that others have done to me have defiled me; and the way that the longing of my heart to be beautiful, to be seen as beautiful, has not been fulfilled, is itself a sign that I am not truly so." O lovely bride of God, do not say this of yourself, for it is a lie! However darkened you may be, you are indeed the loveliest of all in the sight of God! Yes, say that you are dark, that you have been blackened, but recognize that this is not your true color, and that the deepest beauty within you has in no way been destroyed, and that it indeed still shines through the darkness, enough to ravish any heart that can truly see!

The bride cries out, "Do not gaze at me, because I am swarthy, because the sun has burned me!" She fears the gaze that will only see the surface—and indeed will see only certain aspects of the surface—and will turn away in dismissiveness. One look, and you don't want to look again! Is that how it is? But the maiden companions of the bride do look at her, and they do not call her ugly, they do not call her blackened; they rather praise her as "the loveliest of women" (Sg 1:8). Precious heart, reading these words…do you recognize that, in the eyes of our loving God (and remember that what God sees is the truth!), in his eyes you are indeed the loveliest?

Yes, you have not tended your own vineyard, you have not cared for the inner sanctuary of beauty within you—this virgin-space within your heart created for intimacy with God alone. And thus you have found yourself in exile on the surface of your being, caught up in multiplicity, perhaps trying to foster external beauty, to put on a show, or simply hiding yourself from the piercing gaze of others. You have been enslaved to tend the vineyards of others, seeking for the love you desire where it cannot be found, and thus your face has been burned—burned with sin, burned with misunderstanding, burned with wounds and insecurities. But dearly beloved, precious bride! Only cry out to the One whom your soul loves, and who loves you, and he will answer, leading you into the sacred space of intimacy, where you will touch and experience your virginal beauty, as he touches you tenderly in this place!

Yes, and it is thus that she cries out to the One whom her souls loves, calling out to him to show her to the place of intimacy and rest. And in response, the Bridegroom, the Beloved of her heart, for the first time in the Song, makes his voice heard:

I compare you, my love,
to my mare, harnessed to Pharaoh's chariots.
Your cheeks are lovely with ornaments,
your neck with strings of jewels.
We will make you ornaments of gold,
studded with silver.
(Sg 1:9)

In other words: My love, though you are harnessed like a mare to the enslaving chariots of Egypt—to the fears, wounds, insecurities, and sins which keep you from surrendering yourself entirely to me—you are *my* mare, my dearly beloved and precious one. Thus even in the "ornaments" of slavery, the "strings of jewels" that cause you such pain and anxiety, I see and admire your immense loveliness. And I reach out to touch this loveliness, in the very place where you need my love the most, to awaken it and to set it free, that it may radiate forth from within and permeate all! Yes, we will make you "ornaments of gold, studded with silver," we—the Father, Son, and Holy Spirit—will transform the very burdens of your slavery into the space of intimacy and grace! And this is what immediately happens! He needs only to touch her in the place of her woundedness—in that deeply vulnerable place where she thirsts, naked and defenseless, for love—and he immediately draws her into the intimacy of union. Thus she cries out:

While the king was on his couch,
my nard gave forth its fragrance.
My Beloved is to me a sachet of myrrh,
that lies between my breasts.
My Beloved is to me a cluster of henna blossoms
in the vineyards of Engedi.
(Sg 1:12-14)

What is happening here? The Bridegroom has revealed his very presence "between the breasts" of the bride, that is, in her most intimate heart. And when she senses him here, tenderly loving her, her nard gives forth its fragrance—her whole self exudes as a loving gift surrendered to the One whom she loves, and whose loves enfolds her on every side. Yes, as Paul Claudel says of the bride in this most intimate encounter:

> In this embrace, under this strong, patient, penetrating, intelligent demand, the soul feels itself surrendering and dilating little by little, and its intimate essence, so long repressed, compressed, and hardened, is unfolded and breathed out. ... My nard, she says, that which is in me the most intimate, the most personal…the testimony that my very self gives spontaneously through the means of this vital spirit torn away from my flesh.[9]

And yet in her very act of loving surrender, as her nard yields up its fragrance—as her unique and unrepeatable beauty offers itself to the One who alone is worthy of it—she immediately experiences the very fragrance of her Beloved surrendered to her! She experiences his presence as a "sachet of myrrh" emitting such a powerful fragrance, or a "cluster of henna blossoms." His fragrance is so powerful, his ravishing love so deep, that it both overwhelms her with its intensity and yet gently touches and pervades her senses and her entire being with its delicacy.

And what then? Smelling, feeling, and breathing give place to sight—to the joy of mutual beholding, as the Bridegroom looks tenderly into the eyes of his bride, and she looks into his eyes in return. The

Bridegroom says to his bride: "Here you are, my love! Behold, you are beautiful, your eyes are doves." And she replies spontaneously: "Behold, you are beautiful, my Beloved, and how delightful" (Sg 1:15-16). In their eyes all is communicated, all is shared. Though they express this amazement in words—this joy in the beauty of one another—what is communicated through their eyes is beyond words, beyond expression. Here his Heart pours itself out into her heart, and her heart surrenders itself back to him—two hearts beating together as one in an endless symphony of praise and mutual delight.

ישוע

THE MOST INTIMATE EMBRACE

What a beautiful union we glimpsed in our previous reflection! There is so much to say about this loving and intimate encounter between Bridegroom and bride—about their mutual beholding, their shared surrender, their blessed repose—and yet also so little to say, since the mystery surpasses expression in speech, and is known most fully in the reverence of silent and contemplative awe. To preface what I want to say, however, let me express shortly the "heart-strings" that these sacred words of the Song are seeking to pluck, so they may resound under the touch of the divine Bridegroom.

There are two things for which each human heart longs more than for anything else: to be *seen* and to be *held*. And yet these two desires —both on the natural, physical level, as well as on the level of the spirit which the body itself simply mediates—are but expressions of the desire *to be known and loved as I am, and to be welcomed into a constant and enduring intimacy with another, into the shelter of their love.* But whenever I experience this tenderness of sheltering love offered to me—enveloping me completely both through the gaze and the arms of another—I also spontaneously experience the deep desire to offer to the other the same love that they have offered to me. In a word, while my own beauty is revealed to me through their loving gaze and my own heart dilates freely within the safety of their embrace, I also come to be touched, wounded, and ravished by the beauty of the other which I come to see and experience in their very love offered to me. Thus I yearn to offer to them what I myself have received: *to receive and shelter them, in turn, within my own loving gaze and tender embrace.*

How true this desire is even on the natural level, between two human hearts that encounter in authentic mutual understanding and reverent love! And yet how much more true it is, how much more intimate and profound, when the One with whom my heart falls madly in love is God himself, the divine Bridegroom who sees me completely and, in seeing me completely, loves me totally, sheltering me without ceasing in the tenderness of his embrace! In authentic love, in this most tender of encounters between two hearts, there is a mutual "drawing," in which each is drawn near to the other by the very love that attracts them, and also draws the other close in turn. This is manifest both in the "magnetism" of the eyes which invites to a deeper and more intimate gazing, an interlacing of hearts that occurs through a sharing of gazes, as well as through the very embrace in which both are drawn into proximity with one another, holding each other close.

To let myself be drawn into intimacy with another person—whether it be a human person or the very Person of the divine Bridegroom himself—is to let myself be drawn into *mystery*. And mystery always surpasses my ability to grasp and control; rather, it is a matter of surrendering my control through the ardent thirst for a defenseless and vulnerable union with the Beloved, in which two hearts beat together as one, where neither grasps nor controls, but both simply belong to one another in mutual surrender. Yes, mystery is something in which I must participate, something within which I literally must allow myself to be intimately wrapped. Knowledge of God, therefore, is not something that can be manufactured, but rather flowers in the ever deeper and more trusting nakedness of my heart to the gaze and the embrace of God, even as he approaches me in a Mystery that I can never grasp and fully comprehend. Rather, my ever-deepening knowledge of him comes about precisely through allowing myself to be drawn into his Mystery, by letting myself be enfolded and cradled in his embrace. It is only then—not standing-back and analyzing as a scientist would in a laboratory, but letting myself be swept up into the song of eternal Love that ever surpasses—that I will truly come to know, feel, and experience God. Then I will truly "taste and see how good the Lord is," and will "be inebriated with the goodness of his house and flooded with the torrent of his delight" (Ps 34:8; 36:8).

This divine embrace of knowledge and love is a mystery within which I participate and which I know not from a distant perspective, but precisely through intimacy—the intimacy of communion, of friendship, of a hug…an embrace…a spiritual kiss. This is not something I can grasp, take, or own for my private use. The reality of the hug itself requires that I not only include another person but expose myself through open arms to embrace them and thus to draw our two hearts closer together.

And here in this intimate space, indeed, *do not the acceptance of the other and the gift of oneself in some way become one?* Let me quote some words written by a friend of mine in a different context, in which this reality of spiritual embrace, of mutual drawing into intimacy, is beautifully expressed:

> "Here in this intimate space, indeed, do not the acceptance of the other and the gift of oneself in some way become one?" How true this is in the embrace of friendship! It is not difficult to call to mind hugs that have become things; such as when the hug becomes obligatory as a quick greeting or salutation. There's the quick hug where each person simply taps the other on the back without touching their chest or stomach, there's the side hug with its timid and rather awkward nature, and (on the flip side) there is the overbearing hug where one person nearly smothers the other in an embrace that is not opened to be received and not reciprocated with the same intensity. The embrace of friendship, however, has such tenderness, such mutual understanding, such yearning. The embrace is an embodiment of the union of two hearts that pulse and throb together. Often preceded by a knowing gaze and gentle smile, I open my arms wide to expose my heart to you as you do the same for me. Completely defenseless, unguarded, and exposed, it is an invitation to draw near and to be drawn near. A mutual invitation and movement that sweeps each person together into a single embrace. Each is pulled closer by the other, not to own and grasp, but to give of oneself even more, while receiving the gift of the other in the same embrace. I feel your heart as you feel mine, I feel your chest breathing as you feel mine, and I am not simply holding you nor you simply holding me…rather, we are held, we are braced, together in the divine em-brace.

Do not these words pluck the "heart-strings" within us, reverberating in us and getting us in touch with our deep longing for precisely such an intimate embrace? The embrace of human friendship, when two hearts are united within the single divine embrace, is such a blessed gift. And yet this gift itself flows forth from the divine embrace itself, which already perfectly cradles each friend, bestowing the blessedness of union with the fullness of God's Mystery, with the pulsating love of his Heart and with the tenderness of his gaze. It is in the pulsation of this divine Heart, within the shelter of this loving gaze, that friends can then behold one another truly, bathed in the light of God's own vision, and in which they can draw one another close into a shared embrace, breathing together and sharing a single heartbeat, within the Heart in which they are, and always will be, inseparably united.

In the light of these words on the embrace of friendship—in the echo of the reverberation of our deep longing to be seen and to be held, to see and to hold—let us turn back to the Song of Songs. Let us try to see how this mystery reaches it deepest blossoming in the union between the Bridegroom and his precious bride—between Christ and each one of us, uniquely and unrepeatably loved. As the Bridegroom transforms the chains of my burdened slavery into ornaments of joy and love, into a shimmering necklace of gratitude and praise, so too does my loneliness and longing pass into the experience of communion. Or rather, the very openness of my thirst for happiness and love—the hollow cavern of my yearning heart, dilated by love and crying out for my Beloved—is filled with the radiant beauty of his intoxicating presence: "While the King was on his couch, my nard gave forth its fragrance" (Sg 1:12). And this very couch on which the King rests is "between my breasts," in other words, on my own heart. In this most intimate place, the Bridegroom listens to, and feels, my own heartbeat without ceasing, and such a sound brings him joy and gladness. But as I let him listen to the beating of my heart—a heart made for him and beating, therefore, for him alone—he also presses me tenderly against his own breast and lets me hear and feel the throbbing of his own Heart, ever sounding its hymn of perfect tenderness and love.

Thus I experience the closest and most intimate embrace of the divine Bridegroom, as "his left hand is under my head, and his right arm embraces me" (Sg 2:6). In other words, he is cradling me in his arms, somewhat like a mother would cradle her infant as she nurses her at the breast. "His left hand is under my head": he upholds my head within his own hand, such that I can say with the psalmist: "You, O Lord, are a shield about me, my glory, and the One who lifts my head" (Ps 3:3). I need not protect myself, I need not lift up my own head through my own efforts; rather, I feel the gentleness of his hand upholding my head, as he pours into me the torrent of his goodness, just as a mother pours out the nourishment of her own life, from her breast, into her child. Yes, and just as he upholds my head with his left hand, so I can rest peacefully in his arms, for "his right arm embraces me," wrapped around my body and holding me tight and close to himself. Thus my heart is close to his Heart, as he feels my heart beating and I feel his, as he feels the rising and falling of my chest as I breathe, and I in turn feel his breathing too. What greater intimacy is there than this, what greater unity, what greater sharing of what is deepest and most precious?

Yes, in the intimacy of the Bridegroom's love I experience the true and everlasting fulfillment of my two deepest desires: to be seen and to be held. For this intimate embrace—in which our bodies are close to one another, communicating and mediating the very gift of the inner heart, the very breath of life—is preceded by a shared gaze of love, in which the Bridegroom says to me, "Here you are, my love! Behold, you are beautiful!" and I respond to him, "How beautiful you are, my Beloved, and how delightful!" (Sg 1:15-16). Or indeed, it would be more accurate to say that, with such a Lover as this, seeing and holding, gazing and embracing are not mutually exclusive. He can hold me close to his breast, his left hand under my head and his right arm embracing me, while simultaneously gazing lovingly into my eyes.

Jesus, my Beloved, my Life, my All…! Let me ever allow you to gaze upon me in this way, and let me ever gaze, in response, into the infinite wells of your own tender eyes, seeing pour forth from within them the unspeakable goodness, kindness, and delight that you bear in your Heart for me! And yet let me not only read the beauty of your Heart through your eyes, let me not only experience the sheltering and encompassing safety of your cherishing gaze… Rather, as you gaze upon me, so may you hold me close to yourself, that this very Heart, seen in our mutual gaze, may also be felt, beating, throbbing, pulsating, as it is pressed up close against my own—two hearts beating together, unceasingly, a single hymn of our shared love and our unbreakable unity.

ישוע

EVEN AS I LOOK UPON YOU, YOU ARE WITHIN ME

In my enthusiasm to explain the intimate embrace shared by the Bridegroom and the bride, I have perhaps gotten a little ahead of myself in explaining the text! On the other hand, it is probably good to have seen the "big picture" of the narrative unfolding before our eyes: how the Bridegroom, touching his beloved in the very depths of her woundedness, draws her out of exile and into intimacy with himself. And he draws her through the tenderness of his own loving gaze, which is thrown like a bridge on which she can walk into the vulnerability of self-surrender; he draws her out through the gentleness of his touch, his spiritual embrace in which he tenderly draws her close and presses her to his own breast, so that she may be cradled within his embrace and experience the joy of his love.

We have therefore seen, or at least glimpsed, the blessed repose of union for which the heart of the bride thirsts, and which the Bridegroom thirsts even more to bestow, and indeed which he himself yearns to experience by welcoming his bride into his own sheltering arms. The Song describes this movement of mutual surrender as the exuding of the perfume of Lover and beloved: the nard of the bride giving forth its fragrance, while itself being evoked by the inebriating fragrance of her Beloved, who rests upon her heart like a sachet of myrrh or a cluster of henna blossoms. As she inhales the ineffable sweetness of his scent, his own love permeates her senses and her very being, and draws forth spontaneously from within her the fragrance of her own unique beauty, made a gift for the One whom her soul loves.

Then this imagery of the fragrance—the profound permeation of the sense of smell—gives way to the joy of *sight*, of mutual beholding of Lover and beloved. As their eyes interlock in a sustained gaze of tenderness and delight, their hearts themselves pour forth and are knitted together in a single joy, a single embrace of ineffable love. And both exult with joy at this single experience: they rejoice in the beauty of the one whom they love, and whom they are graciously allowed to behold in this shared gaze of vulnerability and surrender. "Here you are!" the Bridegroom exclaims, "you are beautiful!" This "here you are" (which is what the Hebrew text literally says) so wonderfully, so touchingly, expresses his awe and delight at the woman whom he is allowed to look upon, just like the words of Adam upon seeing Eve, pronounced in the Garden of Eden before his gaze was ever marred by sin: "This at last is bone of my bones and flesh of my flesh!" (Gen 2:23).

And, as he looks deeply into the eyes of his precious and beloved one, what does the Bridegroom add? He says that "your eyes are doves." Notice, he doesn't say, "your eyes are *like* doves." He is not comparing; he is simply stating what he sees. But these are not literal, physical doves; rather, her eyes, glistening and dancing under the shelter of his own loving gaze, and awakened by the glance of his own eyes, are pure and limpid, meek and humble, innocent and modest as doves. In one respect, we could say that these are Spirit-eyes that the Bridegroom sees in his beloved—for the Spirit is the true dove, the harbinger of peace after the flood of purification, the bond of intimacy that descends on Jesus as he rises from the water after his baptism in the Jordan. And now Jesus sees in the eyes of his bride—in my eyes—the reflection of the Spirit's presence. He sees the very yearning of the Spirit bursting forth from within my own longing gaze. And in my eyes he discerns the deepest prayer of my heart, a prayer that is awakened, sheltered, and carried by the presence of the Holy Spirit, so that it may find itself cradled in the very intimacy of the Bridegroom himself: "The Spirit helps us in our weakness; for we do not know how to pray as we ought, but the Spirit himself intercedes for us with sighs too deep for words. And he who searches the hearts of men knows what is the mind of the Spirit, because the Spirit intercedes for the holy ones according to the will of God" (Rom 8:26-27).

What this means is that my encounter with the loving gaze of my divine Bridegroom is not an encounter with something that is merely *outside of me*. Yes, this gaze is radically other, radically new and surprising in its depth and intensity; and yet at the same time I already bear this gaze etched into the depths of my heart, and it seeks to burst forth from within my eyes and to make contact with its source. Thus my encounter with God's love is never merely an in-breaking into myself from without, but an encounter between *the grace within me* and *the grace outside of me*, as these two meet and intermingle in the space of intimate communication between my Beloved and I—this space which is the very Holy Spirit himself, the Gaze, the Kiss, the Breath of Love who is shared between us and who unites us.

The bride, in response to the loving exclamation of her Beloved, also comments on his beauty in turn. But she speaks in her own unique way: "Behold, you are beautiful, my Beloved, and delightful!" She does not exclaim, "here you are," for he has already done so. In his words, "here you are," the Bridegroom has already opened up the sacred and safe space of their mutual encounter. In saying "here you are," in a way, the Bridegroom is saying, "Here we are, you and I together, and you can be certain that you are sheltered in the safety of my loving gaze." Thus there is no need for the bride to say the same, to exclaim "here you are," for her own recognition of his presence is contained within his prior recognition of her—indeed, within his cradling of her presence within his own gentle and abiding presence. Their mutual presence, in other words, is already melding together into intimacy—their "I" and "You" intermingling into the "We" of communion.

Therefore she simply says, "Behold, you are beautiful, my Beloved!" How bold and confident she is to call the God of hosts her beloved! And yet there is no name that fits him better than this…for he is the One who is truly known only in being truly loved, and yet who is truly loved only because he is first the perfect Lover! And she adds: "and how delightful." In this she seems to be commenting on the way in which this beauty of her Beloved, rather than just merely remaining outside of her, an object to be looked upon in contemplative wonder, is also a reality that enters into her and permeates her being, becoming her own and filling her with delight and delectation. Is this not, after all, an essential characteristic of the beauty of God? It can never remain merely "outside," to be looked at from a distance. Rather, the moment it is glimpsed, it enters within, it takes up its abode within our heart, pervading our whole being with the ineffable sweetness of the One who cannot be contained but who contains all things within himself. Yes, it is indeed the case that whenever we glimpse the love of God and his beauty approaching us, it is just as true that it is welling up from within us and making itself felt "from the inside out."

The bride, again, has already known and felt this when she exclaimed that her Beloved was a sachet of myrrh and a cluster of henna blossoms between her breasts, resting in the most intimate place of her heart. And now she exclaims that the same is true even in their mutual beholding. This gaze of love, in which eyes are locked in a ceaseless interchange of grateful and contemplative wonder, occurs simultaneously with the intimacy of embrace in which both Lover and beloved hold one another, living in the shelter of each other's most intimate heart.

ישוע

THE BED OF VIRGINAL CREATION

I have said that, in this sacred encounter between the Bridegroom and the bride, *smell* gives way to *sight* and sight gives way to *touch*. And yet this very perfume of her Beloved is smelled only because it is first felt, as he rests upon her heart and cradles her in his arms. Is not the love of this divine Bridegroom, indeed, something which surpasses the grasp of any single sense (whether physical or spiritual) while also making itself known through all of them together? To feel him is to see him, to smell him is to taste him, to taste him is to hear him. This is because the touch of his love is truly deeper—it occurs in a deeper place—than any of the senses themselves, and is felt by the senses only as it overflows from this sacred virgin-space at the core of my being. Here, in my innermost heart, all of my spiritual senses are unified at their root. This heart—which is what I refer to when I say

"I"—is the indivisible core of my being where I surpass all multiplicity in the unity of my personal identity. It is this place where, as I said, I am pure self-reception and self-communication before God, where I am pure relationship with the Trinity because he is always pure relationship with me.

Indeed, in this virginal-space at the core of my being, my three "spiritual faculties"—my *mind, will,* and *affectivity* (emotion)—are unified in a single reality. And this single reality is the direct, unmediated, and "intuitive" contact of my spirit with reality. When I touch God in this place, therefore, I am not merely thinking about him (with my mind); I am not merely choosing him (with my will); neither am I merely feeling the resonance of his love (with my affectivity or emotion). Rather, all three of these spiritual faculties of mind, will, and affectivity are unified in a single experience of *my direct heart-contact with the beauty and love that approach me and touch me so tenderly and yet so powerfully.* Is this not true, indeed, even on the natural level, when I am deeply moved by an encounter with beauty—whether it be in nature, or music, or another person? The "distance" between me and the other breaks down, and I am no longer reasoning about the experience at arm's length; neither am I deliberately choosing to love or respond to the other; neither am I having a merely affective experience of delight, or attraction, or admiration.

Rather, my *mind* is totally "harnessed" in a direct and spontaneous contact with the other; and in this way my "knowing" becomes identical with my loving. I know through love and to the degree that I love. This is the fullest activity of my mind, an activity which is not abstract, which is not parceled out into logical steps, but which is rather the naked touch of my mind with the one whose beauty touches and ravishes my heart.

The same is true with my *will*. The highest exercise of my freedom, the full blossoming of my power of choice, is not made when I stand at a distance and choose between two possible options. It rather occurs when I allow my will to be "gripped" by the innate attraction and power of true spiritual beauty, goodness, and truth, which lifts me up outside of myself and dilates my will to act with a greater freedom than I have ever known before.

The same is true for my *affectivity*. My emotional responses to the realities in my life, spontaneous as they are, cannot be manufactured by me. They are rather evoked by the true values that I encounter, and they are authentic insofar as they truly correspond with what these values deserve. For example, in witnessing an act of heroic virtue, my proper emotional response is admiration and gratitude; in encountering one of my suffering brothers and sisters, my proper response is compassion and pity. In my direct encounter with the beauty of another—and ultimately with the beauty of the divine Beloved—my affectivity is so harnessed, so lifted up, that it offers a super-response to what so intimately touches me, a response of unified reverence, gratitude, tenderness, desire, and humility which can only go by the name of *love*.

This is what the ineffable beauty of the divine Bridegroom evokes in me, as he tenderly touches me in the most intimate, virginal place of my heart. Here we can understand more deeply the words of Paul Claudel that I quoted above:

> In this embrace, under this strong, patient, penetrating, intelligent demand, the soul feels itself surrendering and dilating little by little, and its intimate essence, so long repressed, compressed, and hardened, is unfolded and breathed out. ... My nard, she says, that which is in me the most intimate, the most personal...the testimony that my very self gives spontaneously through the means of this vital spirit torn away from my flesh.

After this exclamation of the Bridegroom and bride as they behold one another's beauty, after this mutual surrender in the delectable perfume that each is for the other, the bride says: "All green is our bed," and the Bridegroom immediately responds: "The beams of our house are of cedar, the paneling of cypress" (Sg 1:17). What is the significance of this, and what are the "bed" and the "house" to which they are referring? Clearly this is the bed of marital union. And yet this union is utterly chaste, utterly virginal, free from any concupiscent passion—while burning with an ardor and a passion much deeper, if also much more restrained—for it is simply *the mutual communication of hearts effected through the tenderness of their mutual beholding, in which the innermost spirit of each is communicated to the other totally through the very flesh, made a virginal gift for the beloved.*

The bride says that their bed is green—and we will soon see that she is compared to the flowers that spring up from the green earth. She is, in other words, the feminine creation in its inherent receptivity to the divine gift (manifest in the rain that pours from heaven or the seed that is implanted in the soil). And yet, much more, she is the human heart, gathering up in herself the whole of creation, making herself a receptive space, a space of virginal and bridal love, for the outpouring of God's love incarnate in Christ. Therefore, the "bed" that she is offering to her Beloved is nothing but the verdant pasture of her own being; she offers herself as a sheltering space in which he may come to lie, in order to consummate his marriage with humanity.

How can we not think here of the Virgin Mary—in whom each one of us can also discern the contours of our own unique intimacy with God? As Saints Augustine and Gregory the Great said: "The bed of the Bridegroom was the womb of the Virgin. For in this virginal womb they united together, the Bridegroom and the Bride, the Bridegroom Word and the Bride flesh." "When, in the mystery of the Incarnation, the heavenly King celebrated the wedding of his Son by giving him Holy Church as a bride, the womb of Mary served as a nuptial bed for the Bridegroom" (quoted in Arminjon, p. 135).

While gratefully accepting this bed offered to him by the bride, the Bridegroom immediately speaks of the bed that he himself creates: "the beams of our house are of cedar, the paneling of cypress." In other words: Even though you, my bride, can only offer me the virgin earth to be my resting place—and I delight in the beauty and simplicity of this gift—I myself will offer to you a sheltered house, the temple of my divine presence, the Holy of Holies, to be our meeting-place and the space of our union.

Here we see very vividly how the bride is Israel, offering to God the very earth of the Holy Land to be his resting place and the bed of their union (this Holy Land which was itself first his gift to her!). But God comes to this Land and he builds for himself a house, a temple, into which he admits the one whom he loves, drawing her into communion with himself. Thus, when the bride exclaims, "The King has brought me into his chambers," she is referring to his temple, and to the holiest place of the temple, where the divine presence dwells.

How easy it is, however, to pass beyond this imagery and into the more enduring, more rich realities of Christ and the Church, of Christ and every individual soul! For where, now, is the true tabernacle of God's presence among us, in "the house of cedar with paneling of cypress?" Where is it that the Bridegroom unites himself to us in an everlasting marriage bond, giving his very Body and Blood and uniting us to himself in the eternal covenant? God no longer needs a physical temple to contain his divine presence, for the Church is the new temple "built of living stones" (1 Pet 2:5). And indeed this Church is the very Bride and Body of Christ, the space opened within his Risen Flesh where each one of us can come to dwell, made one with him in the mystery of a single life and love. Therefore, wherever the Eucharist is offered and received, there the Bridegroom unites with his bride. Wherever the Eucharist is given and accepted, I am offering the virgin earth of my spirit, my heart, my body as a bed on which my Beloved can repose, and I in turn am allowing him to welcome me into the House of the Father, where we, together, make our home, already now in the shadows of this life, and, at the final consummation, in the full light of the eternal Day.

ישוע

IN THE SHADOW OF HIS LOVE

After speaking of the "green bed" of creation that she willingly offers to her Beloved, the bed which, so touchingly, is described as "*ours*," the bride then says:

I am the rose of Sharon,
the lily of the valleys.

And her Bridegroom responds:
As a lily among thorns,
so is my love among maidens.
(Sg 2:1-2)

Now the precious bride is being compared, and indeed comparing herself, not only to the green earth, carpeted bright in the springtime as a resting place for the Bridegroom, but to the most beautiful and delicate flowers of the Holy Land. Scholars seem to think that the "rose of Sharon," as this has traditionally been translated, is a bright red tulip-like flower, which blossoms prolifically in the hills of Sharon, and the "lily of the valleys" is a blue hyacinth. Thus, the bride is comparing herself to flowers that blanket the Holy Land and transform it into a dance of beautiful colors, red and blue swaying on a background of green.

The Bridegroom takes up this refrain and intensifies it. It is as if he says: You are not only the rose of Sharon, the lily of the valleys, but for me you are utterly unique, "a lily among thorns." We have already glimpsed how often, how constantly the Bridegroom reminds his bride that she is his "only one," as if he never tires of telling her this, and never tires of hearing it himself. Of course, here too our mind can go immediately to the Virgin Mary, who was told by her cousin Elizabeth, "blessed are you among women" (Lk 1:42). And this is not a wrong impulse to follow, for she is indeed a lily among thorns, immaculate in the midst of a world marred by sin. She is the "flawless" one, born so from the very womb of her mother (cf. Sg 4:7; 6:9). And yet Mary was given this great gift, not in order to separate her from all of humanity, as if her brightness would then eclipse our own light and dim us in the eyes of God. The opposite is really the truth. What God has worked so lovingly in the Virgin Mary has opened up and intensified his activity in each one of us, and the graces he has poured out upon her are intended to flow freely into us. Saint Thérèse understood this well when she wrote of Mary:

> She is sometimes described as unapproachable, whereas she should be represented as easy of imitation. She is more Mother than Queen. I have heard it said that her splendor eclipses that of all the saints as the rising sun makes all the stars disappear. It sounds so strange. That a Mother should take away the glory of her children! I think quite the reverse. I believe that she will greatly increase the splendor of the elect... Our Mother Mary... How simple her life must have been.[10]

"How simple her life must have been..." Are we comfortable with this? To think of our Virgin Mother as simple and ordinary? For indeed she was, and is, a "little one" in the eyes of the world, and yet infinitely precious in the eyes of God. Her greatness, her nobility, her beauty does not consist in external feats of greatness that sparkle in the eyes of the world, or in being separated from the mass of humanity. Rather, her greatness is simply the greatness of love—of God's love within her and tenderly enveloping her, which evokes and sustains her own love in response. It is the greatness of being simply a green bed for the heavenly Bridegroom to lay down and rest, a flower springing from the earth and offering its beauty and fragrance, undimmed, to the One whom her soul loves.

And in this way Mary is not distant from any of us. Indeed, it is not holiness which separates and creates division. It is sin alone which divides, sin alone which creates estrangement and misunderstanding. Holiness and love always unite. Therefore, the Virgin Mary is intimately more close to each one of us than we can imagine; she is indeed closer to the aching heart of every sinner than the hearts of sinners are to one another. This is because her purity allows her to understand sin, and the heart of the sinner, more than the sinner does himself. She is able, as it were, to enter into the abode of darkness without her light being eclipsed—for she is always cradled in the undying light of God. Therefore, from the heart of her purity and innocence, she intimately understands our burdens, our wounds, our darkness. For when she lost Jesus in the temple in his adolescence, was she not able to cry out: "I am dark but lovely"? When she stood at the foot of his Cross, was she not able to say: "I am black but beautiful"? As Georges Bernanos has so beautifully said of her:

> The eyes of Our Lady are the only real child-eyes that have ever been raised to our shame and sorrow. ... they are not indulgent —for there is no indulgence without something of bitter expe-

rience—they are eyes of gentle pity, wondering sadness, and with something more in them, never yet known or expressed, something that makes her younger than sin, younger than the race from which she sprang, and though a mother, by grace, Mother of all graces, our little youngest sister.

Mary is our "little youngest sister" because she is "younger than sin," younger than Eve who grew old by eating of the fruit of false maturity that God had warned her not to eat. And if Mary is younger than Eve—indeed, if she is the New Eve in whom God restores what was lost by the first sin—then Jesus is younger than Adam, the New Adam in whom our race is renewed and made young again. Indeed, the Song of Songs itself expresses this parallelism between the tree in the Garden of Eden and the tree of intimacy between Bridegroom and bride—in other words, the tree of the Cross. For in the verses that immediately follow, the bride says:

As an apple tree among the trees of the orchard,
so is my Beloved among young men.
In his longed-for shade I am seated
and his fruit is sweet to my taste.
He has taken me to his banqueting house,
and the host that overwhelms me is his love!
Sustain me with raisins,
restore me with apples;
for I am wounded by love!
His left hand is under my head,
and his right arm embraces me.
(Sg 2:3-6)

How rich these verses are in imagery referring to the Paschal Mystery: to the Eucharist, Cross, and Resurrection of Jesus Christ! Ah yes…how much more deeply, now, we understand the depths of intimacy which we glimpsed in our previous reflections on this most intimate of embraces! The bride has offered the virginal creation for her Bridegroom-God to come and to dwell. She has offered the verdant pasture of her being to him, and surrendered her fragrance and beauty as a flower to the One she loves. And in response what does her Beloved do? He welcomes her into the shelter of his shade, protecting her, as it were, "under the shadow of his wings" (Ps 91:4). Now he becomes the one with eyes as doves, just as the cloud of God's presence led the Israelite people as they wandered through the desert of Sinai, as it overshadowed the mountain of the covenant where which God espoused his people to himself. But he does this, above all, when he himself overshadows his bride again—as the Spirit descends upon Mary and overshadows her, so that the child born of her is the Holy One, the Son of God (cf. Lk 1:35). Indeed, he takes his beloved to sit under the shadow of his care as under a tree, and here he gives her to eat of the sweet fruit of his love—this tree of the Cross which, through the offering of his Body and Blood in the Eucharist, through the tender laying down of his life for his beloved, and through the Resurrection that will soon follow, is transformed into the space of most intimate nuptial love and self-giving. Here truly the bride finds herself sheltered in the shadow of God's own compassionate presence, cradled in the infinite mercy of his Heart, and nourished by the outpouring of his love which satisfied her every hunger and satiates her every thirst.

How can we not think, in this context, of Psalm 23, in which the verdant pasture offered to the Bridegroom is now made a gift for the very bride who first offered it? Mary offered her heart as a welcoming-space for Christ at the Annunciation, and now at the Cross, Jesus offers his Heart as a welcoming-space for her, and, in her, for each and every one of us. And thus we can sing, with Mary and with all of those souls throughout history who have stood at the foot of the Cross and experienced, in the opened Heart of Jesus, the shelter of compassionate love and tender mercy for which they ardently thirst.

The LORD is my shepherd, I shall not want;
he makes me lie down in green pastures.
He leads me beside still waters;
he restores my soul.
He leads me in paths of righteousness
for his name's sake.
Even though I walk through the valley
of the shadow of death,
I fear no evil; for you are with me;
your rod and your staff, they comfort me.
You prepare a table before me,
in the presence of my enemies;
you anoint my head with oil,
my cup overflows.
Surely goodness and mercy shall follow me
all the days of my life;
and I shall dwell in the house of the LORD for ever.

Yes, this Psalm vividly expresses exactly the same reality that we see in these verses of the Song of Songs. We see the same blessed repose in green pastures; we see the same safety and shelter that the human heart feels within the tenderness of her Beloved; we see the same feeding and restoration for which she asks in the Song (and which, of course, she receives); we see her being brought into his house, there to dwell forever.

When I gaze upon the tender and loving face of my beloved Jesus, when I look into his gentle yet piercing gaze, when I draw near enough to feel the reverberations of his Sacred Heart, then I truly come to experience the truth of his words:

> I know my own and my own know me, as the Father knows me and I know the Father; and I lay down my life for the sheep. ... My sheep hear my voice, and I know them, and they follow me, and I give them eternal life, and they shall never perish, and no one shall snatch them out of my hand. My Father, who has given them to me, is greater than all, and no one is able to snatch them out of the Father's hand. I and the Father are one. (Jn 10:14-15, 27-30)

ישוע

I AM WOUNDED BY LOVE

As an apple tree among the trees of the orchard,
so is my Beloved among young men.
In his longed-for shade I am seated
and his fruit is sweet to my taste.
He has taken me to his banqueting house,
and the host that overwhelms me is his love!
Sustain me with raisins,
restore me with apples;
for I am wounded by love!
His left hand is under my head,
and his right arm embraces me.
(Sg 2:3-6)

There is a profound and mysterious dynamic in these words of the bride, which can give us a deep and intimate access into the abyss of divine love and into the way that it ravishes the human heart. I spoke in the previous reflection of the great peace and rest that is bestowed on the bride by her Beloved, a rest given through the overshadowing of his presence that shelters her under the tree of his self-giving love, and from which he bestows upon her the succulent fruit of his own being. The bride, in other words, finds herself being gently and tenderly encompassed in the loving kindness of God, cradled in his all-enfolding embrace. It is thus that she sings a hymn of gratitude and praise to the One whom her soul loves, radiant as she is in the joy and gladness that she has at last found the repose for which her heart longs.

And yet, within the very joyful repose of his love, which never ceases to cradle, protect, and shelter her, she also begins to experience another movement. For she exclaims that he not only feeds her with his fruit, but takes her into the banqueting house (literally, the house of wine) and gives her to drink of the very substance of his intoxicating love, which she has already said "surpasses wine" (Sg 1:2). And this experience is too much for her in her frailty! Sheltered and upheld as she is, she nonetheless cries out—in response to the overwhelming intensity of his love which pours forth into her limited human heart, in response to the beauty of her Beloved which ravishes her and draws her out of herself in ardent longing—"The host that overwhelms me is his love…I am wounded by love!"

What does she mean in speaking of a "host?" For this indeed seems to be the most accurate translation, since the word used here, *degel*, means nothing else than this throughout the entire Bible. Yes, her Bridegroom is indeed *the God of hosts*, Yahweh Sabaoth, the God of armies, who is praised in the *Gloria*: "Holy, Holy, Holy, Lord God of hosts, heaven and earth are full of your glory. Hosanna in the highest! Blessed is he who comes in the name of the Lord. Hosanna in the highest!" And this immense holiness of her Beloved is now directed toward her, pouring itself out without reserve into her being. His hosts—that is, the heavenly armies of God's almighty strength, the infinite glory of the Trinity—are directed straight into the heart of the one whom he loves. And yet she recognizes immediately, by what she feels, that this host which assails her with a peaceful violence and an ardent gentleness *is nothing but Love, Love, and only Love*. "The host that overwhelms me is his Love!"

She has been touched by his gentle touch, by the touch of this divine warrior who is the Prince of Peace, and this touch has impressed upon her heart the indelible image of his Uncreated Love. Therefore she can never rest again; that is, she can never be content to simply remain in the narrowness of her own sin and selfishness, her own fear and shame. She will indeed cry out, at every moment, from now on: "Let him kiss me with the kiss of his mouth!" (Sg 1:2). Yes, she is drawn out, by the very love that has touched her, in order to seek an ever deeper, ever more intimate contact with the One in whom alone her heart will be at rest. It is thus that she cries out without ceasing, "I am wounded by love!" She experiences what Origen so beautifully expressed so many years ago:

> If a man has once burned with the faithful love of the Word of God; if, to speak like a prophet, a man has one day receive the sweet wound, the sweet pain "from the best arrow;" if anyone, one day, has been pierced with the dart of love to the extent that later on, day and night, he sighs with desire and knows nothing else, wants nothing else, is attracted by nothing else except to desire it, want it and hope for it, such a one can rightly say: "I am wounded with love."[11]

Is this not the nature of authentic love? It simultaneously bestows a *blessed rest* and awakens a *restless longing*. It simultaneously allows me to surrender, here and now, into the ever-present embrace of my Beloved, and also draws my heart out in a painful longing to experience this embrace more deeply. Yes, the maturing and flowering of love occurs as a "thirst-within-repose," in which my very encounter with God's love, in which I find myself ceaselessly cradled, awakens in me an ardent thirst that in a certain way never allows me to rest again. And yet this very thirst, this reaching out for the ineffable Beauty that has so radiantly revealed itself to me—which has so profoundly pierced my soul, which has, as it were, drawn my very heart out of itself and into the One whom I love—this very thirst flows forth anew into a yet deeper repose in the embrace of my Beloved. For he is the One who, while hidden from my eyes behind the veil of mortality, while not yet grasped in his fullness, nonetheless bestows himself freely upon me and holds me in the shelter of his embrace, in which I can rest at every moment.

In reading the lives of the saints and mystics, one will encounter their experience of this "wound of love" very frequently. It is, of course, manifested uniquely in the life of each one of us (and by no means needs to be experienced through "extraordinary" mystical experiences). Saint Teresa of Avila explains her experience of this wound of love, for example, when she speaks of what is called her "transverberation":

> I saw an angel close by me, on my left side, in bodily form. He was not large, but small of stature, and most beautiful—his face burning, as if he were one of the highest angels, who seem to be all of fire: they must be those whom we call cherubim. I saw in his hand a long spear of gold, and at the iron's point there seemed to be a little fire. He appeared to me to be thrusting it at times into my heart and to pierce my very entrails; when he drew it out, he seemed to draw them out also, and to leave me

all on fire with a great love of God. The pain was so great, that it made me moan; and yet so surpassing was the sweetness of this excessive pain, that I could not wish to be rid of it. The soul is satisfied now with nothing less than God. The pain is not bodily, but spiritual; though the body has its share in it, even a large one. It is a caressing of love so sweet which now takes place between the soul and God. During the days that this lasted, I went about as if beside myself. I wished to see, or speak with, no one, but only to cherish my pain, which was to me a greater bliss than all created things could give me.[12]

John of the Cross speaks of this sacred wound as a kind of "cautery," as if a fire is being applied to the human spirit which simultaneously wounds and heals, consoles and causes pain. And he recognizes spontaneously, as does the bride, that the only remedy for this holy pain is to let oneself be wounded yet more by love, until the soul itself becomes one single wound of love, all aflame with and transformed in the divine fire!

The wound made by an iron heated in the fire of love cannot be healed by any other medication except by the same cautery that made it and will cure it. Because each time the cautery of love touches the wound of love, it enlarges the wound, and, in this way, the more it wounds, the more it binds and heals. For the one who loves is all the more healthy in that he is wounded; and the cure brought by love is to wound and to add one wound on top of the other, and in the end the wound becomes so large that the whole soul is turned into a wound of love. ... O happy wound caused by the one who alone knows how to heal![13]

Each one of us has experienced such a wound, in one way or another, have we not? Perhaps it has not yet penetrated us with such intensity, perhaps it has not yet gripped our whole being with the ravishing beauty of the divine Beloved. And yet the seal of his love has been impressed upon us from our very conception in our mother's womb—and we have glimpsed love, glimpsed beauty, glimpsed goodness throughout our life—and so we yearn, we thirst, we reach out, as grace always goes before us and draws us, until this wound of grace dilates ever more deeply into a consummate union with our heavenly Bridegroom in eternal life.

Is not all love a wound, even on the natural level? When my heart truly glimpses the unique and unrepeatable beauty of another person, is not my heart touched both with a repose in grateful awe and with a wound of painful longing? When my heart is touched by profound beauty, it is spontaneously dilated, torn out of its sinful complacency, torn out of the isolation of fear and self-preoccupation, drawn as it is into the realm of love. It expands, it dilates, it stretches—or rather it is stretched by the very beauty that ravishes it gently yet powerfully from the outside. If this is true even on the created plane, how much more is it true in the encounter with our ineffably beautiful God! In unveiling his unspeakable Beauty, Goodness, and Truth to us, he awakens in us a holy restlessness that can find security and abiding peace only in the tenderness of his everlasting embrace.

ישוע

THE WOUND OF LOVE
THAT HEALS ALL WOUNDS

The Bridegroom has tenderly embraced his bride, and while holding her in his arms—while sheltering her in the shade of his love—he communicates to her the depth of his goodness, he unveils before her the unspeakable radiance of his beauty. And even though the bride is being upheld, she finds this communication to be overwhelming, such that she faints under the powerful torrent of her Bridegroom's majesty, through the outpouring of his glory into her own heart and senses. Thus she cries out: "The host that overwhelms me is his love," and therefore "I am wounded by love!" And yet in the same breath she is able to whisper: "His left hand is under my head, and his right arm embraces me." This is the most gentle assault of love, the most tender and reverent of self-communication, in which the Bridegroom responds to the bride's deepest longings for beauty, for intimacy, for love; and yet, knowing her frailty, he upholds her in his arms so that she can sustain the intensity of this self-communication of the divine Mystery into a tiny human heart!

I have tried to express very clearly the nature of this self-communication of the Bridegroom to the bride, and have emphasized the utter respect and reverence with which he bestows himself upon her. He never does anything for which she is not ready; he never does anything to which she has not first consented. But even when she asks for this outpouring of love, even when she implores him to bestow this wound upon her, he knows that she must always be sustained by grace, cradled at every moment in his sheltering and upholding love.

Perhaps, however, this image of being assailed by love, being wounded by love, can be difficult for some. This is especially true if one has, for example, suffered from abuse at some point in their life.

They have experienced themselves being assailed, yet not out of the fullness of tender love, out an abundance of reverence, goodness, and compassion. Rather, they have experienced their own sacred mystery in some way being invaded, violently intruded upon by another for whom they are a mere "object." The kind of wound that such an experience leaves is very different from the wound left by the touch of the heavenly Bridegroom. Indeed, they could not be more different! When one is wounded by abuse—whether verbal, physical, or sexual—one suffers from a profound sense of insecurity, a sense of shame and guilt, and the feeling that one's sacredness has been desecrated by the irreverence of another. And yet when one is wounded by the gentle touch of God—which is never forceful, never violent, never intrusive—one suffers from an excess of gratitude, an overwhelming sense of one's beauty in the eyes of God, and an ardent longing, springing spontaneously from within the heart, to experience anew, and ever more deeply, his sacred touch in the innermost place of one's own sacredness in his eyes.

Indeed, an essential difference between these two wounds—the wound of abuse or pain that truly *hurts* the human heart, and the "wound of love" which is truly no wound at all, but a *healing* touch—is that the first causes the heart to collapse in on itself in fear and shame, whereas the second opens wide the heart to ever deeper love, dilating it with longing, hope, and aspiration. It is thus, indeed—directly opposed to one another as they are—that the wound of love alone can truly and definitively heal the wound of brokenness and sin. Yes, the only way to heal my broken and fearful heart from a lack of love—from past or present experiences of rejection, abandonment, disrespect for the person that I am, or any other wound—is not to try to "fix" myself, but to welcome the true and authentic love that comes to me from the outside. I need—I absolutely need—to experience healing as a gift that comes to me from another. It is not something that can come forth merely from within me. But when I experience myself sheltered in the very places of my woundedness by another, when I experience the light of another's loving gaze in the very places of my darkness, when I experience the cherishing, affirming, and reverent embrace of another in my vulnerability—it is then that the walls of protection that I have built up around myself break down, and my heart freely dilates into the ever-deepening joy of loving relationship.

We need only think of the drama that has unfolded up to this point in the Song to understand the utter reverence and respect that the Bridegroom has for his bride. He found her, indeed, enclosed fearfully within herself, chained in slavery to the "chariots of Pharaoh," and he drew near in order to liberate her. And he heard her cry of complaint, her longing for this liberation and this union with him. Therefore he was able to reach out and to touch her in her place of bondage; he tenderly gazed upon her in the midst of her suffering and darkness. He offered his own loving gaze as a safe space in which she felt secure, in which she could begin to step out of the barriers of fear and shame and to let herself be bathed in the light of his compassion. And when she did this, she experienced the joy of mutual beholding, in which he gazed upon her beauty and exclaimed how precious she was in his eyes, and she responded with the same delight and wonder at the beauty of her Beloved. This mutual gazing in tender and reverent love, I said, is the preface to an intimate touch, in which the two, Lover and beloved, draw one another close into a single embrace, where their hearts beat together as one and their breath mingles together in a single symphony of intimacy and praise.

But even though the Bridegroom has loved so tenderly, manifesting the immensity of his love as the sheltering space for the very littleness and frailty of the bride, she is still overcome by such love. For he is God after all! And thus she still faints in his embrace, overcome by the ocean of tenderness that pours forth from him into her own receptive heart. And it is precisely this experience of being "overcome by love" which, she realizes, is the true victory. And thus she wholeheartedly consents to being "conquered" in this way by the gentleness of divine love, surrendering herself carelessly into the care of the One who loves her perfectly and forever. "His left hand is under my head, and his right arm embraces me."

And the Bridegroom himself, holding his bride as she sleeps, says to those who would awaken her:

I adjure you, daughters of Jerusalem,
by the gazelles, by the hinds of the field,
not to stir my love, nor rouse her,
until she is pleased to awake.
(Sg 2:7)

Thus ends the first of five poems contained in the Song: with the Bridegroom cradling the bride in his arms and sheltering her from all that would disturb her. This is a refrain that we will hear twice more in the Song, once bringing another poem to its conclusion and once in the concluding epilogue. In these words we recognize that the bride still has a journey to walk, she still has more to grow—since she has been overcome by the Bridegroom's love, unable yet to sustain it! And yet at the same time we see the Bridegroom's great patience, in that he upholds and protects her in her very frailty, knowing that only in eternal life will she be able to receive the full outpouring of his generosity, face to face in the consummation of the eternal marriage, without being overcome by what she encounters. It is then that she will exclaim, definitively, "his left hand is under my head, and his right arm embraces me," while he will have no need to say, "Stir not up my love." This is because their hearts and lives will be so intimately knitted together as one that they will share a single existence of intimacy and joy. Bridegroom and bride will breathe forth together the same breath of the Spirit, and will share the same heartbeat of love, which is the throbbing tenderness of the Trinity himself, whose very life has become the life of the bride, caught up as she is in the innermost intimacy of the Father, Son, and Holy Spirit.

SECOND POEM

THE SPRING OF BETROTHAL

ARISE, AND COME TO ME

The voice of my Beloved!
Behold, he comes,
leaping upon the mountains,
bounding over the hills.
My Beloved is like a gazelle, or a young stag.
Behold, he stands behind our wall.
He is looking through the windows,
gazing through the lattice.
My Beloved speaks and says to me:
"Arise, my love, my beautiful one, and come to me,
for behold, the winter is past,
the rain is over and gone.
The flowers appear on the earth,
the time of singing has come,
and the cooing of the turtledove
is heard in our land.
The fig tree puts forth her first figs,
and the vines, with their blossoms,
give forth fragrance.
Arise, my love, my beautiful one, and come to me.
O my dove, in the clefts of the rock,
in the hidden places of the cliff,
let me see your face,
let me hear your voice,
for your voice is sweet,
and your face is lovely."
(Sg 2:8-14)

How clear and powerful these verses are, even without any explanation! But they also burst in upon us unexpectedly—for just a moment ago we were witnessing the bride resting in the arms of her Bridegroom, overcome by his love and yet sheltered in his embrace, even in her frailty. But now it is as if she awakes and realizes that the Bridegroom is no longer present. Rather, she is alone "in the clefts of the rock, in the hidden places of the cliff." What has happened? Did he forsake her while she slept? No, it seems that what she is experiencing is something else entirely. In order to understand the drama of this second poem, it is necessary to recognize that the One whom the bride loves can never be far away, he can never forsake or abandon the precious one of his Heart—even if she herself cannot always feel his presence in the shadows of this life. He is indeed still holding her, as we will see. But within his very embrace, he is also inviting her to immerse herself ever more deeply, more radically, more vulnerably into his welcoming arms.

Yes, he has not withdrawn from her…but he is nonetheless calling her deeper. We already saw, indeed, that she still needed to grow in order to fully receive and reciprocate the awesome love of her Bridegroom. This is because she was still to some degree closed within her frailty, still nestled within the false comfort that she had build up to protect her in her wounds. And while the Bridegroom touched her, while he held her in his arms, because her heart was not yet totally and unreservedly surrendered to him, she could not sustain the immensity of his tenderness, and so she fainted under his touch. So now he is inviting her to deeper vulnerability in love, asking her to expose her heart to the gaze of his love yet more totally, in order to experience the healing and transformation it effects within her. Therefore, he comes to her, bounding over the hills like a giant, leaping over the mountains, and calling out to her ardently yet tenderly: "Arise, my love, my beautiful one, and come to me." And yet, even as he comes as a giant bounding across the face of the earth, he also comes intimately and secretly: "Behold, he stands behind our wall. He is looking through the windows, gazing through the lattice."

Is this not an essential trait of God? Whenever he comes to me it is as though he bounds toward me from the most distant expanses of the universe, reaching out in his immensity—he who upholds the entire universe by his word of power!—to touch me with his love. And yet in the same moment, he who is so great and uncontainable is also the most gentle, kind, and reverent of all. Thus, even in his transcendent greatness he is intimately close, standing right behind "our wall." That is, he enters in as deeply as I will allow him, and when he finds a wall, he stands right there, pressing his head up against it and listening for the beating of my heart, listening for my voice, hoping perhaps to hear its sweetness…even to hear it speaking lovingly of him! Yes, he looks in through the windows, gazing upon me through the lattice, like a shy lover who wants to draw near, to make himself visible, but does not want to frighten me or to have me turn him away. And in this intimate yet deeply reverent posture, he calls out to me: "Arise, my love, my beautiful one, and come to me…" Yes, he says:

O my dove, in the clefts of the rock,
in the secret places of the cliff,
let me see your face,
let me hear your voice,
for your voice is sweet,

and your face is lovely."
(Sg 2:14)

There I am, hiding like a dove in the hidden places of the cliff, while he bounds toward me in ardent haste; there I am, enclosed in my room, as he presses against the wall and gently whispers my name. Yes, I have experienced my beauty in his eyes before; I have tasted his love and his goodness. But I find myself still burdened by fear and shame, by hesitation, doubt, or guilt. And so the One who so ardently loves me calls me out anew, so that he may renew this experience within me again, and in renewing it, deepen it. In this way my heart is ever more deeply healed in the light of his loving gaze, and I come to live, spontaneously, from my true identity as his beloved, in the joy and playfulness of knowing myself to be seen, known, and loved by him, and unceasingly cradled in the arms of his perfect love:

"Arise, arise my love! Arise and come away...draw near to me by letting me draw you out of your fear and shame, your anxiety and sadness, your darkness. You are my precious dove, uniquely beautiful in my eyes. And so I call you out; I call you out, beloved, only because I want to hear your voice, I want to see your face...for (I will never tire of telling you!) your voice is sweet and your face is lovely."

ישוע

A HEART FILLED WITH LIFE ANEW

What is being referred to when the Bridegroom calls his bride out of "the clefts of the rock," out of "the hidden places of the cliff?" It is interesting that an ancient mystical tradition has actually come to understand these dwelling-places cut in the rock as *the open wound of the Heart of Christ*. Saint Bernard expressed this when he said: "How can one not see, through these openings, the secret of his Heart that is bared in the wounds of his body?" This is absolutely true, but a step must be made first—for clearly this cannot be the primary meaning of the text. Why? Because the Bridegroom is calling his beloved *out* of these places in order to look upon her and to unite her to himself. If she were already nestled safely within his Heart, there would be no need for her to come out in this way. Or, rather, she *is* nestled within this Heart, but she does not yet *know* it, for she is still closed in upon herself and unable to see beyond the blinding fog of her own fear and shame, unable to step out of the rocky cleft where she is hiding. Protecting her vulnerability from the eyes of others, afraid of being hurt, she is also making herself incapable of seeing the One who is gently calling out to her. Yes, it is the Bridegroom's ultimate goal to welcome his precious one into the open wound of his Heart, into the true "cleft in the rock" where she is forever safe and sheltered.

Where, then, is she that he cannot gaze freely upon her, that he cannot shelter her freely within the infinite security of his own Sacred Heart? I would say that *she is hiding in the burden of her own wounds, rather than taking refuge in the liberating wounds of Christ.* Does this not resonate with our own experience—perhaps in relationships with others who appear trapped within their woundedness and are unable to experience the tenderness of our love for them, if not in our own relationship with God himself? Are there not so many persons in this world who, deeply wounded either by the sins of others or by their own sins, seem incapable of seeing anything else than the distorted perspective offered by these wounds? Indeed, the very rigidity and hardness of their heart, built up with many defenses and walls, seems to them to be the only safe place where they can dwell—the "clefts" in the rocky hardness of their fearful heart where they can avoid the vulnerability of possibly being hurt again by another person.

It is thus that the Bridegroom comes to his aching bride, trapped as she is in her fear, in her terror of opening her heart vulnerably to another—afraid that she will not be loved, sheltered, and cherished as she deserves, but rather abused or disregarded, hurt or dismissed. So he comes to her in her very fear, and he speaks with utter tenderness, affirming her beauty in his eyes, affirming that she is safe within his sheltering gaze and in the embrace of his love. Yes, his love pours out through his words and gestures, which simply express his deep yearning to lay open his own Heart in vulnerability so as to shelter the vulnerability of his beloved, who feels so alone and completely unprotected in her nakedness.

He hears the cries of her heart aching for love and yet unable to receive such love when it is offered to her. Since she has been deeply wounded in her vulnerability before, she has spent so long protecting her heart that she has forgotten just how utterly beautiful it is. Her heart yearns and pleads so much for a home to rest in safety, free to expose and air her painful wounds through healing love. But without the protection of a home, she turns toward a preservation which is stale, isolating, and ultimately becomes hardened and petrified through such an intense need to protect herself. Aiming to preserve what is "left" of her heart, she lets nothing and no one near because she is frozen in terror of being wounded even more. Unable to move, breathe, or open, her heart remains profoundly stuck in its woundedness. Petrified, no life is able to touch it and just like anything that has become stiff, frozen, or rigid, it maintains its shell and outward appearance without the interior fullness that breathes life into it. Her heart is aching with longing for love and intimacy, and yet she finds herself stilled gripped by the fear caused by her wounds.

Therefore, it is only with the most tender and gentle pulsations of love that the hollow yearning of her heart can gradually be filled without being cracked or shattered in the process. In other words, she needs another heartbeat, utterly gentle, utterly loving, utterly reverent, to slowly fill the emptiness of her own heart, until it comes to beat again with the hymn of love for which it was made. This is why the Bridegroom comes as he does—this is why the Crucified Christ comes, with a Heart radically open and vulnerable, aflame with an intense desire to love and shelter his beloved who so deeply needs this healing embrace. In his own wounded Heart, pierced by a lance—but much more, torn open by the very ardor of compassionate love itself! —Christ carries precisely this tender and gentle love. This most loving pulsation of his Heart is the only thing which can both shelter the vulnerable heart of his bride, as well as gradually fill her emptiness with the throbbing of the very heartbeat of eternal love and the endless life of intimacy and joy.

ישוע

SHELTERED IN THE WOUND OF HIS HEART

In the last reflection I tried to show how the dynamic movement of this part of the Song is the Bridegroom's tender invitation for the bride to step out of hiding and into vulnerability before him, in order that he, in turn, may welcome her into the perfect shelter of his loving embrace. Indeed, this is a movement out of her own wounds, which trap her in herself and in which she creates a false sense of security, and into the welcoming wounds of Christ, which are wounds of pure love in which she can truly rest and be protected. I explained how these wounds of the bride can be wounds received from others or the wounds of her own sin. But these are not the only wounds to which the Song can be referring. We have already seen that there is also the wound of love itself, which has struck the bride so powerfully at the end of the first poem.

Perhaps now, then, the bride is simply experiencing the yearning of her love-wounded heart for her Beloved who seems absent. But even then, he comes to her and calls her out, inviting her to come to himself: "You yearn for me, my dear one, but I yearn for you so much more. And so I invite you to step out of your own yearning—indeed, use your yearning as a spring-board—to get in touch with my deeper yearning for you. Do not be enclosed only within the pain of your own longing, but see that your longing is a mirror-image of my longing for you. Indeed, even as your wound, your longing, your thirst reflects my thirst for you, it is still only a fraction, like a small lake trying to reflect the entirety of the night sky, blazing with billions of stars! Therefore, look beyond the wound of your own heart to see the greater wound within my own—the wound of my infinite love for you. There you will find refuge, as your wound of love is sheltered within my wound of love, and together these two wounds, touching, become the joyful fullness of mutual self-giving."

John of the Cross has given this interpretation to these words of the Song, as he so beautifully says:

> Beholding that the bride is wounded with love for him, because of her moan he is also wounded with love for her. Among lovers, the wound of one is a wound for both, and the two have but one feeling. Thus, in other words, he says: Return to me, my bride, because if you go about wounded with love for me, I too, like the stag, will come to you wounded by your wound.[14]

Here we see the tenderness of the Heart of Christ, who cannot bear to see his beloved one wounded without being wounded by her wound, without reaching out to her and making her wound his own, in order, through his very compassion, to unite her to himself in this very place of woundedness. This is indeed true for all kinds of wounds, whether they be wounds of abuse, misunderstanding, rejection, sin, or isolation, or even of love: Christ has taken all of the bride's wounds into the wound of his own Sacred Heart. And there she is totally understood, totally sheltered, within the wound of his love which is the true victory, the transparent gap in the veil of creation through which Love freely pours in order to touch, illumine, and heal all with its radiance.

How can this not immediately direct our minds to the powerful events following Christ's Resurrection? The disciples are afraid, enclosed within the narrowness of their fear-filled hearts, locked in the upper room. They have not yet realized that the One whom they love, and whom they feel that they have irrevocably lost, has not disappeared, but rather *has entered forever into the sphere of limitless self-communication*. And they will only be able to see him, experience him, touch him, when they too enter with him into this open and expansive place of love. Only when their hearts, too, become pure relationship—and to the degree that they do—will they be in touch with the living Body of Christ which surpasses the limitations of time and space while filling all of time and space with his radiant presence.

But first he comes to them, first he draws near to them in their very place of fear and anxiety, entering into their closed and narrow hearts. He enters without needing to knock, for nothing can now limit the flow of his self-giving, since his entire being, his very body, has become nothing but Love in the ceaseless movement of giving and acceptance:

> On the evening of that day, the first day of the week, the doors being shut where the disciples were, for fear of the Jews, Jesus came and stood among them and said to them, "Peace be with you." When he had said this, he showed them his hands and his side. Then the disciples were glad when they saw the Lord. Jesus said to them again, "Peace be with you. As the Father has sent me, even so I send you." And when he had said this, he breathed on them, and said to them, "Receive the Holy Spirit." (Jn 20:19-22)

The divine Bridegroom comes and breathes upon his fearful bride the Breath of his Holy Spirit; he bestows upon her the Kiss of Peace. And her heart rejoices when she sees him, delighting to encounter the one whom she had thought forever lost. But his delightful touch, his loving kiss, draws her heart out of itself in ardent longing—and if she wants to remain in touch with him, she must enter into him, she must make her abode within him, she must "be with him where he is, to behold his glory which was given to him by the Father before the foundation of the world" (Jn 17:24). In other words, she is invited to step out of the narrowness of her sinful and fear-filled life, the life marked by anxiety and death, and let herself be drawn into the fullness of his own Risen Life. But how can she do this? How can she let herself be drawn, in the heart of her very woundedness, into the expansive openness of the Heart of her Beloved, which cradles her and the whole universe unceasingly within itself? The answer is this: *she enters through his wounds*, which even in his Resurrection he has retained. And yet these wounds are no longer a sign of hurt, of defeat, of weakness, but rather are *the symbol and expression of the pure openness of Love, indeed, of the victory of Love over all darkness, hate, and pain, and over the very dissolution of death itself*. His wounds are now but the witness to the enduring constancy of his loving embrace, from which nothing can separate the bride, sheltered as she is in the most intimate vulnerability of his own receptive Heart:

Now Thomas, one of the twelve, called the Twin, was not with them when Jesus came. So the other disciples told him, "We have seen the Lord." But he said to them, "Unless I see in his hands the print of the nails, and place my finger in the mark of the nails, and place my hand in his side, I will not believe." Eight days later, his disciples were again in the house, and Thomas was with them. The doors were shut, but Jesus came and stood among them, and said, "Peace be with you." Then he said to Thomas, "Put your finger here, and see my hands; and put out your hand, and place it in my side; do not be faithless, but believing." Thomas answered him, "My Lord and my God!" (Jn 20:24-28)

In this experience—in being drawn out of her hesitation, her fear, her doubt, and letting her very life be inserted into the receptive space opened up in the wounds of Christ—the bride experiences the shelter for which her heart thirsts. She enters into the dimension of eternal Love and discovers, cradled as she is in the "cleft of the rock" of the Sacred Heart of Jesus, the very expansiveness of the life of the Father, Son, and Holy Spirit, which will forever be her enduring gladness and her perfect joy.

ישוע

THE ABSENCE WHICH IS A DEEPER PRESENCE

The Bridegroom comes to his fearful bride and tenderly calls her out of hiding, imploring her with a gentle ardor: "Arise, my love, my beautiful one, and come to me. O my dove, in the clefts of the rock, in the hidden places of the cliff, let me see your face, let me hear your voice, for your voice is sweet, and your face is lovely" (Sg 2:13-14). How touching are these words, in which he does not force, does not compel, but draws her only by the very ardor of his own love and his desire for her! Indeed, we can see here too the same theme that the bride expressed at the end of the first poem: "The host that overwhelms me is his love!" Is she hiding because she does not want to be overwhelmed in this way again, because the intensity of his great love causes her fear? Or is she rather hiding because she has come to believe the lies that his love is not true, not authentic, not enduring? Is she tempted even to feel that the Bridegroom's love will not be enough for her?

After all, he cannot be grasped, cannot be contained within her hands, within her mind, within her own desire to control and possess.

If she were to try to hold him, he would slip through her fingers. How can such an elusive Lover, never grasped, never possessed, but always fleeing from my desire to lay hold of him, ever fulfill the longings of my heart? Ah, lovely bride, you have not yet come to know—but soon you will!—that your Beloved never flees. It is impossible for him to withdraw from you. And yet...and yet he is continually drawing you deeper, into the hidden places in the depths of his own Sacred Heart. Indeed, he slips through your fingers only in order to take up his abode in the innermost place of your own heart, where alone he can be virginally united to you in this inmost virgin-space.

Yes, do you see? You cannot lay hold of him; you cannot reduce his mystery to your own size; and yet you can surrender to him, you can let yourself be laid hold of by him and enveloped in the most intimate embrace of his mysterious Love. It is thus that the union that you seek will flower ever more deeply until its perfect and everlasting consummation in heaven! He reaches out to take you in his arms, exposing his defenseless Heart to you, and he gently draws you close. Receive this embrace, and let yourself be drawn. Indeed, you too can draw him close, not through possessiveness, but through the very longing of your heart to experience him in the fullness of his mystery!

Yes, in the first poem the bride still found herself surrounded by darkness, her own beautiful face blackened by the sun, and her countenance surrounded with the chains of slavery. But the Bridegroom looked upon her and saw her beauty; his Heart was spontaneously drawn to her, as he saw beyond her brokenness to her immense loveliness, deeper than everything. And so he came, he came to her and exclaimed how beautiful she is! He came and rested against her heart, exuding his own inexpressible perfume of love, touching the inmost substance of her own soul and causing it to pour itself forth as the rich and precious fragrance of nard in return. In this mutual surrender of self, in this mutual beholding of love and delight, Bridegroom and bride were drawn together and united, and she found herself resting in the shade of the tree of her Beloved, eating of the sweetness of his fruit and drinking the inebriating wine of his love. Ah! But she was still so weak, and so she fainted under to impetus of this great love—and yet even so, she found herself upheld and cradled in the arms of the One who loves her, his left hand under her head and his right arm embracing her.

Now she awakens at the beginning of the second poem, and things look somewhat different. Before, even in her frailty he was close, even in her darkness she glimpsed his light. But now its seems as if he is entirely absent. But there is another difference too. While earlier it was she who called out to him, ardently longing to know where he pastures his flock in the fullness of noonday light, now it is the Bridegroom himself who comes to her and asks her to show herself to him. What is this? An absence which is an even deeper form of presence! He has seemed to withdraw, but only in order to come to her more deeply, more intimately. And he calls out with those beautiful words, claiming that the winter of her exile has ended, inviting her to step forth into the springtime of love and intimacy:

"Arise, my love, my beautiful one, and come to me,
for behold, the winter is past,
the rain is over and gone.
The flowers appear on the earth,
the time of singing has come,
and the cooing of the turtledove
is heard in our land.
The fig tree puts forth her first figs,
and the vines, with their blossoms,
give forth fragrance."
(Sg 2:10-13)

These words make us think of the words that the Bridegroom will later pronounce, when he has taken the bride's flesh as his own, becoming her Brother and sharing her land as truly "our land." And how intimately does he speak of this land, how often does he use the images of our earth to describe the mysteries of his love! In this case he says: "From the fig tree learn its lesson: as soon as it branch becomes tender and puts forth its leaves, you know that summer is near. So also, when you see all these things, you know that he is near" (Mt 24:32-33). What is the bride witnessing—hiding as she is, chilled and in darkness, in the clefts of the rock—which heralds for her the coming of her Beloved? Here indeed we encounter one of the greatest paradoxes of the life of prayer: that as the Bridegroom draws ever nearer he seems to be harder to grasp, and as we come to be united to him more intimately, it seems even harder to lay hold of him!

But this will not be forever! No, even in this life you can come, lovely bride, to hold him in an enduring embrace, but only by letting yourself be held by him in mystery. You can remain always united to his enduring and ever-present light, if only your heart remains always open in its vulnerability to his gaze. Then, even if it feels that you walk in the darkness, you are nonetheless enfolded in his radiance—for you have cast yourself into the burning Hearth of Love, which will warm you in your chill and illumine you among the shadows of this life: "He who follow me will not walk in the darkness, but will have the light of life" (Jn 8:12). Yes, the light burns within you, and already now you find a deeper, abiding presence—the enduring embrace of your Beloved, even deeper than feeling and thought—which remains even in the seeking and finding, the loss and seeking, that recurs throughout the journey of this life. And this enduring and ever-present light will carry you, at the end, into the fullness of light in the consummation that awaits you in the eternal noonday of his Love!

What is the cause of this holy restlessness that causes the bride, once she seems to lay hold of her Beloved, to immediately feel the pain of his absence and to reach out for him anew? Ah, this is not indeed the pain of his absence, even if for the bride this seems to be what she feels, but rather the aching longing for the fullness of his presence! Is this not the case even on the natural level in the love of two persons? The more my heart falls in love with another person, the more keenly do I feel their absence! Indeed, before I loved them in this way, before my heart allowed itself to be touched by their unique beauty, I didn't even realize that they were not present. But once they become precious to me, once I let my heart be drawn out of itself as a gift for them, our hearts are knitted together in a deep unity. But then how much more vividly do I experience the imperfection of this union! However close we may be, we do not truly live in one another, in a perfect mutual indwelling in which all is shared, all is understood, in an intimacy that is enduring and unbreakable. But if I truly love, then this is what I desire! Thus, the very presence of the one whom I love is experienced as an "absence," that is, as the lack of the fullness of presence. But the mysterious thing is that, precisely through experiencing this absence, I am drawn deeper into the awareness of the other's presence, as they are welcomed more intimately into the depths of my heart, and my heart more radically gives itself to them in love and longing.

It is precisely in this way, through the ravishing glimpse of the Beauty of my Beloved, that I come to experience the space between us that is meant to be filled by the fullness of love and mutual self-communication. And then, precisely through experiencing this space of "absence" which is to be filled with presence, this very space itself between us begins to be crossed over by the vibrations of love that reverberated in the air and fill it with a mysterious, impalpable presence! I experience this very space sounding with the hymn of our mutual breathing, I feel it throbbing with heartbeat of our union, in which our hearts, even through the veil of this mortal life, are woven together as one in a single mystery of everlasting consummation.

ישוע

CATCH US THE FOXES

In my previous words on the "absence" which is a deeper form of presence, and which opens up the path into a deeper intimacy, I have already led into the verses that follow in the Song, where the bride arises in ardent longing to seek for her absent Beloved among the streets of the city. However, there are a few verses that intervene between the Bridegroom's ardent call, "Arise, my love, my beautiful one, and come to me," and her arising in the night to search for him. He makes one more comment:

"Catch us the foxes,
the little foxes,
that bind the vines,
for our vines are in blossom."
(Sg 2:15)

What are these "foxes" that bind the vines and keep them from bringing to maturity the sweet grapes that are already beginning to blossom? Is this not yet another way in which the Bridegroom is tenderly calling his bride out, out of her hiding in fear, shame, and sin, so she may let herself be looked upon and let her voice be heard? Yes, the blossoming of these vines is but another way of expressing the trusting surrender to which the Bridegroom invites her, her loving abandonment into his welcoming arms and into the shelter of his Heart.

But there are these pesky little foxes that bind her to her fear, that keep her paralyzed in hesitation and doubt! "Catch the foxes!" he cries out. In other words, don't allow these fears and hesitations and attachments keep your heart far from me. Whether it is shame and self-hatred which hinders you from receiving my love; whether it is your grasping for the things of creation to cover over your nakedness, just as Adam and Eve "hid from the face of the Lord God among the trees of the garden;" whether it is your fear of the unknown, of the darkness of a mystery which you have not yet come to see as nothing but the Mystery of Love; whatever it may be, my love, do not let these little foxes bind you and keep your heart from bringing forth the full blossoming of its surrender to me!

It is important to note, however, that the Bridegroom's call does *not* imply that the bride herself should become preoccupied in trying to grasp and control these foxes herself, as if through her own efforts she could "fix" the things that are broken and astray within her own heart. The call to "catch" the foxes rather reveals the profound vision of the Bridegroom, who, as he draws near and lovingly calls the bride to step out into his tender gaze, recognizes that her thoughts immediately go to the "foxes" of fears and insecurities that would keep her closed in herself! "Catch the foxes" therefore means: "Do not allow these thoughts to bind you, do not allow them to grow, for they will suffocate your heart and hold it back from a naive and childlike surrender to me. Catch them by stopping them in their tracks and moving immediately beyond them, letting go of them into my care as you turn your gaze from yourself to me. My gaze will set things right; my gaze will truly catch the foxes, healing the very wounds from which they arise. All you need to do is to turn away from them, to not cling to or foster these thoughts, and to direct your trusting gaze to me, that I may look at you as you look at me, our eyes interlocking and bringing profound healing within the depths of your soul."

In the light of these words of the Bridegroom to "catch the foxes," I would like to emphasize an important point. There is a danger in the spiritual life of becoming preoccupied with secondary things, with superficial matters that cause us to lose sight of the central reality of God's immense love, and to lose our trust in the way that his love is ceaselessly at work healing and transforming us in ways that we often do not see or feel. It is not, in the end, a matter of us detaching ourselves from our disordered dependence on created things through our own effort, or even from the inordinate responses of our own hearts. Yes, it is important to be aware of these movements within us, to refuse to foster them, and to turn away from them; this is what the Bridegroom's call to "catch" the foxes means. And this interior attitude of "catching" also applies in our external actions, in what the tradition has called "asceticism," that is, a way of reorienting our actions into authentic freedom and love through a certain persevering practice of good habits. Here is where the traditional practices of Lent—fasting, prayer, and almsgiving—find a part of their meaning.

However, these things—both our interior and our exterior "asceticism"—are really very small in comparison with what God does, and even very small in the light of the whole dynamic of our relationship with him. How sad it is, then, when someone is so preoccupied with trying to grow in virtue and to overcome faults, or even trying to understand and heal their wounds, that they lose sight of the "big picture" of God's tender, passionate, and unique love for them, and of the divine romance that is ever unfolding between them and their divine Beloved! It is indeed only the experience of this unique love, and of the reciprocal love that it awakens within the passionate union of this romance, that can truly heal and transform the human heart. The wise words of a Carthusian monk are very pertinent here, and can well summarize what I have been trying to say:

> In speaking of detachment I am afraid of giving too much importance to what is of little consequence. Certainly detachment from things is an essential element of the spiritual life. This does not mean that we are obligated to make a continual effort of the will to be detached. A continual preoccupation such as this is unhealthy and sometimes results in a negative attitude and bitterness that has little to do with Christian simplicity and joy. And, in the end, it puts too much emphasis on secondary matters. To be continually preoccupied with denying ourselves something is to feed the desire to possess and give it importance. The kingdom of God is not made of such things, 'not food and drink but righteousness and peace and joy in the Holy Spirit' (Romans 14:17). The true contemplative doesn't need to make a constant effort to mortify the senses. Only love is necessary, the heart turned to God and the things of God; or rather, he realizes that things are leaving him and detaching themselves from him. He quickly forgets them, so fascinated is he with the discovery of the wondrous Mystery. Let us not be like the fearful people who, on the mountain, did not take their eyes from their feet for fear of stumbling and were thus unable to revel in the broad horizon and vast expanses. Let us be bold enough to be joyful. Christ, and the love of God, are worth this.[15]

After hearing the Bridegroom's tender call to come out, like a dove hidden in the clefts of the rock, allowing him to see her beautiful face and to hear her sweet voice, the bride says:

My Beloved is mine, and I am his;
he pastures his flock among the lilies.
Until the day breathes
and the shadows flee,
encircle me, my Beloved,
like a gazelle or a young stag,
upon the mountains of the covenant.
(Sg 2:16-17)

In the next reflection I will speak in much more depth about these words of the bride, but let me only note, in bringing this one to a close, that these word directly mirror the words of the Bridegroom. The Bridegroom has already come like a gazelle or a young stag, bounding over the mountains as he approaches her, calling her forth in the midst of the night of her fear in order to draw her into intimacy with himself. But she still feels her fears, and she still experiences the darkness of the night enshrouding her. And she also acknowledges immediately that she cannot fully come out on her own; her surrender must be evoked by his own presence, by the security created by his tender and inviting gaze. Indeed, she immediately sees that she cannot catch the foxes either. And thus the Bridegroom's own words of invitation are mirrored by her invitation to him:

"Without you, my Beloved, I can do nothing. Therefore, while the night remains—before the rising of the sun dispels the darkness and the day breathes is warm breath over me—I implore you to encircle me with your own presence. Cradle and uphold me as you once did when your left hand was under my head and your right arm embraced me. When you do this, then I shall be able to draw near to you as you desire—and as I desire too!—for all, in the end, is your gift, your grace…awakening, sustaining, and bringing to full flower my own response of trust and reciprocal love."

ישוע

ENCIRCLE ME, MY BELOVED

My Beloved is mine, and I am his;
he pastures his flock among the lilies.
Until the day breathes
and the shadows flee,
encircle me, my Beloved,
like a gazelle or a young stag,
upon the mountains of the covenant.
(Sg 2:16-17)

These verses of the Song can be a little difficult to understand, and have been interpreted in different ways within the tradition. A large part of this depends on the way in which the word *sabab* is translated. I have translated it as "encircle," since the word in Hebrew can mean to turn about, to go around, to surround, etc. Often in this verse the word is translated as "return" or "turn," as if, after calling the bride so ardently, the Bridegroom has left now her alone, and so she must seek him, since he has disappeared. I have already said, however, that the Bridegroom does not know how to go away; he does not know how to flee from the face of his bride. But he does nonetheless seek to go always deeper, to draw her ever further into intimacy with himself, and in this sense he must, as it were, draw her out into the night of longing so that there she may encounter and love him more deeply as he truly is in his radiant beauty.

It can be said that the translation "encircle" brings out another possible meaning of the text which seems to unveils a different dynamic, or at least a deeper dimension of the same dynamic. Indeed, it reveals again the reality that I have already spoken of which encompasses and sustains the continual movement of thirst, of seeking and finding, that is experienced by the love-wounded heart. This all-encompassing dynamic is the bride's awareness of being always already enveloped and sustained within the Bridegroom's embrace, even as she searches more deeply for him through the shadows of this life. Understood in this way, the bride's words here also more naturally follow from the Bridegroom's words that immediately precede them, namely, his invitation to "catch the foxes." In other words, she is not ignoring his caution, but rather recognizing the only way that she can truly be safe: by belonging totally to him in covenant love, and by being encircled and sustained by his ever-present grace. Before explaining this more deeply, however, let me note another word whose translation is important for understanding the text.

This other word is *bether*, which is translated here as "covenant," as in "mountains of the covenant." The literal translation would actually be "the mountains of the pieces." But unless we understand the culture and the covenantal experience of Israel, this would be entirely unintelligible. This is why the Jerusalem Bible interprets the "pieces" as a sign of the covenant, referring to the pieces of the animal that would be passed through when a covenant was made, as a sign of the radical commitment and mutual belonging. We see this, for example, in the covenant God makes with Abraham:

> And [the LORD] brought [Abram] outside and said, "Look toward heaven, and number the stars, if you are able to number them." Then he said to him, "So shall your descendants be." And he believed the LORD; and he reckoned it to him as righteousness. And he said to him, "I am the LORD who brought you from Ur of the Chaldeans, to give you this land to possess." But he said, "O Lord GOD, how am I to know that I shall possess it?" He said to him, "Bring me a heifer three years old, a she-goat three years old, a ram three years old, a turtledove, and a young pigeon." And he brought him all these, cut them in two, and laid each half over against the other; but he did not cut the birds in two. And when birds of prey came down upon the carcasses, Abram drove them away. As the sun was going down,

a deep sleep fell on Abram; and behold, a dread and great darkness fell upon him. Then the LORD said to Abram, "Know of a surety that your descendants will be sojourners in a land that is not theirs, and will be slaves there, and they will be oppressed for four hundred years; but I will bring judgment on the nation which they serve, and afterward they shall come out with great possessions. As for yourself, you shall go to your fathers in peace; you shall be buried in a good old age." When the sun had gone down and it was dark, behold, a smoking fire pot and a flaming torch passed between these pieces. On that day the LORD made a covenant with Abram. (Gen 15:5-15, 17)

The symbolic passage of the Lord through the midst of the pieces symbolizes God's pledging himself to everlasting fidelity to his covenant; it is his promise that he will indeed fulfill what he has said. And indeed God passes through also on behalf of Abraham and his descendants, whom, he knows, are frail and inconstant. If this translation of the Song is indeed accurate, then, it is very illuminating, since it reveals for us what the bride is thinking of in the darkness of the night she is now experiencing. Her mind goes back to that night so long ago in which God pledged himself to Abraham and to all of those who would place their faith in God just as he did. She is therefore calling out, in her own darkness and longing—and with the same radical faith in God's fidelity to his promises—that he will truly show forth this faithfulness anew in her present circumstances. In other words, she experiences the turmoil caused by the "foxes" that are within her, but she immediately cries out to her Beloved to come to her, to encircle her with his own strength, for in him alone can she be free, and her own fidelity is nothing but the mirror of his own prior and enduring fidelity to her.

The Revised Standard Version tries to overcome the uncertainty of the word *bether* translating the phrase as "rugged mountains." This assumes that the text must be somehow inherently obscure, and that a meaning needs to be supplied to a word whose meaning is unclear. But I think that the interpretation of the mountains here as the mountains of the covenant is very beautiful, and unlocks a great deal of meaning for us. Perhaps the Hebrew text is indeed obscure, not because of some textual difficulty, but because of the deliberate intentions of the author. This indeed is the case in a number of places throughout the Song, in which the veil is, as it were, pulled back a little from the allegory and we are able to glimpse, laid bare before our eyes, the undimmed history of Israel in her romance with her God. We will soon see this, in the third poem, in the description of the throne of Solomon that comes up out of the desert. This throne sure looks a lot like the ark of the covenant leading the people out of the desert of the Exodus and into the Promised Land!

We can see the same kind of veiled imagery here, in that the bride describes the mountains as "mountains of the pieces," referring to the act of covenant-making. And she asks the Bridegroom to encircle her upon these mountains. A few verses from the Psalms immediately jump to mind. For example, Psalm 125 says: "As the mountains encircle Jerusalem, so the LORD encircles his people, from this time forth and for evermore" (cf. v. 2). Who then is the bride but Jerusalem, asking that God come to her by bounding over the mountains that surround her, and that these mountains themselves may be signs of his own encircling and protecting love? As another Psalm says: "I lift up my eyes to the mountains; from where shall come my help? My help shall come from the Lord, who made heaven and earth" (121:1-2-*Grail*).

Thus the bride both knows herself to be encircled, she knows herself to be betrothed to God in covenant-love, and yet she asks him to do so even more: to encircle her more deeply, more intimately, in his love, and to consummate with her this marriage covenant. This way of reading the text automatically sheds light on the first words spoke by the bride in response to her Beloved. He requests that she catch the foxes, and she immediately replies: "My Beloved is mine, and I am his. He pastures his flock among the lilies." How often, when referring to his covenant with his people, does God not use these same words? "You shall be my people and I will be your God" (Ez 36:28). "I will be their God and they shall be my people" (Jr 31:33). Marie of the Incarnation comments on this: "It is a continuous renewal of the covenant between my soul and its beloved. O God, how great is this union! It is a mixture of love and love, and one can say with God: 'My Beloved is mine and I am his.'"

Therefore, even if foxes still roam about in her garden, she knows that she is a garden that belongs entirely to the Lord. She knows that he has already espoused her to himself and taken her as his own in covenant love, and so she reaffirms her awareness of this belonging, her confidence in his protection of her and his activity within her. And only within this perspective does she then add: "Encircle me." In other words:

"I know that you have already united me to yourself, you have encircled me upon the mountains of the covenant. But now I feel the pain of your absence and yearn ardently for you. Indeed, now I hear you calling out to me in order to draw me into a deeper intimacy with you. But I know my frailty, my inconstancy—that I cannot keep my half of the covenant, and that you alone can bind me to yourself in an enduring way, by encircling me in your own sustaining grace. As long as the night of this life lasts, my Beloved, encircle me as a gazelle or a young stag, upon the mountains of the covenant, that I may be faithful to you as your are faithful to me, until you draw me at last into the radiant noonday light of the everlasting consummation of this Covenant of Eternal Love."

ישוע

I SOUGHT HIM WHOM MY HEART LOVES

As we come to the climax of the second poem of the Song, we encounter a mysterious movement, the final surge of love and longing, which is deeply rooted in the reality that I have repeatedly spoken of until now. After inviting her Beloved to encircle her, and in this way to give her the courage and confidence to step out into vulnerability in order to be united to him, the bride says:

Upon my bed, at night,
I sought him whom my heart loves;
I sought him, but found him not.
So I will arise now and go about the city;
in the streets and in the squares
I will seek him whom my heart loves.
I sought him, but found him not.
(Sg 3:1-2)

This poem began with the bride recounting her experience of the Bridegroom bounding towards her and inviting her to "arise" and to come to him. And now she speaks about how this same Bridegroom is being sought by her; she describes her own going out to search for the One whom she does not see. She has first been seeking him upon her bed, which seems to symbolize the same thing as the "clefts of the rock" in which she has been hiding. In other words, she has been seeking him in a place of false security, rather than stepping out in vulnerability in order to be bathed, in complete openness, in the outpouring of his healing and transforming love.

But once she realizes that this is not working, her love for the Bridegroom spurs her on, and so she says to herself: "I will arise now." Yes, the Bridegroom himself has invited her to do this! He has said to her, "Arise, my love, my beautiful one, and come to me." And now she does precisely that. But how mysterious it is, that as she pursues the face of the One whom she loves, it is as if he is nowhere to be found! I have already spoken about how this kind of "losing-seeking-finding" dynamic is played out in our spiritual life, how the Bridegroom does not hide, but nonetheless draws us ever deeper, and thus is experienced as slipping from our grasp as he pulls us more intimately into the depths of his own Sacred Heart.

But now I want to speak about another dimension of this seeking and finding, another profound aspect of the bride's anguished longing for her absent Beloved. These verses, indeed, only reveal their deepest meaning when we read them in the light of the Paschal Mystery. Yes, John the Evangelist himself did precisely this in writing his Gospel. When he recounts the scene of Mary Magdalene coming to the tomb on Easter morning, he explicitly portrays her as the longing bride looking ardently for the Bridegroom whom she feels that she has forever lost:

> Now on the first day of the week, Mary Magdalene came to the tomb early, while it was still dark, and saw that the stone had been taken away from the tomb. So she ran, and went to Simon Peter and the other disciple, the one whom Jesus loved, and said to them, "They have taken the Lord out of the tomb, and we do not know where they have laid him." Peter then came out with the other disciple, and they went toward the tomb. They both ran, but the other disciple outran Peter and reached the tomb first; and stooping to look in, he saw the linen cloths lying there, but he did not go in. Then Simon Peter came, following him, and went into the tomb; he saw the linen cloths lying, and the napkin, which had been on his head, not lying with the linen cloths but rolled up in a place by itself. Then the other disciple, who reached the tomb first, also went in, and he saw and believed; for as yet they did not know the Scripture, that he must rise from the dead. Then the disciples went back to their homes.
>
> But Mary stood weeping outside the tomb, and as she wept she stooped to look into the tomb; and she saw two angels in white, sitting where the body of Jesus had lain, one at the head and one at the feet. They said to her, "Woman, why are you weeping?" She said to them, "Because they have taken away my Lord, and I do not know where they have laid him." Saying this, she turned round and saw Jesus standing, but she did not know that it was Jesus. Jesus said to her, "Woman, why are you weeping? Whom do you seek?" Supposing him to be the gardener, she said to him, "Sir, if you have carried him away, tell me

where you have laid him, and I will take him away." Jesus said to her, "Mary." She turned and said to him in Hebrew, "Rab-boni!" (which means Teacher). Jesus said to her, "Do not hold me, for I have not yet ascended to the Father; but go to my brethren and say to them, I am ascending to my Father and your Father, to my God and your God." Mary Magdalene went and said to the disciples, "I have seen the Lord"; and she told them that he had said these things to her. (Jn 20:1-18)

How rich are the parallels between this passage and the verses of the Song of Songs! Let us read them again now, in the light of this scene from the Gospel of John, and indeed read the verses immediately following:

Upon my bed, at night,
I sought him whom my heart loves;
I sought him, but found him not.
So I will arise now and go about the city;
in the streets and in the squares
I will seek him whom my heart loves.
I sought him, but found him not.
The watchmen found me,
as they went about in the city.
"Have you seen him whom my heart loves?"
Scarcely had I passed them,
when I found him whom my heart loves.
I held him fast, and would not let him go,
until I had brought him into my mother's house,
into the chamber of her who conceived me.
(Sg 3:1-4)

Mary Magdalene comes to the tomb early in the morning (to anoint the body of the Lord, as the other Evangelists note). Perhaps she was tossing and turning all night upon her bed, seeking to lay hold in her memory and in her heart of the One whom her heart loves! And so she rises early in the morning, before dawn, drawn by the greatness of her love for Christ, for the One beside whose Cross she stood as he lovingly poured out his life. She, the woman from whom seven demons had been driven out, who had experienced the immense mercy of God, she who had washed Jesus' feet with her tears and wiped them with her hair—she is all aflame with love. Yes, she who has been forgiven much now loves much. She is drawn by the irresistible longing of love, the longing of the bride for her heavenly Bridegroom.

Just like the restless and longing bride, Mary goes out at night to search for her lost Beloved, and yet in her search she does not immediately encounter him, but only the "watchmen." Mary first speaks with Peter and John (the watchmen of the Church!), who join her in her ardent haste, but then return to their homes. But she, on the other hand, remains at the tomb, weeping and longing for the love of her life. And here she encounters the angels sitting like watchmen at either side of the Lord's tomb. And how amazing is her response to them! "They have taken away my Lord, and I do not know where they have laid him" (Jn 20:13). Who is this *"Lord,"* who is this *"him"* whom you do not even think it is necessary to name? It is as if, in the passionate love of your heart, you presume that everyone already knows him, that he is the only one, the "one whom your heart loves."

And once Mary Magdalene utters her own cry, just like the bride in the Song, she turns around and sees Jesus. "Scarcely had I passed them when I found him whom my heart loves." But she says to him, too, those mad words of love: "Sir, if you have carried him away, tell me where you have laid him, and I will take him away" (Jn 20:15). He tenderly pronounces her name, "Mary," and thus strikes her to the very core, vibrating the sinews of her heart with the touch of his own love. And what does she do in response? She holds on to him! "I held him and would not let him go…"

How beautiful is the parallelism of these two passages! Mary doesn't even see the need to describe the One whom she seeks, to even mention his name. Just as for the Beloved in the Song, he is simply "mine," simply "the One whom my heart loves." Doesn't everyone know him? How could anyone not know him, who is the fairest of the children of men, who is Beautiful above all beauty? And indeed the angels understand her. She begs them, the "watchmen," for the presence of her Beloved, but only when she "passes them" does she encounter him, does she find him whom her heart seeks. But at first she doesn't recognize the Lord; her eyes are not yet opened to see him. "She turned around and saw Jesus standing, but she did not know that it was Jesus. … Jesus said to her, 'Mary.' She turned and said to him in Hebrew, 'Rabboni!' (which means teacher)" (Jn 20:14, 16). Ah yes, didn't Jesus say, "I know my own and my own know me, as the Father knows me and I know the Father"? Didn't he say that the sheep "hear his voice, and *he calls his own sheep by name* and leads them out" (Jn 10:14-15, 3)?

A simple word: *Mary*. She hears her name, her name falling from the lips of the divine Beloved—and how sweetly he speaks it. In this simple word is contained all the force of love. It is as if, through his loving gaze and his tender voice, he reaches across the space of her fear, her hesitation, her longing, and plucks the strings of her inmost heart, causing them to vibrate with the joy of his presence, and with the certainty of experiencing herself to be seen, known, and uniquely loved by him. Is this not precisely what I have said so frequently in these reflections? *My identity comes precisely from the love of God for me.* Yes, he alone truly knows my name and can reveal it to me—and he does so with a simple look, a simple word, touching my innermost heart with his goodness—and thus fills my being with joy!

He says: You love me, Mary, and you seek me. But do you not see that I love you yet more? I seek you even more deeply, more lovingly, more ardently. *Mary.* The word envelops her whole being, the mystery of who she is in the eyes of God, in the tender gaze of her Lover. And this awareness causes her being to blossom. Experiencing the love of God, she yearns to be united forever to him in this love, to belong to him, to cling to him so perfectly that nothing will ever be able to tear her from him—from him to whom her heart has been surrendered. As we will see, this theme recurs again at the very climax of the Song, in some of the most beautiful verses in the whole Bible: "Set me as a seal upon you heart, as a seal upon your arm; for love is strong as death, jealousy as relentless as Sheol. Its flashes are flashes of fire, a flame of God himself" (Sg 8:6).

"I held him, and would not let him go" (Sg 3:4b). Mary throws herself down before the Lord and grasps his feet, those feet which she washed so lovingly before. Or perhaps she even embraces him fully, made bold by the ardent desire of love! But he says, "Do not hold me, for I have not yet ascended to the Father; but go to my brethren and say to them, I am ascending to my Father and your Father, to my God and your God" (Jn 20:17). I am indeed yours forever, Mary, as you so deeply desire. But you do not yet understand the full nature of our union, for it is even deeper, even more intimate than you yet grasp or comprehend. It is an enduring embrace, but an embrace of another order. In my Death and Resurrection I have opened up a new way of being, a new depth of intimacy. I have entered wholly into the sphere of pure Love, and I want to lead you here, so that you can be united with me as I truly am in the fullness of my Mystery. Therefore, in departing to be with the Father—who is both my Father and yours—I am not really leaving you, but drawing near in the most profound way. In me you will know yourself to be his beloved child, just as I am his beloved Child. Yes, you will be with me where I am, nestled deeply in the inmost recesses of my Heart, and in the bosom of the Father, in faith, hope, and love… Bridegroom and bride united in a single embrace, within the all-enveloping embrace of the Father of them both!

And even now, my beloved, I will never cease to come to you in the deepest way, a way made possible only by my being wholly in the Father. In him I can penetrate all things and fill them with my presence. This Body that I have taken as my own, it is no longer limited like you imagine. No, opened utterly on the Cross, and, even more, glorified in victory over death and sin, it now embraces the entire world and gives itself without hindrance or limitation. Dearly beloved, my Body is now the perfect nuptial gift—a gift which envelops you even when you do not sense it. This is a gift which communicates the deepest truth of my being and of my intimacy with the Father, a gift to which you draw near in the Holy Eucharist and in the mystery of the Church, in the truth of every moment of your life, throbbing with your love and longing which is but a reflection of my love and longing for you.

And here I welcome you, my bride, here I take you into myself and hold you to my Heart. Here I give myself to you without reserve, and, through this gift, you experience my happiness and the peace and joy of my Father—my Father and yours. In his love we are forever united, brother and sister, husband and wife, in a union beyond all earthly union, in a virginal embrace in which I am yours and you are mine—uniquely and unrepeatably.

Because of my love, dearly beloved, the abiding truth of joy is already beginning to be fulfilled in you, and will be perfectly fulfilled at the end: "Enter into the joy of your Lord" (Mt 25:21). You enter in, you are enveloped in my perfect embrace, as in an ocean of joy and gladness, as a drop of water in the chalice of wine, transformed in my Blood, my Presence, my very Being as beloved Son of the Father and Bridegroom of your heart. Yes, in all truth, you are enfolded as my beloved in the undying tenderness of my embrace, and you repose, as a beloved child, in the bosom of the loving Father.

ישוע

EVEN IN THE SHADOWS OF THIS LIFE, I REST IN YOUR EMBRACE

After the bride expresses her ardent search for the Bridegroom, and recounts her encounter with him, in which she holds him fast and does not want to let him go until she brings him into her mother's house, into the "chamber of her who conceived me," the Bridegroom interjects, and repeats the refrain that brings this second poem to a conclusion: "I adjure you, Daughters of Jerusalem, by the gazelles or the hinds of the field, that you stir not up nor awaken my love until she is pleased to awake" (3:5). And so we see that this poem ends in the same way as the first, with the bride sleeping, and the Bridegroom sheltering her in her repose from all that would disturb her.

Has she perhaps been dreaming this whole time? This is what a number of commentators think: that the entire search of the bride has occurred only in her own dreams, and that she has actually never left her bed at all! How impoverished an understanding this would be, though, if we were to imagine that she is only dreaming, and that she has really had no contact with her Beloved, and indeed that she is not even fully conscious! Is not the opposite rather the case? She is gradually awakening ever more deeply to the living presence of her Bridegroom, she is gradually becoming more and more awake as the drama of the Song of Songs progresses. She is awakening through this ever deepening movement of seeking and finding, which unfolds within the sheltering embrace of the absent Beloved who is intimately present even in his apparent absence, and who, even when he is present holding his bride, surpasses her experience in the depth of his mystery.

This mysterious dynamic of the life of prayer alone can adequately explain the paradoxical unfolding of the Song of Songs, and the way in which the Bridegroom and the bride both ardently seek one another, embrace, and then seek one another anew with an even greater longing. We encounter here the romance of two love-wounded hearts which are ever discovering one another's beauty more deeply, ever letting themselves be captured by the other and drawn toward them, ever embracing and giving themselves to one another, and yet in this very surrender experiencing that such a surrender can be perpetually renewed throughout this life until it is consummated in eternity.

We have seen how the Bridegroom comes to his bride, calling out to her as she hides within her wounds, afraid and vulnerable, scared of being hurt again. And yet in calling her out he casts a bridge of safety and security in his own gaze, in the tenderness of his words. Yes, he opens to her the wound of his own Sacred Heart and invites her to step out, naked and defenseless, in order to allow herself to be gazed upon, to be heard, and to be received in this way into the true and perfect shelter of his enduring Love. Thus her wounded heart encounters his wounded Heart. Her vulnerable heart encounters his vulnerable Heart. And thus, gradually, she is nestled ever more deeply into his Heart, and her wounds of fear, of sin, of shame, are eased, purified, and healed by the touch of the wound of love that he bears in his own Heart through his ardent compassion and tender longing for her.

Thus she finds herself standing close to the wounded Heart of her Redeemer; she finds herself bathed in the sheltering love of the One who, in his very woundedness, heals. She experiences the bond of covenant-love that allows her to pronounce, "My Beloved is mine and I am his" (Sg 2:16). And she asks to be always encircled in the security of this enduring love, in the shelter of his Crucified Heart, which has been torn open by compassion and pours forth living streams of grace. And so she is cradled, she is held, she is sheltered. And in being sheltered she is also given to drink. By standing at the foot of the Cross of the One who cried out in this place, "I thirst!" she herself learns how to drink. And in drinking she satisfies the very thirst of the divine Beloved, for he is the Thirsty Fountain whose deepest longing is precisely that his precious one will let herself be loved, that she will let herself be sheltered in the open space of his Heart, which he has opened, in its nakedness and vulnerability, precisely in order to receive and hold her in the place where she needs it the most.

But this union in the place of greatest vulnerability, this union effected through two hearts sharing in a single passion of love—this union of com-passion in which the ardent passion of God's love awakens the passionate love of the human heart, and unites the two together in an enduring intimacy in the Sacred Heart of Christ—this union is not brought to its full flowering and consummation until the Resurrection. Yes, the bride's heart is surrendered to her Beloved. She experiences the binding-together of covenant-love in the very place where she stands at the foot of the Cross of her Bridegroom as he pours out his life lovingly for her salvation. But then he is laid in the tomb, hidden in the clefts of the rock from which he had previously called her, and in which she is still hidden. He has united himself with her in the very sleep of death, but only so that, taking her up in his arms in this very place, he may draw her out into the light of enduring Day. Yes, by uniting himself so intimately with her, he gives her the confidence to step out in ardent longing in order to unite herself with him. And so she comes, early in the morning while it is still dark, yearning ardently for her Beloved and searching for him in anguish. And there she encounters him, radiant in the beauty of his Risen Body. But she only recognizes him when he tenderly pronounces her name, when his own Name is an oil poured out to penetrate the deepest fibers of her being until it makes contact with her own most intimate and true identity. What a blessed union!

And in response to this, she lays hold of him, wrapping her arms around him and holding him close to her heart. Have not these two hearts already beat together as one, sharing a single pulsation of love?

Have not these two lovers already shared a single breath? Why then does he tell her not to hold him, to let him ascend to the Father? He is not rebuffing her desire for union, for an enduring intimacy. Rather, he is directing her to the only space in which that intimacy can truly endure, to that space in which the union of their hearts, the sharing of a single breath, can be unbroken at every moment of time. He is inviting her to immerse herself—in faith, hope, and love—into the very realm of eternal Love, into the space opened up within his Risen Body. He is inviting her into the clefts of the Rock!

Yes, he goes to the Father, and she stays behind, if only for a time. But he also brings her with him, already, by nestling her within the shelter of his own Crucified and Risen Heart as he ascends into the everlasting intimacy of the Father's embrace. Therefore, she is already "hidden with Christ in God" until he "who is her life appears," and then she will at last "appear with him in glory" (Col 3:3-4). And until that day their union is true, even if hidden behind the veil of mortality, sheltered in the sacred space of faith, hope, and love. Therefore, the bride can sleep, can rest, already now in the shadows of this life, even as her heart is ever seeking the embrace of her Beloved more deeply, more intimately. For she knows that she is already cradled at every moment within this embrace, until she experiences it perfectly, in the full and undimmed light of the eternal Day, when she at last passes from this life and into the radiant communion that her Beloved eternally shares with the Father and the Holy Spirit.

THIRD POEM

THE SUMMER OF THE WEDDING

WHAT IS THIS?

The third poem begins with a cry of surprise, or amazement, or awe, and at first we are uncertain about who is speaking:

What is this coming up from the desert,
like a column of smoke,
breathing of myrrh and frankincense,
with all the fragrant powders of the merchant?
(Sg 3:6)

What is this column arising from the arid desert, this pillar of cloud and fire? In this description, how can we not think immediately of the Exodus, in which God led his people with a column of fire by night and a pillar of cloud by day, until they passed at last into the Promised Land?

> And the LORD went before them by day in a pillar of cloud to lead them along the way, and by night in a pillar of fire to give them light, that they might travel by day and by night; the pillar of cloud by day and the pillar of fire by night did not depart from before the people. (Ex 13:21-22)

"What is this?" There is a cry of uncertainty here, but also a cry of awe, a heartfelt expression of the trembling amazement that fills the human heart when it encounters the *mysterium tremendum* of God. The heart always cries out in awe whenever God pulls back a little the veil of his unspeakable Beauty that so that it may touch the contemplative gaze of the one whom he loves. Ah, what is this? And how mysterious is the nature of this column, forbidding in its mystery and yet inviting in its sweetness! How is it that it is both a column of smoke, and yet breathes forth—literally, emits smoke as a burning sacrifice—the fragrance of myrrh and frankincense and all the other powders of the merchant?

In the covenant on Mount Sinai, it seems that the mystery of God's transcendence is especially emphasized, as his bride is not yet ready to realize that the only true greatness of God is the greatness of his infinite Love. She must first learn to turn away from the idols of Egypt and to recognize that "God is the LORD, and there is no other. Beside him there is no other god" (cf. Is 45:5). Only in the New Testament will the forbidding majesty of God be revealed as nothing but the unspeakable tenderness of Love...the radiant beauty of the One who pours himself out without reserve and who welcomes the beloved totally, taking her to himself. We need think only of the difference between the two following passages, and we can see the newness that Christ brought in his Incarnation and his Paschal Mystery, as he has unveiled for us the true face of the Father and the tenderness of his compassionate heart:

> And the LORD said to Moses, "Behold, I am coming to you in a thick cloud, that the people may hear when I speak with you, and may also believe you for ever. ... On the morning of the third day there was thunder and lightning, and a thick cloud upon the mountain, and a very loud trumpet blast, so that all the people who were in the camp trembled. Then Moses brought the people out of the camp to meet God; and they took their stand at the foot of the mountain. And Mount Sinai was wrapped in smoke, because the LORD descended upon it in fire; and the smoke of it went up like the smoke of a kiln, and the whole mountain quaked greatly. And as the sound of the trumpet grew louder and louder, Moses spoke, and God answered him in thunder. And the LORD came down upon Mount Sinai, to the top of the mountain, and Moses went up. And the LORD said to Moses, "Go down and warn the people, lest they break through to the LORD to gaze and many of them perish." (Ex 19:9, 16-21).

> For you have not come to what may be touched, a blazing fire, and darkness, and gloom, and a tempest, and the sound of a trumpet, and a voice whose words made the hearers entreat that no further messages be spoken to them. For they could not endure the order that was given, "If even a beast touches the mountain, it shall be stoned." Indeed, so terrifying was the sight that Moses said, "I tremble with fear." But you have come to Mount Zion and to the city of the living God, the heavenly Jerusalem, and to innumerable angels in festal gathering, and to the assembly of the first-born who are enrolled in heaven, and to a judge who is God of all, and to the spirits of just men made perfect, and to Jesus, the mediator of a new covenant, and to the sprinkled blood that speaks more graciously than the blood of Abel. (Heb 12:18-24)

What was only anticipated in the Sinai covenant—what could only be shown as a transcendent mystery that, in its greatness, terrified—was at last unveiled as the inviting call of the One who beckons his bride into an everlasting intimacy of love, and into the heavenly Jerusalem in which there is celebrated the eternal marriage feast! We see the same thing in the words of Saint Paul in his Second Letter to the Corinthians:

> You yourselves are our letter of recommendation, written on

your hearts, to be known and read by all men; and you show that you are a letter from Christ delivered by us, written not with ink but with the Spirit of the living God, not on tablets of stone but on tablets of human hearts. Now if the dispensation of death, carved in letters on stone, came with such splendor that the Israelites could not look at Moses' face because of its brightness, fading as this was, will not the dispensation of the Spirit be attended with greater splendor? For if there was splendor in the dispensation of condemnation, the dispensation of righteousness must far exceed it in splendor. Indeed, in this case, what once had splendor has come to have no splendor at all, because of the splendor that surpasses it. For if what faded away came with splendor, what is permanent must have much more splendor.

Since we have such a hope, we are very bold, not like Moses, who put a veil over his face so that the Israelites might not see the end of the fading splendor. But their minds were hardened; for to this day, when they read the old covenant, that same veil remains unlifted, because only through Christ is it taken away. Yes, to this day whenever Moses is read a veil lies over their minds; but when a man turns to the Lord the veil is removed. Now the Lord is the Spirit, and where the Spirit of the Lord is, there is freedom. And we all, with unveiled face, beholding the glory of the Lord, are being changed into his likeness from one degree of glory to another; for this comes from the Lord who is the Spirit. (2 Cor 3:2-18)

What has made this difference? What has truly unveiled the face of eternal Love before our eyes, giving us a radical childlike confidence to gaze, without hesitation, on the radiant beauty of our Beloved? What has impressed the law of God so deeply upon our hearts that we experience it no longer as an external burden, but as the spontaneous flowering of our hearts in the freedom of love, in the joy and playfulness of confident trust in the One who loves us and has taken us for himself? It is, as Saint Paul immediately explains, "the light of the knowledge of the glory of Christ, who is the likeness of God." And then he adds: "For it is the God who said, 'Let light shine out of darkness,' who has shone in our hearts to give the light of the knowledge of the glory of God in the face of Christ" (2 Cor 4:4, 6). What a blessed light has dawned upon us in the radiant and beautiful face of Christ, in whose tender countenance we see the very glory of the heavenly Father!

In these words we are standing at the heart of the New Testament revelation. For here we encounter the Beauty of eternal Love laid bare before our eyes, and we are awakened, through this Beauty that ravishes us and tenderly touches our inmost heart—like oil poured out and pervading our entire being, or the sweetness of perfume inebriating our senses!—to step out into the welcoming embrace of the One who calls. "Arise, my love, my beautiful one, and come to me" (Sg 2:10). Yes, the bride is being asked to remove the veil that covers her face, so that her own countenance, in gazing upon her Beloved, may be bathed in the healing light of his own loving gaze! In this radiant light of contemplative love, in this mutual surrender of shared knowledge—in which eyes interlock and hearts themselves communicate—the bride is "transformed from glory unto glory," into the very likeness of her heavenly Bridegroom.

Just as a bride, on their marriage day, takes the name of her husband as her own, so the same is true with the spiritual bride of Christ. When she lets herself be drawn to her Beloved and espoused to him, her own unique identity is sheltered in his embrace, and yet this name is cradled and sheltered in the very Name of her Spouse, and precisely there it finds its true home and its radiant expansion in its authentic beauty! This makes me think of a story from the life of Saint Teresa of Avila, whose religious name was *Teresa de Jesús*, Teresa of Jesus. This is how Arminjon describes it:

> One day, on the staircase of the novitiate of the Carmelite Convent of the Incarnation in Avila, young Teresa, who was then between eighteen and twenty years old, met a boy about ten years old. She was not too surprised at first. In those days, monastic discipline was very lax, and the kin and friends of the nuns moved about freely in the monastery. The time of Teresa the reformer had not yet come! But the child approached her daringly and asked her, "What is your name?" "Teresa of Jesus," she replied, rather surprised. Who was that boy to interrogate her so freely without the usual ceremony? "And you," Teresa went on rather abruptly, "who are you?" "Jesus of Teresa," the child replied, and he vanished. Teresa of Jesus, Jesus of Teresa: same identity, same name, same seal.[16]

What is striking here is that, not only is the bride's name that of her Beloved, but the Bridegroom himself takes the name of his bride as his own. "I am Jesus of Teresa…" In other words, I belong to you completely. I am yours, totally and forever, just as you, my love, are mine. "I know mine and mine know me," Jesus said in the Gospel of John, "and I call them by name and they follow me" (cf. Jn 10:14, 3-

4). But we can even say something similar to him! How astounding this is! It should make us cry out with an even greater amazement than that evoked by the Sinai epiphany. "I know my Beloved and he knows me," we can say, "and I call him by Name and he answers me!"

יְשׁוּעַ

THE ARK OF HIS PRESENCE

"What is this?" We heard this cry at the start of the third poem, a cry that seems to come from the Daughters of Jerusalem—that is, the chorus of maiden companions who accompany the bride and witness her journey throughout the Song. And we saw the mysterious awe awakened by God, who is both cloud and fire, who is both mystery and revelation, who is both immense in his majesty and yet intimately near in his love. Or rather, we saw that God's greatness, his mystery, his immensity, is simply identical with his eternal Love. And this Love is but the everlasting embrace of the Father, Son, and Holy Spirit, who have created, desired, and chosen each one of us to share forever in the joy of their own life of perfect communion and joy.

God's presence is coming up out of the desert at the start of this poem like a column of smoke, and yet this is not the smoke of a burning animal or even of a bonfire, but a smoke that is simply breathing forth the sweet and yet pungent perfume of myrrh, frankincense, and all the perfumes. My mind also go at this point to the gift given by the wise men from the east to the Christ Child: "When they saw the star, they rejoiced exceedingly with great joy; and going into the house they saw the child with Mary his mother, and they fell down and worshiped him. Then, opening their treasures, they offered him gifts, gold and frankincense and myrrh" (Mt 2:10-11). Is this not what is being evoked now by this vision of God's glory coming out of the wilderness? "They rejoiced exceedingly with great joy!" What an amazing, superlative way of expressing the experience of joy! They not not only rejoice. They not only rejoice exceedingly. Rather, they rejoice exceedingly with great joy! Many times through the New Testament, human language is pushed to its utmost limits in trying to express the inexpressible depth of God's love, and the great joy brought by his inestimable gift. I think of another phrase, this time by Saint Paul, which is so beautiful:

I bow my knees before the Father, from whom every family in heaven and on earth is named, that according to the riches of his glory he may grant you to be strengthened with might through his Spirit in the inner man, and that Christ may dwell in your hearts through faith; that you, being rooted and grounded in love, may have power to comprehend with all the saints what is the breadth and length and height and depth, and to know the love of Christ which surpasses knowledge, that you may be filled with all the fullness of God. (Eph 3:14-19)

How could he express with any more ardor and expansiveness the depth of God's love, and the amazing intimacy that he effects by pouring out this love into us? The heavenly Father wants us to know the "breadth and length and height and depth" of the Love that surpasses all knowledge, this Love that cannot be limited or contained and yet fills all of creation with its fullness, pervading all like an oil poured out or a perfume penetrating everything with its fragrance. And the ultimate desire of this ardent and passionate Love that fills all with its presence? "That you may be filled with all the fullness of God!" We do not just touch the fullness of God. We are filled with this fullness...and not just filled with this fullness, but filled with *all* of this fullness!

I could go on and on like this, since the New Testament is full of such exuberant expressions of praise and jubilation at the great love of God. But let us return to the text of the Song. This column of smoke is seen coming up out of the desert, emitting the sweetest of perfumes. But what is within this column? What is being both shrouded and revealed by the smoke of this epiphany of God?

Behold, it is the throne of Solomon!
About it are sixty champions
of the champions of Israel,
all belted with swords
and expert in war,
each with his sword at his side,
against alarms by night.
(Sg 3:7-8)

What is this throne, this "litter," that is progressing up out of the wilderness, carried upon the shoulders of men and surrounded by these "champions of Israel?" Yes, the king of Israel himself had champions in his retinue to protect him, men trained and experienced in battle. But there is something different here. This is not just the king of Israel, not just Solomon the son of David. For David had thirty champions who surrounded him, but this Solomon has twice as many. But more than that, there is something deeply mysterious about this explanation of the throne. For one, why is this litter of Solomon enveloped in the cloud of God's presence, and why is Solomon himself not seen? Only his throne is described, but it is as if the throne is empty.

This brings us immediately to our answer. The Solomon being described here is the true King of Israel, the God of hosts himself, veiled under the thin imagery of king Solomon. For what indeed, in the historical Exodus, was surrounded with the cloud of God's presence as the Israelites marched through the desert toward the Promised Land? *The ark of the covenant!* Let us read some of the descriptions of this ark, which was the visible presence of God on earth throughout the Old Testament. God said to Moses:

> They shall make an ark of acacia wood, two cubits and a half shall be its length, a cubit and a half its breadth, and a cubit and a half its height. And you shall overlay it with pure gold, within and without shall you overlay it, and you shall make upon it a molding of gold round about. And you shall cast four rings of gold for it and put them on its four feet... You shall make poles of acacia wood [for carrying the ark], and overlay them with gold. The poles shall remain in the rings of the ark; they shall not be taken from it. And you shall put into the ark the covenant which I shall give you [i.e. the tablets of the law]. Then you shall make a mercy seat of pure gold... And you shall make two cherubim of gold; of hammered work shall you make them, on the two ends of the mercy seat. ... The cherubim shall spread out their wings above, overshadowing the mercy seat with their wings, their faces one to another; toward the mercy seat shall the faces of the cherubim be. And you shall put the mercy seat on the top of the ark... There I will meet with you, and from above the mercy seat, from between the two cherubim that are upon the ark of the covenant, I will speak with you of all that I will give you in commandment for the sons of Israel. (cf. Ex 25:10-22)

Recall that God had forbidden the Israelite people to craft images to worship, since they were still immersed in the process of purification from the idol-worship of Egypt and the surrounding nations. They were tempted again and again to try to reduce the invisible God to something that they could touch, see, and grasp in their own size and according to their own limitations. But God transcends all of this! Even in his intimate closeness he cannot be grasped by human hands or by human gaze. Only in Christ will this prohibition of images be dissolved, since in Jesus God himself takes the initiative of making himself visible, touchable, and graspable! As Saint John writes in his First Letter:

> That which was from the beginning, *which we have heard, which we have seen with our eyes, which we have looked upon and touched with our hands,* concerning the Word of Life—*the Life was made manifest, and we saw it, and testify to it, and proclaim to you the eternal life which was with the Father and was made manifest to us*—that which we have seen and heard we proclaim also to you, so that you may have communion with us; and our communion is with the Father and with his Son Jesus Christ. And we are writing this that our joy may be complete. (1 Jn 1:1-4)

Yet now we are getting off track, and have almost forgotten about the ark! God would come to the Israelites by descending upon the ark and "taking his seat" upon the mercy seat (his throne!) that was built between the overshadowing wings of the two cherubim. But God himself would not be seen! Rather, he remained invisible and his presence was known only through the pillar of cloud or fire that would rest upon the ark:

> Then the cloud covered the tent of meeting, and the glory of the LORD filled the tabernacle. And Moses was not able to enter the tent of meeting, because the cloud abode upon it, and the glory of the LORD filled the tabernacle. Throughout all their journeys, whenever the cloud was taken up from over the tabernacle, the people of Israel would go onward; but if the cloud was not taken up, then they did not go onward till the day that it was taken up. For throughout all their journeys the cloud of the LORD was upon the tabernacle by day, and fire was in it by night, in the sight of all the house of Israel. (Ex 40:34-38)

This is what is seen, in the Song of Songs, coming up from the wilderness enveloped in a column of smoke: the "throne" of the true Solomon. It is the ark of the covenant of the invisible God who has entered into a lasting union with his people and has come to dwell among them in their desert journey. But, in saying this, I have not said all that needs to be said about the ark. For the material ark made of acacia wood overlaid with gold—containing the tablets of the law, an urn containing the miraculous bread called manna, and the staff of Aaron that had miraculously flowered—is still but a sign of greater things. It is still only a symbol and a promise of the lasting dwelling of God with his people—the true Word and Law of God made flesh, the Bread of Life giving himself as our food, and the Priest, Prophet, and King who rules, guide, and teaches us with the tenderness of his eternal Love. Yes, this union between God and humanity will be accomplished fully only in the Incarnation of Christ within the womb of the Virgin Mary, and in his Eucharist, Passion, and Resurrection. But that is for the next reflection.

ישוע

I PLEDGED MYSELF TO YOU

In the previous reflection I spoke in depth about the ark of the covenant and its role in the Old Covenant. There is much more I could say, but I don't want to be led too far afield from our reflections on the Song of Songs, so let me speak now about the way in which the symbol of the ark is fulfilled in the New Testament. Let me note especially the spousal imagery of the covenant and the ark, especially in the light of the Song of Songs. In a number of places in the Old Testament, the covenant between God and his people is described as a marriage. This is especially, though not exclusively, true of the books of the Prophets. Indeed, the Song of Songs fits precisely within the context of this prophetic tradition, taking it to the next level with the depth of its prolonged allegory of the marital union between the Bridegroom-God and his beloved bride. Let us take one example. In the book of Ezekiel, God says:

> Thus says the Lord GOD to Jerusalem: Your origin and your birth are of the land of the Canaanites; your father was an Amorite, and your mother a Hittite. And as for your birth, on the day you were born your navel string was not cut, nor were you washed with water to cleanse you, nor rubbed with salt, nor swathed with bands. No eye pitied you, to do any of these things to you out of compassion for you; but you were cast out on the open field, for you were abhorred, on the day that you were born. And when I passed by you, and saw you weltering in your blood, I said to you in your blood, "Live, and grow up like a plant of the field." And you grew up and became tall and arrived at full maidenhood; your breasts were formed, and your hair had grown; yet you were naked and bare. "When I passed by you again and looked upon you, behold, you were at the age for love; and I spread my skirt over you, and covered your nakedness: yes, I pledged myself to you and entered into a covenant with you, says the Lord GOD, and you became mine. Then I bathed you with water and washed off your blood from you, and anointed you with oil. I clothed you also with embroidered cloth and shod you with leather, I swathed you in fine

linen and covered you with silk. And I decked you with ornaments, and put bracelets on your arms, and a chain on your neck. And I put a ring on your nose, and earrings in your ears, and a beautiful crown upon your head. Thus you were decked with gold and silver; and your raiment was of fine linen, and silk, and embroidered cloth; you ate fine flour and honey and oil. You grew exceedingly beautiful, and came to regal estate. And your renown went forth among the nations because of your beauty, for it was perfect through the splendor which I had bestowed upon you, says the Lord GOD. (Ez 16:3-14)

In these words we see the delight that the Bridegroom-God has in his bride, who is simultaneously the whole of his chosen people and each individual person. He draws her out of her loneliness since he sees great beauty in her. He gradually prepares her for himself and, when she is at the age for love, pledges himself to her in a covenant of love and, through his own tender care and his loving gift, makes her radiate with a beauty that is perfect, renowned through all the nations. Indeed, this is a reflection of the splendor of the Bridegroom himself shining forth from within the bride, as he says: "it was perfect through the splendor which I had bestowed on you." We will see this theme of the woman bearing the beauty of her Beloved soon in the Song, this woman indeed who is received like a crown by her Beloved and radiates with beauty and splendor which capture his heart and fill it with awe.

But what does this have to do with the ark, and with its presence in the New Covenant? In the book of Ezekiel the bride has been deeply unfaithful, playing the harlot with many other lovers—many false gods—and yet God says to her: "I will remember my covenant with you in the days of your youth, and I will establish with you an everlasting covenant" (Ez 16:60). As he explains much later: "I will sprinkle clean water upon you, and you shall be clean from all your uncleannesses, and from all your idols I will cleanse you. A new heart I will give you, and a new spirit I will put within you; and I will take out of your flesh the heart of stone and give you a heart of flesh. And I will put my spirit within you, and cause you to walk in my statutes and be careful to observe my ordinances. You shall dwell in the land which I gave to your fathers; and you shall be my people, and I will be your God" (Ez 36:25-28). Here we see the same theme of purification by water, and something even more amazing: that this covenant will be impressed on the very heart of the bride, since his love will give her a new heart, no longer of stone but of flesh. In other words, her heart hardened by sin and guilt and shame, enclosed upon itself and afraid, will be melted by the tenderness of God's own love so that it may flow back to him in a fluid response of spontaneous reciprocal love.

The presence of the divine Bridegroom which was once present among his people through the tablets of the law, through the external commandments, will be interiorized as this law is written on their very heart. Thus the covenant which God ordered to be kept in the ark is now being situated, not in a material box of wood and gold, but in the very heart of the human person. And let us remember that for the Israelite mind, the heart was the inner core of personal being, the very center of one's existence, where body and spirit were inseparably joined together. Thus the human person in her entirety, flesh and spirit, becomes a dwelling place of the covenant-love of God. But if this is true, do we see other elements of the epiphany of God associated with the ark manifest in his relationship with the human body? Yes. There are too many to recount here. Let us only note the most significant one: "The Holy Spirit will come upon you," the angel Gabriel says to the Virgin Mary, "and the power of the most high will overshadow you, and therefore the child to be born of you will be called the Holy One, the Son of God" (cf. Lk 1:35). Here is the true pillar of cloud and fire that overshadows the ark of the covenant and makes God truly present at the heart of creation. Here is the true Emmanuel, God-with-us, incarnate within the womb of the Virgin Mary. She is the Ark of the Covenant in the fullest sense, the one that was but symbolized by the ark of old; she is the true meeting-place of God and humanity, and the dwelling-place of his presence. Saint Luke understood this very well, as he explicitly (though subtly) portrays Mary as the Ark of the Covenant when, immediately after the Annunciation, she makes haste to visit her aunt Elizabeth. He draws a direct parallel (or rather many parallels!) between Mary's visit and the incident in which David, finally making Jerusalem his home, takes the ark of the covenant up into the city. Let me quote the scene with David first, and then I will quote the Visitation scene:

> David arose and went with all the people who were with him from Baale-*judah*, to bring up from there the ark of God, which is called by the name of the LORD of hosts who sits enthroned on the cherubim. And they carried the ark of God upon a new cart, and brought it out of the house of Abinadab which was on the hill; and Uzzah and Ahio, the sons of Abinadab, were driving the new cart with the ark of God; and Ahio went before the ark. ... And David was afraid of the LORD that day; and he said, *"How can the ark of the LORD come to me?"*

So David was not willing to take the ark of the LORD into the city of David; but David took it aside to the house of Obed-edom the Gittite. And the ark of the LORD remained in the house of Obed-edom the Gittite *three months*; and the LORD *blessed* Obed-edom and all his household. And it was told King David, "The LORD has blessed the household of Obed-edom and all that belongs to him, because of the ark of God." So David went and brought up the ark of God from the house of Obed-edom to the city of David with *rejoicing*... And David danced before the LORD with all his might; and David was girded with a linen ephod. ... As the ark of the LORD came into the city of David, Michal the daughter of Saul looked out of the window, and saw King David *leaping and dancing before the LORD*... And they brought in the ark of the LORD, and set it in its place, inside the tent which David had pitched for it; and David offered burnt offerings and peace offerings before the LORD. And when David had finished offering the burnt offerings and the peace offerings, he blessed the people in the name of the LORD of hosts. ... And David *returned to bless his household*. (cf. 2 Sam 6:2-20)

Now let us read the scene of the Visitation, with the parallels highlighted just as I have done above:

In those days Mary arose and went with haste into the hill country, to a city of *Judah*, and she entered the house of Zechariah and greeted Elizabeth. And when Elizabeth heard the greeting of Mary, the babe *leaped in her womb*; and Elizabeth was filled with the Holy Spirit and she exclaimed with a loud cry, "*Blessed* are you among women, and *blessed* is the fruit of your womb! And *why is this granted me, that the mother of my Lord should come to me?* For behold, when the voice of your greeting came to my ears, the babe in my womb *leaped for joy*. And *blessed is she* who believed that there would be a fulfillment of what was spoken to her from the Lord." And Mary said, "*My soul magnifies the Lord*, and my spirit rejoices in God my Savior..." And Mary remained with her about *three months*, and *returned to her home*. (cf. Lk 1:39-56)

So what's the point? Mary is being revealed as the Ark of the New Covenant, who lets herself be overshadowed with the very fullness of God's presence such that God himself becomes incarnate within her heart and her womb. Yes, she is his true throne, the *sedes sapientiae*, the "Seat of Wisdom" on which the Incarnate Word of God himself is seated. *But let us remind ourselves that everything that God does in Mary he desires also to do in us!* She is the true bride of Christ who consents to the marriage proposal of God; she is the one who welcomes and allows to be realized in her very flesh the fullness of the New Covenant. Yes, we see her again and again in the unfolding of both the Old and the New Testaments, in the whole narrative of salvation history. And yet, sheltered within her maternal tenderness, within the depth of her own intimacy with God, we find nestled the unique personal identity, and the unrepeatable path, of each one of us, who is each directly willed by God and unspeakably beautiful in his eyes.

ישוע

THE CORONATION WHICH IS A MARRIAGE

Does Mary appear anywhere else in Scripture as the Ark of the Covenant? Let us turn our gaze to the book of Revelation, to the climax of the whole history of God's relationship with humanity. Here the veil of heaven is opened before our eyes and we are gradually drawn into the awesome *marriage* that is eternally consummated in the new Jerusalem, the glorified Church in whom every human heart finds its home. John the Evangelist writes:

> Then God's temple in heaven was opened, and the ark of his covenant was seen within his temple; and there were flashes of lightning, voices, peals of thunder, an earthquake, and heavy hail. And a great portent appeared in heaven, a woman clothed with the sun, with the moon under her feet, and on her head a crown of twelve stars; she was with child and she cried out in her pangs of birth, in anguish for delivery. And another portent appeared in heaven; behold, a great red dragon, with seven heads and ten horns, and seven diadems upon his heads. His tail swept down a third of the stars of heaven, and cast them to the earth. And the dragon stood before the woman who was about to bear a child, that he might devour her child when she brought it forth; she brought forth a male child, one who is to rule all the nations with a rod of iron, but her child was caught up to God and to his throne, and the woman fled into the wilderness, where she has a place prepared by God, in which to be nourished for one thousand two hundred and sixty days. Now war arose in heaven, Michael and his angels fighting against the dragon; and the dragon and his angels fought, but

they were defeated and there was no longer any place for them in heaven. And the great dragon was thrown down, that ancient serpent, who is called the Devil and Satan, the deceiver of the whole world—he was thrown down to the earth, and his angels were thrown down with him. And I heard a loud voice in heaven, saying, "Now the salvation and the power and the kingdom of our God and the authority of his Christ have come, for the accuser of our brethren has been thrown down, who accuses them day and night before our God. And they have conquered him by the blood of the Lamb and by the word of their testimony, for they loved not their lives even unto death. Rejoice then, O heaven and you that dwell therein! But woe to you, O earth and sea, for the devil has come down to you in great wrath, because he knows that his time is short!" And when the dragon saw that he had been thrown down to the earth, he pursued the woman who had borne the male child. But the woman was given the two wings of the great eagle that she might fly from the serpent into the wilderness, to the place where she is to be nourished for a time, and times, and half a time. The serpent poured water like a river out of his mouth after the woman, to sweep her away with the flood. But the earth came to the help of the woman, and the earth opened its mouth and swallowed the river which the dragon had poured from his mouth. Then the dragon was angry with the woman, and went off to make war on the rest of her offspring, on those who keep the commandments of God and bear testimony to Jesus. (Rev 11:19-12:17)

This passage is too rich for us to even begin to do justice to it here. We see here, however, the beautiful identification of Mary as the true Ark of the Covenant, and also as the archetype of the Church. She is both the Mother of Christ and the Mother of all who believe in him, "those who keep the commandments of God and bear testimony to Jesus." Yes, this Ark of God is both Mary and the Church! This single, twofold woman, this Virgin Bride and Immaculate Mother, is the dwelling-place of God with his people, and the space in which each one of us can discover our true, unique beauty in the eyes of God, awakened and reflected in the tenderness of her own loving, maternal gaze. Ah! But we see in this passage even more. Mary is the one who, enveloped in the column of smoke, comes up out of the wilderness and into the fullness of the "promised land" of heaven, conquering over the serpent by the grace of God and entering into the everlasting marriage of eternity. And in her each one of us conquers, provided only we let ourselves be conquered by the Love of God that assails us so tenderly yet so powerfully!

As we will see, the bride of the Song of Songs is described as "terrible as an army with banners" (Sg 6:4, 10), since in her very ravishing beauty, cradled in the beauty of her Bridegroom, she overcomes the temptations of the evil one and finds herself caught up to God and to his throne. *His* throne! Yes, she is—each one of us is—his throne! But, while he makes his home within us already in this world, he wants to take us to be with him where he is for all eternity, to sit upon his throne, to adorn him like a crown upon his head:

> Then I saw a new heaven and a new earth; for the first heaven and the first earth had passed away, and the sea was no more. And I saw the holy city, new Jerusalem, coming down out of heaven from God, prepared as a bride adorned for her husband; and I heard a loud voice from the throne saying, "Behold, the dwelling of God is with men. He will dwell with them, and they shall be his people, and God himself will be with them; he will wipe away every tear from their eyes, and death shall be no more, neither shall there be mourning nor crying nor pain any more, for the former things have passed away." And he who sat upon the throne said, "Behold, I make all things new." (Rev 21:1-5)

Yes, in these words we see the true and ultimate fulfillment of those mysterious words of the Song of Songs which we have now reached:

King Solomon made himself a throne
from the wood of Lebanon.
He made its posts of silver,
its back of gold, its seat of purple;
it was lovingly wrought within
by the daughters of Jerusalem.
Go forth, O daughters of Zion,
and behold King Solomon,
with the crown with which his mother crowned him
on the day of his wedding,
on the day of the gladness of his heart.
(Sg 3:9-11)

After coming up out of the desert and into the land of promise, the true Solomon builds himself a throne, radiant in beauty, and there his Mother crowns him on the day of his wedding. But what is going on here? This is not an ordinary marriage, nor an ordinary coronation... For a king is not crowned on the day of his wedding! And it is not his mother who crowns him! Then what King is this who is crowned by his Mother on the day of his marriage, and what crown, then, is this that he receives? This crown is nothing but his bride herself, who is the only adornment he desires, and the one alone in which his Sacred Heart delights, as he cries out:

Behold, you are beautiful, my love,
behold, you are beautiful!
(Sg 4:1)

Yes, after the King ascends his throne and takes his seat, and after his Mother crowns him with his true crown, the people await his coronation speech. Ah, and how touching it is to see the deepest desires of this King's Heart, to witness the way in which he himself understands his reign. His eyes are fixed entirely on the bride, on the love of his Heart, so totally that it is like he is inebriated by gazing tenderly upon her. And thus his coronation speech is not a matter of assuring that all understand his authority, or his prerogatives, or even his plan of action. Rather, he simply sings forth a prolonged hymn of praise for his lovely one, the one who is truly "the gladness of his Heart." For is this not the only desire of the true King: to pour forth his love upon his beloved one, so that she may know how beautiful she is in his eyes, and may welcome the tenderness of his embrace by which he wants to take her completely to himself?

ישוע

YOU HAVE RAVISHED MY HEART

After ascending his throne and receiving his crown, the true King opens his mouth and speaks. And he does nothing but praise the beauty and lovableness of his bride:

Behold, you are beautiful, my love,
behold, you are beautiful!
Your eyes are doves behind your veil.
Your hair is like a flock of goats,
moving down the slopes of Gilead.
Your teeth are like a flock of shorn ewes
that have come up from the washing,
all of which bear twins,
and not one among them is bereaved.
Your lips are like a scarlet thread,
and your mouth is lovely.
Your cheeks are like halves of a pomegranate
behind your veil.

Your neck is like the tower of David,
built for an arsenal,
whereon hang a thousand bucklers,
all of them shields of warriors.
Your two breasts are like two fawns,
twins of a gazelle,
that feed among the lilies.
Until the day breathes and the shadows flee,
I will hasten to the mountain of myrrh
and the hill of frankincense.
You are all fair, my love;
there is no flaw in you.
(Sg 4:1-7—RSV2CE)

How beautiful are these words of the heavenly Bridegroom, expressing his joy and delight as he gazes upon his bride. Of course, on the literal level of the text, the imagery can seem a little bizarre, since it is intended to convey the spiritual truth of Israel's marriage to God. Notice that the bride is described in terms of the flora and fauna of the Holy Land, with the exception of her neck, which is described as the "tower of David." This Bridegroom is therefore the God of Israel gazing upon the people whom he has made his own and rejoicing in the land that, because of his love, has become "our land."

And this hymn of praise of the Bridegroom climaxes in his answer to the bride's plea from the previous poem: "Until the day breathes and the shadows flee, encircle me, my Beloved, like a gazelle or a young stag, upon the mountains of the covenant" (Sg 2:17). Mirroring this, he says now: "Until the day breathes and the shadows flee, I will hasten to the mountain of myrrh and the hill of frankincense" (Sg 4:6). And as he approaches, he exclaims anew, summarizing all that he has said: "You are all fair, my love; and there is no flaw in you" (Sg 4:7).

What is this mountain to which the Bridegroom hastens, desiring to arrive even before the dawn has come and dispelled the darkness of the night? It's literal meaning in the text seems to refer to the temple mount, the mountain in Jerusalem on which the temple is built. This is apparent in the play on words that is made in the Hebrew between the "mountain of myrrh" and "Mount Moriah," which is not only the mountain on which Abraham was willing to sacrifice his son Isaac, but was also traditionally understood as the very mount on which the temple was built. Thus God is expressing his ardent desire to come and dwell in the heart of his bride, at the center of his people, already during the shadows of this life, before the breath of the eternal Day comes.

Yes, the King is therefore coming into his city! He is coming to make this mountain truly the mountain of the covenant! This mountain, this city, is nothing but the dwelling-place where he wants to unite himself to his loved one forever. We can see in these words of the Bridegroom, therefore, a foreshadowing of the coming of Christ into the city of Jerusalem at the height of his ministry and on the verge of his Passion:

> When he drew near to Bethphage and Bethany, at the mount that is called Olivet, he sent two of the disciples, saying, "Go into the village opposite, where on entering you will find a colt tied, on which no one has ever yet sat; untie it and bring it here. If any one asks you, 'Why are you untying it?' you shall say this, 'The Lord has need of it.'" So those who were sent went away and found it as he had told them. And as they were untying the colt, its owners said to them, "Why are you untying the colt?" And they said, "The Lord has need of it." And they brought it to Jesus, and throwing their garments on the colt they set Jesus upon it. And as he rode along, they spread their garments on the road. As he was now drawing near, at the descent of the Mount of Olives, the whole multitude of the disciples began to rejoice and praise God with a loud voice for all the mighty works that they had seen, saying, "Blessed is the King who comes in the name of the Lord! Peace in heaven and glory in the highest!" And some of the Pharisees in the multitude said to him, "Teacher, rebuke your disciples." He answered, "I tell you, if these were silent, the very stones would cry out." (Lk 19:29-39)

We can hear in these words of Christ the same emotion, the same ardor, the same tenderness that we hear in the voice of the Bridegroom of the Song: "I tell you, if these were silent, the very stones would cry out!" Yes, it is with ardent desire and loving exultation that the Bridegroom exclaims: "I will come to the mountain of myrrh and the hill of frankincense." I will offer myself life on this mountain (Golgotha was one of the many smaller hills that made up Mount Moriah), I will give myself up to death in such a way that my body itself will be anointed with myrrh and frankincense. These two precious perfumes, used to anoint the body of Christ after his Passion, are precisely the perfumes associated with the temple liturgy. Thus, in these verses we are seeing the body of Christ as the new temple, as the new and enduring place of encounter with God and the gift of "living worship" that offers the whole human being to God as a hymn of perfect love and ceaseless praise.

And indeed, by being taken up into the tender embrace of Christ and transformed in him, my life too becomes a pleasing fragrance: "Be imitators of God, as beloved children. And walk in love, as Christ loved us and gave himself up for us, a fragrant offering and sacrifice to God" (Eph 5:1). Yes, this is why the body of the bride was explained in such detail by the Bridegroom, because it is this body which, fashioned by the very hand of the Creator and filled with the breath of life, is "offered as a living sacrifice, holy and acceptable to God," her "spiritual worship" (Rom 12:1).

The body of the bride is not an incidental part of who she is, as if her divine Bridegroom wanted to be united with her only in the spirit, only in a merely intellectual or volitional union. No, he wants to take her very body to himself, and to give his Body to her. Does not Saint Paul say "the body is for the Lord and the Lord for the body?" (1 Cor 6:13). What is this chaste, virginal union in which Christ and the human person become "one spirit" and "one flesh?" (Cf. 1 Cor 6:14-17; Gen 2:24). What is this intimacy in which I am drawn close to Jesus, into the vulnerability of mutual self-giving, and find myself "betrothed to Christ, as a pure bride to her one husband?" (cf. 2 Cor 11:2).

These passionate words of the Bridegroom have the potential to radically transform my understanding of the way that God himself sees me and loves me. Perhaps I too often think that I am the only one seeking; that I am longing for him, whereas he, of course, could not possibly be drawn to and attracted to me. After all, look at what I am! But his loving words give the lie to this doubt and hesitation!

Come with me from Lebanon, my bride;
come with me from Lebanon.
Turn your gaze from the peak of Amana,
from the peak of Senir and Hermon,
from the dens of lions,
from the mountains of leopards.
(Sg 4:8)

In other words, the Bridegroom gently calls me from the space in which my gaze is turned away from him, preoccupied with others things. He calmly and tenderly redirects my glance to himself, away from the lions and leopards of temptation, doubt, and fear. Yes, he tells me to lower my gaze from the heights, since I do not need to climb these heights in order to find him. No, I do not need to be more, to be someone different, to attain, after much effort and performance, the reward of being at last lovable in his eyes. Rather, the exact opposite is the truth! I am already lovable, and it is precisely the certainty of his love that allows my life to flow freely in joy and gladness, to flower in playfulness and rest.

And indeed this experience of my loveliness truly lifts me up, unshackling me from all that is inauthentic, all that holds me bound, so that I may arise and be joined inseparably to my Beloved. But I arise, not to the heights that I expected, those places of "greatness" which would have compensated for my fear of weakness and littleness. Instead, I arise into the very shelter of the Heart of Christ, in which I know myself to be his "little one," loved and cherished precisely in this way, my weakness sheltered in the vulnerability of his own love. And indeed I realize that my weakness is but the flip side of a deep spiritual sensitivity to his touch, the very expression of the ardent longing of my heart for him! And I discover that my littleness is but the flip side of my greatness and nobility, a sign of the truth that my heart is inherently ordered to him, and indeed is sustained by his ever-cradling love at every moment!

So what does he say to me, my divine Beloved, in this intimate place, where my heart touches his Heart in the place of greatest vulnerability? He says to me those words of passionate love which unveil the profound tenderness of his Heart, and how he truly sees me:

You have ravished my heart, my sister, my bride,
you have ravished my heart with a glance of your eyes,
with one jewel on your neck.
(Sg 4:9)

What is this? The heavenly Bridegroom is ravished by his bride, such that he cries out in the experience of being overwhelmed by her beauty! Indeed, even if before he enumerated the beauty of her features in detail, now he says that even this is not necessary to touch him so deeply. Rather, there is a kind of restraint, a subtlety in these words, which contrasts with the exuberance of his previous words. A single glance…as if our eyes meet for only a single moment and it is enough to cause vibrations throughout the whole of his being! Indeed, he glimpses simply my neck in passing, and it is enough to bring before him the whole mystery of who I am in his eyes, to make me present in the fullness of my being. It is not until the final poem that he will enumerate my beauty fully, from my feet to my head, but already now and at every moment he sees me in my entirety, and, seeing me entirely, he loves all of me without reserve.

ישוע

IN HIS AFFIRMING LOVE

In these words of the Bridegroom, as he calls forth his precious bride and enumerates all the many ways in which she is beautiful in his eyes, we encounter the fulfillment of the deepest desires of the human heart. He comes to her where she is, yearning for love and affirmation, and he sees in her the inherent beauty that is her own, the unrepeatable personal mystery that spontaneously attracts his Heart. After exclaiming how she ravishes his Heart, the Bridegroom proceeds:

How sweet is your love, my sister, my bride!
How much your love surpasses wine,
and the fragrance of your oils any spice!
(Sg 4:10)

Do these words remind us of anything? They call to mind the very opening stanza of the Song, in which the bride had exclaimed to her Beloved: "Your love surpasses wine, your anointing oils are fragrant, your name is oil poured out" (Sg 1:2-3). The Bridegroom, therefore, is finding in the bride the same joy and sober inebriation that the bride had first found in the Bridegroom! He is delighting in her unique name which is an oil poured out, more delectable for him than anything else. And this name of the bride, which is given to him in tender love, delights his Sacred Heart and fills it with joy—for it in turn is corresponding with the true desire that he bears within himself: to be allowed to love the bride freely, and to receive her love in return.

How sweet, then, is this mutual self-giving of Lover and beloved, in which both inhale the sweet perfume of each other's name, and drink the inebriating yet utterly sober drink of the other's love! Through her Bridegroom's love, the bride's most intimate desires have begun to be fulfilled—and will be perfectly fulfilled when she passes at last into the eternal Day—namely, to know her true identity, bathed in the light of his loving gaze, and to experience a deep and lasting intimacy with the One whom her heart loves. Even on the natural level, this is an absolute need for each human heart. Even in our relationships with our brothers and sisters, we each have a deep need for affirmation in our unique identity, and for the experience of being able to open wide our hearts to receive and to give love, entering thus into deep relationships of love, mutual understanding, and friendship. As the Catholic psychiatrist Conrad Baars beautifully writes concerning what he calls the "miracle of affirmation:"

> I lead the affirming life by being *continuously present* with the full attention of my whole being to everything that is; by being fully

capable of being *moved emotionally* by all I encounter in the world around me; and by *allowing the delight and joy that I experience to be revealed* naturally and spontaneously so that the object of my delight can be moved too by his or her own goodness. It is in this way of being present to another, prior to my doing anything, that the other is born psychologically, delivered from the prison of his loneliness and self-centeredness, is strengthened and made firm in the realization that he may be who he is and may become who he is meant to be in his own way and at his own pace. It is in this process that the other is gradually opened to the goodness of all creation and to God Himself.

It is in being affirmed that a person's psyche is allowed to flower fully in its own unique way, to become open to its own goodness and that of others. Thus affirmation can be said to be truly life-giving, and as such is the source of another's psychic [psychological] birth. [I compare] the affirming process to the effect water has on something immersed in it. The water respects the object and lets it be. The water surrounds it perfectly and adjusts itself faithfully to the exact contours of the object without destroying it. It allows the object, if a living one, like fish, coral or plant, to grow and develop without hindrance by adjusting its own weight in relation to it. Moreover, it hides its defects from view.[17]

If this is true even on the basic human level—in the realm of nature which provides the substratum for the activity of grace, and which is not destroyed, but rather purified, elevated, and transfigured by grace—how much more true is it on the supernatural level in the intimate relationship between Christ and each human heart! Yes, how much we have already witnessed this truly affirming love in the attitude, gestures, and words of the Bridegroom of the Song! Even when the bride is afraid, even when she is enclosed in the "prison" of her own fear, anxiety, and shame, her Lover never ceases to tenderly delight in her. He never ceases to cradle her in the enveloping embrace of his Love, which is truly like the water that upholds and protects a child in the womb of her mother. Here alone is the full, infinite, and utterly unique affirmation for which I long! Here is that radical tenderness that sees into the very depths of who I am, here and now, and touches that sacred space in the core of my being, and affirms, delights in, desires, and gently shelters me here at every moment!

Let me add that, even though God alone can truly see and affirm each person in their entirety, in the fullness of their unique mystery, I too—from the heart of my own security in God's affirming love—can open my heart to see, know, love, and affirm others in his name. In this way my own sheltering love can become a kind of "womb" too, a kind of sacrament of the love of God himself. My love can help to heal my brothers and sisters and to open their hearts to the love of God himself, in whom they experience their true identity, as well as the intimate relationships of love in which they find true happiness. Let me continue on this track for the remainder of this reflection and the following ones, before continuing with the text of the Song. I allow this digression because I think this is something very important to say, and this is a fruitful and essential way in which the Bridegroom's love may become more visible, and his heartbeat more deeply felt, in our world and our relationships. Baars says further:

> We must learn to be simply present to what is good and to be moved by it…but if I'm rushing around, I can't stand still and be present, for example, to the goodness and beauty of a tree or another person or whatever it may be. If I do take the time and let the goodness of things move me, then I affirm that creation. I become a *co-creator* with God of what He has created. That's another way of saying what an affirmer is: *a co-creator*. … In order for me to live the affirming life, it is necessary that I be present with the full attention of my whole being to all of creation—not just with my thinking, or discursive mind, but also with the attention of my senses, my intuitive or contemplative mind, my spiritual sense, and my emotions [and I would add my spiritual affectivity]. … The discursive mind has to be much less active than the intuitive mind. In our society, the overactivity of our active minds and the overactivity of the utilitarian (assertive) emotions are a tremendous obstacle to leading the authentic human life. The overactivity of our discursive reason and utilitarian emotions also prevents us from being responsive to the other group of emotions that God has given us. We call those the humane emotions, the emotions of love and desire, joy and kindness, affection, compassion, and tenderness. These emotions work directly under the guidance of our intuitive mind. Ennobled by the intuitive mind and guided by reason and will, these humane emotions should be the main source of being present to all of God's creation. [If we do this, then people] will be able to sense our delight in their goodness. When I am moved by the goodness of what I see around me, I automatically feel that I must protect that goodness. I do not wish to do anything that will interfere with this goodness. That is the

source of my developing this love-with-restraint. I do not restrain the love itself; I always let it be and grow. I do restrain myself in the manifestations of my love, however, when I know that those manifestations cannot be received by the other person, when he cannot respond to me, or when I know that those manifestations of my love would be contrary to the moral order. Only in this way of relating do we allow the other person to be who he or she is and allow the other to become what he or she is meant to be in God's plan, both in his own time and at his own pace. At that point the deepest and most unbreakable bonds of friendship are formed, of mutual affirming and loving.

The first need of a person, then, is to be allowed to be himself. The second need is to know the truth. My obligation within this affirming relationship is to help the other to know who and what he is, and what he should do. The other will listen to me only because I have opened him to his own goodness, to the goodness of all creation, and to the goodness of God. When the other is disposed to listen to me, then I can tell him how he must live.[18]

We encounter in Christ this love-with-restraint, this love that in its ardent intensity, if fully expressed too early, would simply overwhelm me, and which for precisely that reason comes to me with unspeakable tenderness, reverence, and gentleness. And yet he never ceases to love, to let his expansive love enfold me in itself, as he yearns for and seeks, with all the desire of his Heart, my authentic good and my enduring happiness. He allows his love full expression within the burning furnace of his own Sacred Heart, and he little by little unveils it before me, insofar as I am open to receive it, until he has drawn me at last into the very fullness of his divine embrace. Is this not the movement that we are encountering as the drama of the Song of Songs unfolds before our eyes? The Bridegroom is unveiling the beauty of his love, and of his own goodness, ever more deeply to the one whom he loves. He is drawing her tenderly and patiently into the openness of mutual self-giving where the two will be united together, perfectly, in an embrace of total belonging for all eternity.

ישוע

AUTHENTIC TENDERNESS

Before plunging back into the text of the Song, I would like to make a few more connections with the theme of the last reflection. I spoke about the gift of *affirmation*, which is not so much a matter of "doing" something (and definitely not of artificially "affirming" other people with inauthentic or forced words, etc.), but is rather *simply a wholehearted contact with the unique goodness and beauty of another person, a delight and joy which I allow to be spontaneously awakened within me by my attentiveness to them, which is then externally expressed in such a way that they may feel it*. It is precisely in this way that I, as it were, co-create with God by mediating to the other person their unique beauty and identity in his eyes. Of course, only God knows this identity fully, but I can nonetheless mediate their experience of his gaze through my own reverent tenderness, my own receptive gaze upon their unique beauty. In this way, I can help the other person to experience a "second birth," which is the birth of awakening to the freedom of securely knowing who they are in the eyes of love, and being able to live within and from this space of love's sheltering embrace.

This gift of affirmation also corresponds with John Paul II's definition of *tenderness*, which is a unique gift of my heart to another person, not in a selfish grasping or a desire for pleasure or possession—as these directly contradict the movement of affirmation—but rather in the ardent desire for the other's happiness. In his philosophical work *Love and Responsibility*, John Paul II defined tenderness as "the ability to feel with and for the whole person, to feel even the most deeply hidden spiritual tremors, and always to have in mind the true good of that person."[19] Authentic tenderness, therefore, is a profound sensitivity of heart to the mystery and beauty of another person. It is not the dominating or demanding desire to appropriate the other to myself, but rather the reverent awe and receptivity before who they are in the eyes of God, awakening in me the desire for their true happiness and well-being. This is where the "love-with-restraint" that Conrad Baars spoke about comes in, in which, precisely because of the fullness of my love for another, I restrain the expressions of my love to what they can truly receive and understand. In other words, I "channel" or "translate" my love in such a way that it meets them where they are at, as a gentle and tender touch upon the heart of another person. It is precisely in this way that the fullness of my own love and the insecure longing of the other person to be loved meet and are united. This gradually creates a space of confident trust in which the other person can open himself or herself more and more to my love, and can experience it more truly as it is in itself. Then there is less and less need for "translation," and more of a spontaneous, profound, and mutual understanding between two hearts. This is the essence of friendship, and what Baars was referring to when he said, "At that point the deepest and most unbreakable bonds of friendship are formed, of mutual affirming and loving."

There are two different paths which open up from these insights that I would like to follow. In neither of them, however, will I rely on my own words, but rather primarily on the words of others. First, in this reflection, I want to listen a little more in depth to this encounter between the love-with-restraint of one heart and the fearful defensiveness of another heart, in order to see how this gradually opens up a growing confidence and vulnerability between two persons, flowering in intimacy. I will quote the words of a friend, who has once already been quoted in these reflections. With these words I will conclude:

> To be seen, to be known, and to be loved become synonymous with each other, and the person to whom this is being communicated intuitively, spontaneously, and most intimately experiences this address…an address in which they are called by their name. The person is, in this moment, not only recognized in their authentic identity but is lovingly engaged, held, and communicated to in this most true identity of which their name speaks.
>
> Though this is rarely explicitly stated by either person, it is known and felt between the two persons. Perhaps this is even what precedes the embrace, or at least the most intimate of embraces. This is jumping ahead, however… When initially encountering someone, there is a distance, a hesitation, a "testing" of the space between them. Even if one is going to the other particularly for guidance and healing, both persons hold the space with hesitancy…perhaps more precisely, with a pause. However the quality of this hesitancy for each is different. For the person seeking healing, the hesitation is primarily rooted in fear, derived from experiences of being hurt in vulnerability, and aimed at protecting oneself through distance and isolation; it is an arm that is extended towards you with one's hand held up to maintain safe independence. For the healer, the hesitancy, or pause, is one of gentleness and patience; with incredible tenderness, accepting the hand that is reached out even as it is thrust upwards, with its palm in your face. For some, they may let their hand be gently touched, maybe even slightly lowered

such that their face can be glimpsed. While for others, this touch may be felt as violent and violating. Rather they must know that their hand is seen, even in its obstructing and distancing position, seen both in its intention to maintain safety and in its reaching out towards you. This hand can only express its yearning to be closer to you in a posture that demands that you keep your distance. It desires but it does not yet trust, yet it calls for you to receive it in both movements, in both gestures.

When this hand is both received in its desire and respected in its demand, it can begin to shift in gesture from rejection to an invitation. The hand whose palm is in the face of the other begins to rotate such that the hand reaches out in invitation. Perhaps it is a subtle and barely audible invitation at first, as if to see if you are really listening, if you can really hear the desires of their heart, if you can make out their goodness and their beauty even as it is obscured by the hand. Over time, perhaps a short time or perhaps a long time, their hand can trust enough to let you take hold of it. You can see their face now, you can hold them, at least by their hand, though their eyes may be cast down. Avoiding your gaze which is too intense, too penetrating, too invasive to receive in full, you cradle their hand with tenderness and their words with wonder. It seems that much of this relationship remains at this place, at least for a while.

But...but the name, what happens when one hears their name! A person speaks, revealing themselves more and more vulnerably, and the other hears, touches, and speaks such that a rare moment occurs...a rare moment in which the love of the one finally reaches across the abyss to pluck the heartstrings of the other. This moment that says, "I see you, and I know you, and I love you, my friend." At the touch of the fingertips upon one's heartstrings, at the moment the name reaches one's ears, spontaneously the person's face is lifted up and their eyes rush over to meet yours. The two share in a gaze, it is no longer one hiding from another, but a mutual gift of vulnerable love. Powerful, intimate, and loving, even if only sustained for a moment.

ישוע

THE "WORD" OF THE HEART

In the last reflection I spoke about the gift of tender love that gently affirms another person, and gradually opens them, through a self-restraining and yet totally self-donating love, to an ever deeper encounter of healing and intimacy. In this reflection, I would like to follow the second path, to which I hinted in the last reflection. This second path that I would like to follow is to take a deeper look at the role of affectivity in human life, and especially in the gift of my heart to another. In this, I want to listen to the words of the great philosopher Dietrich von Hildebrand. First, let me emphasize anew that this gift of the heart to another—whether of my heart to a human person, or to God, or the gift of God's heart to me—is not something that can be manufactured by technique, *or even, for that matter, merely willed.*

Rather, in many ways, it is *the spontaneous movement of my affection* which more deeply reveals, and more totally gives, my heart to another person. If I merely *willed* to love them, without actually feeling this love, without an actual surging of my emotions and affectivity, then they would immediately feel that something is lacking in my love. Of course, if I cannot feel this love for another person, simply to will and to seek their good is sufficient for a morally adequate response to them. But how much more rich and full, and in a real way, more adequate, is the act of my will and my external action when it springs from, and is enfolded within, the spontaneous gift of my affectivity as well! This is why, for example, we spontaneously say, "I love you with all of my heart," and not, "I love you with all of my mind and my will." Only all three together, working in harmony—the mind, the will, and the affectivity—truly speak the undivided and total word of my heart given to the one whom I love. Perhaps in this light, therefore, we can understand why the Song of Songs is so attractive, since it is simply God's way of saying to us: "I do not love you only with my mind, I do not only choose to will your good; rather, I love you, deeply and spontaneously, with the full movement of my affection, as my Heart surges with delight, longing, hope, and desire for you, my beautiful and precious one!"

Allow me now to quote Dietrich von Hildebrand, who spent a great deal of effort throughout his life striving to "rehabilitate the heart" in the realm of philosophical thought, as well as in our concrete experience of life. He knew, sensitive man that he was, that we cannot live our lives only in the sphere of the intellect and the will (thinking and choosing), while our emotional and affective life remains dwarfed or repressed. He understood that the emotions are not merely *physical* feelings that are beyond our control (or are "base," belonging to our "lower nature," needing simply to be subjected to reason). Yes, I admit (as did he) that there are things such as irrational moods and mere physiological or psychological feelings. But there is also another, immensely higher realm of affectivity which is not animal (or psychological), but truly *spiritual*, and which speaks in a unique way the "word of the heart" that is awakened by my living contact with reality. This "word of the heart" spoken through the *spiritual affectivity*—in union with the *contemplative mind* and the *consenting will*—is truly necessary for the full and adequate response of my being to the values that I encounter outside of myself. This heartfelt response, therefore is an expression of the full and radiant "Yes" of my being to the Beauty, Goodness, and Truth that touch and invite my heart. Indeed, as I have said in a previous reflection, in the most profound, most "gripping" encounter with the Beloved, all three of these spiritual faculties respond as one within the inner sanctuary of my heart, where they are undivided in the core of my personal "I." Here is what von Hildebrand says in this respect:

> We must understand that in the affective sphere there are two levels. The one is inhabited by feelings which rank lower than all those acts which are in the immediate range of our freedom [i.e. the activity of our will cooperating with the intellect]. This is the level of the mere affective states, whether bodily ones, such as tiredness, or psychic ones, such as good humor or depression. It is the level of all passions in the strict sense, and even of many affective responses, such as those not motivated by values (for instance, joy over a financial profit). These experiences range ontologically lower than an act of promise or making a contract, or an action in the strict sense, or any work or deed.
>
> But there is also a higher level in the affective sphere. In certain respects this level is above volitional [i.e. willed] acts, though not above the will itself. And it is this part of the affective sphere which has the character of a gift from above; this part, moreover, has the special character of being the "voice" of the heart in the narrower sense of the term. These affective responses come from the very depth of the person's soul. This "depth" must be clearly distinguished from the subconscious. It is a mysterious depth. It is not possessed by us in the way in which we "possess" actions or acts in the range of our immediate power.
>
> Typical of man's createdness is the existence of a depth dimen-

sion of his soul which does not fall under his mastery as do his volitional acts. Man is greater and deeper than the range of things he can control with his free will; his being reaches into mysterious depths which go far beyond what he can engender or create. Nothing expresses this fact more adequately perhaps than the truth that God is nearer to us than we are to ourselves. And this applies not only to the supernatural level, but also analogously to the natural sphere. These affections of the higher level, then, are truly gifts—natural gifts of God which man cannot give himself by his own power. Coming as they do from the very depth of his person, they are in a specific way voices of his true self, voices of his full personal being.

It now becomes more intelligible why in certain domains the heart [i.e. the affectivity] is more the true self than the will. Yet we must add that the full voice of the heart demands the cooperation of the free spiritual center of the person [the will]. ... [T]he deepest manifestation of our freedom is to be found in cooperative freedom [rather than mere self-determination]. However great and admirable free will is as lord and master of our actions, nevertheless, the free cooperation with the "gifts" from above, which as such are only indirectly accessible to our free power, is the deepest actualization of our freedom, the highest vocation and mission of our freedom. The great word in which the meaning and nature of cooperative freedom is contained in its most sublime form is the *Ecce ancilla Domini, fiat mihi secundum verbum tuum*. "Behold the handmaid of the Lord, be it done unto me according to thy word."

The highest manifestation of cooperative freedom is to be found in sanctioning—in the "yes" of our free spiritual center which forms from within our "being affected" by values and, above all, our affective responses to them. In its strictest form it is possible only with affective responses to God... What matters in our context is to understand that these affective experiences which are gifts from above become fully ours, that is to say, they become ultimately valid expressions of our entire personality only when they are sanctioned by our free spiritual center. Our deep love for another person is a gift from above—something we cannot give to ourselves; yet only when we join this love with the "yes" of our free spiritual center does it have the character of a full self-donation. We not only endorse this love, but by this freely spoken "yes" we make it the full and express word of our own. This "yes" of our free center can be spoken only if a high affective experience is granted us. It presupposes the presence of a voice of our heart which is a gift from above.[20]

Obviously, many things could be said about these words, but let me only note that, in the light of what von Hildebrand is saying, we can understand how *authentic human freedom is not merely a matter of self-determination fashioned from within by the effort of the will, but rather a gift of grace that drops down like dew from above*. I am only truly free when I am liberated by the love of another, when I am drawn out of myself by what touches me from the outside. Indeed, in letting myself be touched, in letting myself be "moved" in this way by the beauty and goodness of another, I am truly unified within myself in a "yes" of love that harnesses my whole being as one. My intellect, my will, and my affectivity become unified in a single loving donation of my heart to the one whom I love, and who has ravished my heart.

Ah! Yes…here we can at last come full circle and return to the text of the Song. When the Bridegroom exclaims that his bride has ravished his Heart, he is pronouncing precisely this "yes" of love in which he lets his whole being be harnessed by her beauty, her lovableness, her goodness, and made an unreserved and total gift for her. And, for the bride's part, the entire Song is the unfolding of her journey ever deeper into the Bridegroom's love, in which her heart is made a more total and unconditional gift to the One who, in his ineffable beauty, has ravished her heart and drawn her to himself. Her existence, and indeed her very being, as it is grasped and tenderly held by the unspeakable Beauty, Goodness, and Truth of her beloved—by his infinite Love!—becomes a pure and ceaseless "yes" to him in reciprocal love.

ישוע

THE WAYS IN WHICH THE HEART SPEAKS

In the communication between two hearts, there are many and varied expressions of love and mutual sharing. This is true on a human level, and even more so, with the proper adjustments, on a supernatural and spiritual level. We could say that there are five primary ways in which the heart of one person communicates with another, and in which the other person can perceive, welcome, and experience another's love. As we will see, they are deeply related and interlaced with one another. They are: 1) the eyes, 2) the voice, 3) gesture, 4), touch, 5) silence.

In all of our human relationships, we communicate with one another through these channels, that is, we speak through the "language of the body." Our hearts do not encounter one another directly, in an unmediated space where we spontaneously sense what is going on in one another. (Though because of the activity of grace and our spiritual nature, this too in some way is possible; but I want to focus on the reality of "mediation" at this point.) Rather, the dispositions of our hearts are mediated through these channels, through the vessel of the body which, as it were, make the inner heart in some way visible and palpable. God, on the other hand, communicates with us not only through our senses—through these five channels—but also directly within the core of our being. In a way we could say that, while humans communicate with one another "from the outside-in," God communicates with us most especially "from the inside-out." This is why he is not palpable and present to us in the same way that other created beings are—even though he ceaselessly communicates himself to us through all the goodness and beauty of creation—since he himself cannot be sensed, but only encountered as his touch "wells up" from within the core of our being and irradiates our experience with his light and love.

In the Song of Songs, therefore, these five channels of communication are harnessed very vividly and explicitly, precisely in order to "sensitize" our hearts to the way in which God unceasingly communicates himself to us, both "from the outside-in," through our bodily senses, and "from the inside-out," through our spiritual senses and the faculties of our heart. The path of the bride is one of progressively becoming more and more attuned to the way in which the Bridegroom is present to her: to his gaze, to his voice, to his touch, to his gestures, to his silence. And as she receives this self-communication of her Beloved, she is able to let herself be grasped by his love and to pronounce her "yes" of loving surrender to the One who invites her.

Let us now try to look more deeply at these five ways of communication. I receive another person precisely through my *eyes*, through the way that I look upon them and offer to them a tender and inviting gaze, which is not overwhelming or intrusive, but is nonetheless penetrating in its reverence, since it seeks to communicate to the other that they are seen, not on the surface, but in their unique beauty, and affirmed and desired in this place. I also receive them through my *voice*, not only through its tone, by which I make the very atmosphere of my speaking a sheltered space for them, but also through what I say, in that it reveals my understanding of the other, my compassion, my love, and my desire for their good. Also, by the way that I hold myself in their presence, by my "body language" in the narrower sense of the term, I create a secure and safe place in which another feels sheltered. By the way that I move, I am communicating to them the love that I desire them to experience—by being engaged, by smiling, even by shedding tears, all of which are ways of letting the affections of my heart be manifest in my face and my posture as a gift for the other person. In the proper circumstances, and whenever the other is ready to receive it, I also receive them and give myself to them through touch, revealing my loving tenderness by sheltering and holding them, whether through a hand laid on their shoulder in prayer, through holding their hand within my own, or through a short or more prolonged embrace.

Finally, there is the language of *silence*, which in our culture (and in our fallen world in general) is a very difficult language to discern. But in a way it is silence which surpasses the other modes of expression in its depth and intensity. Or rather, silence pervades them all while enfolding them within its ever present embrace. A word pronounced in silence, a word born from silent receptivity and deep contemplation of the other, reverberates much more deeply than a word born merely on the surface. A gaze of love that is received and reciprocated in a prolonged silence can say more, and can knit hearts together more intimately, than any words can. A long embrace in which two persons hold one another, hearts beating silently together in unity and breath shared as one, is a mode of communication that is unsurpassed, a glimpse of the embrace of eternity in which the eyes, the voice, the body, and the heart will communicate together as one in a ceaseless movement of mutual self-giving and acceptance.

Even in this life, it is a great gift when the spirit and the body are together united in the mutual communication of two hearts, sharing themselves with one another through sight, voice, gesture, and touch, bathed in the atmosphere of reverent silence. This intimacy, glimpsed in this life, will be brought to its consummation in heaven when the body, restored to its full integrity and totally joined to the spirit, will be a pure and transparent communication of the innermost mystery of the person. Then the communication through eyes, voice, gesture, and touch will be full and complete, without any fear, hesitation, or reserve, in which hearts pour themselves out ceaselessly into one another and welcome one another, living a single life of love within the all-enfolding embrace of God who cradles them together within himself. Here indeed our sight, voice, and touch will be united as one in a single gift of love, within the vision, word, and embrace of God himself who binds all together in the shelter of his own welcoming Love and in his total, unreserved self-communication in boundless tenderness.

Yes, the joy of eternity is to truly see the other person, bathed in the light of God's own love, which reveals their unique personal beauty as they truly are in his eyes. It is to truly speak to them and listen to them in the words which are no longer inadequate, but fully express what the heart wants to say. It is to communicate, through the very visibility of the body of each of us, the true inner character of our being, made a gift for the other, radiating for them, as we in turn tenderly receive them too. It is to draw them near, and to be drawn near by them, into a shared embrace in which all is joined together, because all is given and all is received.

This is heaven, this is eternity, the consummation of the intimacy for which I have been created. In this consummation I am finally united to the One for whom my heart has so ardently yearned throughout the shadows of this life: the divine Bridegroom who has so tenderly touched me and drawn me ever deeper into his embrace. And here, too, I am united to all of those whom I have loved during this life, all of those whom God has entrusted to me, as we embrace, as we are united, in the single embrace of the One who holds us within his arms: the Father, Son, and Holy Spirit.

ישוע

A GARDEN ENCLOSED

The Bridegroom has exclaimed his gratitude and awe in response to the beauty of the bride, and has spoken of how her love is for him far surpassing wine, an oil poured out which surpasses any spice. He then proceeds to say:

Your lips distil nectar, my bride;
honey and milk are under your tongue;
the scent of your garments
is like the scent of Lebanon.
A garden enclosed is my sister, my bride,
a garden enclosed, a fountain sealed.
Your shoots are an orchard of pomegranates
with all choicest fruits, henna with nard,
nard and saffron, calamus and cinnamon,
with all trees of frankincense,
myrrh and aloes, with all chief spices—

*a garden fountain, a well of living water,
and flowing streams from Lebanon.
(Sg 4:11-15)*

There is something astounding occurring in these words. Do we not see throughout Scripture the recurring theme of the *garden*, and a garden that contains within it a *stream of living water*? And yet it is usually God who offers this garden, this water, to the thirsting human heart, which has been created to live in the paradise of his own love. Now, however, the movement is reversed, and the bride is the very garden which the Bridegroom comes to inhabit. In other words, she is his paradise!

The word paradise actually literally means garden, an "enclosed park" that is verdant and well watered. The very etymology of this word, when compared with the Bridegroom's words here, show that he is indeed calling his bride his "paradise." For the word paradise, of Persian origin, is transliterated into Greek as *paradeisos*, which is composed of two parts, equivalent to the Greek *peri* and *teichos*. These mean "around" and "wall," referring, in other words, to a space that is surrounded by a wall—but more than just any space, but a verdant and beautiful garden, enclosed and protected. Thus, when the Bridegroom calls his bride an "enclosed garden," he is speaking of her as his *paradise*.

But what connotations does the word "paradise" bring to mind? Indeed, the word "garden" in the first chapters of Genesis—as in "the Garden of Eden"—when translated from Hebrew into Greek, was translated precisely as *paradeisos*. Thus in the beginning God created his beloved in a garden of paradise, a garden of undisturbed happiness, in which she could sit under the tree of his love and eat the fruit of his goodness, in which she could rejoice in the beauty of creation as his awesome gift, and could rejoice especially in his own abiding presence with her at the heart of this garden!

> And the LORD God planted a garden in Eden, in the east; and there he put the man whom he had formed. And out of the ground the LORD God made to grow every tree that is pleasant to the sight and good for food, the tree of life also in the midst of the garden, and the tree of the knowledge of good and evil. A river flowed out of Eden to water the garden, and there it divided and became four rivers. (Gen 2:8-10)

Does not the garden signify the place of undisturbed happiness and innocence, the space of true intimacy between God and humanity, and between human hearts with one another? Was it not in a garden that Adam and Eve were "naked without shame" (cf. Gen 2:25), and in which their childlike relationship with God was undisturbed by sin? Only after sin were they exiled from the garden of paradise. And then they experienced the *desert* rather than the garden, the aridity of dry and arid steppe rather than the flowering fecundity and outpouring fullness of the garden. But God comes to them unceasingly in order to draw them out of the desert of their exile, to lead them into the Promised Land of intimacy that flows with milk and honey (and what does the Bridegroom of the Song say is under the tongue of his bride but "milk and honey!").

> Then the LORD said, "I have seen the affliction of my people who are in Egypt, and have heard their cry because of their taskmasters; I know their sufferings, and I have come down to deliver them out of the hand of the Egyptians, and to bring them up out of that land to a good and broad land, a land flowing with milk and honey." (Ex 3:7-8)

And even after her infidelity and her exile from the Promised Land, God continually promises to bring her back, to renew with her the marriage-covenant he once made with her when he brought her out of Egypt. Through her very experience of the wilderness, he purifies, renews, and transforms her in his love, such that the very desert is made into a garden. And, finally, he promises a new and everlasting covenant, in which the garden of intimacy symbolized by the Promised Land is revealed as *the true interior indwelling of grace in the depths of the human heart*. These themes are so rich throughout Scripture that I cannot possibly express them all. But let me give a few examples:

> The wilderness and the dry land shall be glad, the desert shall rejoice and blossom; like the lily it shall blossom abundantly, and rejoice with joy and singing. The glory of Lebanon shall be given to it, the majesty of Carmel and Sharon. They shall see the glory of the LORD, the majesty of our God. Strengthen the weak hands, and make firm the feeble knees. Say to those who are of a fearful heart, "Be strong, fear not! Behold, your God will come with vengeance, with the recompense of God. He will come and save you." Then the eyes of the blind shall be opened, and the ears of the deaf unstopped; then shall the lame man leap like a deer, and the tongue of the dumb sing for joy. For waters shall break forth in the wilderness, and streams in the desert; the burning sand shall become a pool, and the thirsty ground springs of water. (Is 35:1-7)

> I will faithfully give them their recompense, and I will make an

everlasting covenant with them. ... I will greatly rejoice in the LORD, my soul shall exult in my God; for he has clothed me with the garments of salvation, he has covered me with the robe of righteousness, as a bridegroom decks himself with a garland, and as a bride adorns herself with jewels. For as the earth brings forth its shoots, and as a garden causes what is sown in it to spring up, so the LORD God will cause righteousness and praise to spring forth before all the nations. (Is 61:8b, 10-11)

For I will restore health to you, and your wounds I will heal... And you shall be my people, and I will be your God... The people who survived the sword found grace in the wilderness; when Israel sought for rest, the LORD appeared to him from afar. I have loved you with an everlasting love; therefore I have continued my faithfulness to you. ... Hear the word of the LORD, O nations, and declare it in the islands afar off; say, "He who scattered Israel will gather him, and will keep him as a shepherd keeps his flock." For the LORD has ransomed Jacob, and has redeemed him from the hands too strong for him. They shall come and sing aloud on the heights of Zion, and they shall be radiant over the goodness of the LORD, over the grain, the wine, and the oil, and over the young of the flock and the herd; their life shall be like a watered garden, and they shall languish no more. (Jer 30:17, 22; 31:2-3, 10-12)

The divine Bridegroom lovingly draws his bride out of her slavery to sin, fear, and shame, and leads her, like a column of smoke, out of the wilderness. This is the way that the third poem of the Song began. The Bridegroom, the true Solomon, is coming up out of the desert breathing forth perfumes, and after taking his seat on his throne and receiving his crown, he opens his mouth to exclaim the beauty of his bride! And he describes his bride, not only as the very Promised Land of union, but as the garden of his paradise and the space of his own joy and delight! As Isaiah says:

You shall be called by a new name which the mouth of the LORD will give. You shall be a crown of beauty in the hand of the LORD, a royal diadem in the hand of your God. You shall no more be termed Forsaken, and your land shall no more be termed Desolate; but you shall be called My delight is in her, and your land Married; for the LORD delights in you, and your land shall be married. For as a young man marries a virgin, so shall your God marry you, and as the bridegroom rejoices over the bride, so shall your God rejoice over you. (Is 62:2-5)

This third poem of the Song of Songs almost seems to be a direct commentary on these beautiful words of Isaiah! Therefore, sharing in the wonder and delight of the Bridegroom, we can direct our gaze upon the bride and exclaim with him, using the same words that began this poem: "What is this?" Yes, what is this—this bride who is for God himself a kind of paradise in which he makes his home?

Ah...and this paradise is each one of us! I myself am his paradise, made a dwelling-place for the divine presence through the grace of God. The Bridegroom has come, with the Father and the Holy Spirit, and has entered into the enclosed garden, the sealed fountain, of my inmost being. And by entering in, he causes my being to breathe forth its sweet perfume, to come to life, flowering with beauty and joy for the One whom my heart loves.

ישוע

UNDER THE TREE OF LIFE

In the last reflection, I tried to show how the image of a garden paradise flowing with water stands as a central theme throughout the Old Testament. Indeed, in a certain sense, it is *the* central symbol of the Bible, signifying as it does the radiant beauty of nuptial union with God, and the way that this union transfigures all of creation into a dwelling place of love and intimacy. This is how the Bible begins: with God creating the paradise of Eden and placing there the man and woman whom he has formed. It is there in Eden that the tree of life stands, but also the tree of knowledge of good and evil. This is the primal beginning of human history, the state of innocence before our nature is marred by sin; and it is a state precisely of deep vulnerability in love and profound personal intimacy.

But after our first parents allowed their trust in the goodness and love of their Father to die in their hearts through the deceit of the evil spirit, and grasped instead for the fruit of disobedience, the human race experienced the pain of exile. Their very sin thrust them out of the vulnerable openness of childlike trust before the gaze of God, whom they saw no longer as a tender and loving Father, as an ardent and gentle Spouse, but as a taskmaster and angry judge. The paradise of the garden was then a distant memory, and yet also a hope, a longing etched into the very sinews of the human heart, fallen yet yearning for redemption and consummation. Yes, we have seen how God's whole pedagogy throughout the Old Testament is a matter of preparing his sinful and unfaithful bride to welcome him anew in a true and everlasting marriage-covenant. This covenant, furthermore, is a covenant that, while effected in the very aridity of the desert wilderness (on Mount Sinai), reaches it consummation only whenever the bride experiences the beauty of the true garden-intimacy for which she was made.

This is the meaning of that ever-recurring refrain throughout the Prophets: "I will bring you back to your own land!" Yes, God is saying to his precious bride: "I once delivered you from the wilderness of exile when you found yourselves enslaved to the taskmasters of Egypt, and I led you out to espouse you to myself at Sinai in the desert; and through this covenant I washed you, purified you, and prepared you to enter into the Promised Land of union. Here I truly dwelt with you, the ark of my presence abiding in your midst as your strength and your protection. My very house dwelt in Zion, upon this holy hill of myrrh, breathing with frankincense. But you were unfaithful; you played the harlot with other gods; 'under every green tree you played the harlot' (cf. Jer 2:20). Therefore you have been taken away from your land by an enemy, dragged off into exile. But I assure you that I will bring you back, that I will renew my covenant with you (cf. Bar 4:9-5:9). Yes, again 'I will allure you and bring you into the wilderness, and speak to your heart… I will espouse you for ever; I will espouse you in righteousness and in justice, in steadfast love, and in mercy. I will espouse you in faithfulness; and you shall know the LORD' (cf. Hos 2:14, 19-20). And, my love, my dove, my beautiful one, I will make with you a new and everlasting covenant, 'and you will forget the shame of your youth, and the reproach of your widowhood you will remember no more. For your Maker is your husband, the LORD of hosts is his name; and the Holy One of Israel is your Redeemer, the God of the whole earth he is called.' Yes, 'my mercy shall not depart from you, and my covenant of peace shall not be removed' (Is 54:4-5, 10)."

We see, therefore, that, as the Scripture begins with a marriage in a garden, so indeed the whole trajectory of the Old Testament is a movement of return to this space. It is the yearning of the bride—and even more of her Beloved!—for a true and lasting marriage that can never be broken. But this is not a theme for the Old Covenant alone. Rather, it is precisely the New Covenant of Christ which truly effects this eternal marriage, this everlasting bond of nuptial love between God and humanity. As the bride was corrupted under a tree in the beginning, in the very garden of Eden, and as the bride so often played the harlot under a tree throughout the Old Testament, so the bride will be redeemed and awakened to life also under a tree. But this tree is not like any other. Rather, this is the true Tree of Life—the tree, not of disobedience, of false maturity, of lustful grasping or disordered autonomy, but the Tree of Love, the Tree of the Bridegroom, giving himself to the bride and awakening her reciprocal surrender.

We already saw that the bride exclaims, in the first poem, "As an apple tree among the trees of the wood, so is my Beloved among young men. With great delight I sat in his shadow, and his fruit was sweet to my taste" (Sg 2:3). And we will see this again at the very climax of the Song, where the Daughters of Jerusalem cry out: "Who is this coming up from the wilderness, leaning upon her Beloved?" Ah! Who else could it be but the bride, carried in the arms of her Bridegroom? And then immediately after this the Bridegroom himself speaks and reveals the nature of this liberation, of this final exodus from the wilderness into the garden of endless union: "Under the apple tree I awakened you, there where your mother was in travail with you, there where she who bore you was in travail" (Sg 8:5). At last, the bride is under the Tree of Life, no longer dreaming the fantasies of sin, no longer hiding in shame and fear. Rather, she is finally and fully awakened at the foot of the Tree of her Beloved:

> Standing by the cross of Jesus were his mother, and his mother's sister, Mary the wife of Clopas, and Mary Magdalene. When Jesus saw his mother, and the disciple whom he loved standing near, he said to his mother, "Woman, behold, your son!" Then he said to the disciple, "Behold, your mother!" And from that hour the disciple took her to his own home.
>
> After this Jesus, knowing that all was now finished, said (to fulfil the Scripture), "I thirst." A bowl full of vinegar stood there; so they put a sponge full of the vinegar on hyssop and held it to his mouth. When Jesus had received the vinegar, he said, "It is finished"; and he bowed his head and gave up his spirit.
>
> Since it was the day of Preparation, in order to prevent the bodies from remaining on the cross on the sabbath (for that sabbath was a high day), the Jews asked Pilate that their legs might be broken, and that they might be taken away. So the soldiers came and broke the legs of the first, and of the other who had been crucified with him; but when they came to Jesus and saw that he was already dead, they did not break his legs. But one of the soldiers pierced his side with a spear, and at once there came out blood and water. (Jn 19:25-34)

Yes, this is the true Tree of Life in the midst of a garden, the garden of reconciliation and consummation, in which the true well of living water flows. This is the Fountain opened in the very wounded Heart of the Redeemer, pouring forth blood, water, and the Spirit to wash the bride of all her infidelity and to liberate within her the unique beauty that she bears as his gratuitous gift. And, indeed, as the Bridegroom says: "Whoever drinks of the water that I shall give him will never thirst; the water that I shall give him will become in him a spring of water welling up to eternal life" (Jn 4:14). Yes, he explains: "If any one thirst, let him come to me and drink. He who believes in me, as the Scripture has said, 'Out of his heart shall flow rivers of living water.'" And John adds: "Now this he said about the Spirit, which those who believed in him were to receive; for as yet the Spirit had not been given, because Jesus was not yet glorified" (Jn 7:37-39). But when Jesus is glorified, raised up on the Cross and raised up in the Resurrection, he truly pours forth this living water into the heart of the bride. Yes…he gives himself so totally that he comes, fully and forever, to live in the heart of the one whom he loves and whom he has espoused to himself, such that her own heart becomes his garden, flowing unceasingly with rivers of living water.

ישוע

IN THE PARADISE OF GOD

We have seen the theme of the garden, the tree, and the marriage-union throughout Scripture. It is present at the beginning of the Bible; it is present at its very center (the Song of Songs is situated right in the heart of the Bible); and it is present at its highest climax, in the Gospel accounts of Christ's Passion and Resurrection. Is not Jesus in a garden when he is arrested, when he pronounces the perfect "yes" of love and childlike surrender to his Father, the "yes" of ardent spousal love for his bride? Is he not also buried in a garden, and does he not rise in a garden, such that Mary Magdalene herself mistakes him for the gardener? Ah, no Mary, this is not the gardener, but the Master of the Garden himself, the Bridegroom who comes into the garden of his creation, the paradise of his bride, which has been disturbed by sin and shame and shackled to the fear of death. He comes into this garden and gives himself to the very end, pouring out his very Body and Blood, his very life, as a gift for his precious bride. And he is buried in the earth, only to break the curse of sin and to unleash endless life, rising from the dead into the fullness of boundless and unbreakable Love!

Yes, Mary...by all means, hold on to him! Grasp his cloak, or grasp his legs, or throw your arms around his body and hold him tight! But you must do this in the right way, for he cannot be held by merely human arms. Rather, it is the love of your heart which alone can hold him, the faith and hope that impel you to surrender yourself trustingly into his embrace. You can hold him when you let yourself first be held. Do you see? The Bridegroom has not simply disappeared into the heavenly realm, leaving you alone and isolated. But perhaps you have not yet learned to listen to his silence, to grasp him in his mystery by letting yourself be grasped by him. Nonetheless, he has returned to his Father in such a way that he is enabled, from the fullness of the Trinity's Love, to come into his garden and to dwell here unceasingly. And what is this garden but his Church? What is this garden but your own heart, made a dwelling place of grace? From the boundlessness of his Love, he is ever present to his precious one, ever sheltering her in his embrace, ever upholding her at every instant. He cradles her, his left hand under her head and his right arm embracing her, as he holds her against his bosom, precisely as he is unceasingly held in the bosom of the Father.

If we take a step back, it is clear how we have seen that the theme of the garden as the space of marital union occurs throughout Scripture, in a kind of ever growing crescendo until it finds its climax in the Passion and Resurrection of Christ. But this is not all, is it? In the beginning of the Bible there is a marriage in a garden; in the middle there is marriage in a garden; at the climax of the drama there is a marriage in a garden. But is this not true also at the very conclusion of the Bible? Yes, at the very end of the Bible there is also a marriage in a garden, the true consummation of this Covenant that our hearts yearn for, when the divine Bridegroom will come again the last time, to definitively lead his bride up out of the wilderness and into the Promised Land of everlasting union, the garden of endless and unbreakable intimacy.

As Jesus himself says at the beginning of this last book of the Bible: "To him who conquers I will grant to eat from the tree of life, which is in the paradise of God" (Rev 2:7). I have already quoted the verses that sing forth so beautifully the hymn of consummation effected by the love of God, but let us revisit them now. Let us see them unfold even more beautifully the richness of their meaning, in the light of all that has been said, like a rose opening its petals in the sun. Saint John the Evangelist, in the closing chapters of the book of Revelation, says:

Then I saw a new heaven and a new earth; for the first heaven and the first earth had passed away, and the sea was no more. And I saw the holy city, new Jerusalem, coming down out of heaven from God, prepared as a bride adorned for her husband; and I heard a loud voice from the throne saying, "Behold, the dwelling of God is with men. He will dwell with them, and they shall be his people, and God himself will be with them; he will wipe away every tear from their eyes, and death shall be no more, neither shall there be mourning nor crying nor pain any more, for the former things have passed away." Then he showed me the river of the water of life, bright as crystal, flowing from the throne of God and of the Lamb through the middle of the street of the city; also, on either side of the river, the tree of life with its twelve kinds of fruit, yielding its fruit each month; and the leaves of the tree were for the healing of the nations. There shall no more be anything accursed, but the throne of God and of the Lamb shall be in it, and his servants shall worship him; they shall see his face, and his name shall be on their foreheads. And night shall be no more; they need no light of lamp or sun, for the Lord God will be their light, and they shall reign for ever and ever. (Rev 21:1-4; 22:1-5)

Here at last is that paradise of God in which my yearning heart will find enduring rest! Here is the Tree of Life, no longer marked by suffering or sacrifice, by the aching compassion with which Christ shelters my vulnerability in the wounded vulnerability of his own Sacred Heart. Rather, here all is transfigured in the radiant light of the Trinity, in the perfect love of the Father, Son, and Holy Spirit, who have taken me up into the innermost heart of their own eternal dance of mutual self-giving, their endless delight of most intimate embrace. Now God lives in me and I in God, our being totally interpenetrating such that I am sheltered in the heart of this love, sitting on the very throne of the Father and the Son—that is, like a child on the lap, held in the arms of her Father, or a bride cradled in the arms of her Bridegroom.

And yet, even as I am held, sheltered, and cradled by him, he pours forth into me the streams of living water which are his own love, joy, and eternal delight. He comes to me, drawn by my unique beauty—a beauty which he himself has created in me, and yet which ravishes and draws his Heart. He comes into his garden, enclosed and sealed for him alone, an exclusive gift to the One who has first given himself exclusively to me. He makes his home in me as in a paradise, as I, in turn, live in him, in the Paradise of his own Trinitarian Being, nestled tightly in the embrace of the Father and the Son, my entire being vibrating with the breath of the Holy Spirit whom they share.

Yes, my heavenly Bridegroom, holding me in his arms, has drawn me out of the wilderness of my exile in this life, and, passing beyond the very abyss of death, has admitted me into the life of perfect communion and unbreakable intimacy. No longer is there any loneliness, any painful longing, any fear, any tears of sorrow or anguish. Rather, there is but the passionate delight of eternal Love pervading my entire being, and drawing me into itself, immersed and transformed in the arms of the One who loves me. Jesus holds me, he holds me close to himself, pressing my heart to his Heart, my mouth to his mouth, as he breathes into me the fullness of his love. And then he whispers to me, in delight at having finally consummated this union:

"My love, my beautiful one, I have taken you to myself; I have drawn you into the most intimate space of my love. You need not look back to what has been in the past. You need not fear any more. For look: I have made all things new! Now I will hold you in my arms forevermore. My sister, my bride, I am now perfectly united to you, and you are united to me, as we are together cradled in the embrace of the perfect Father of us both...Lover and beloved held together in the embrace of perfect Love."

ישוע

ONE WITHIN HIS HEART

In the previous reflections, I have been looking at the "big picture" of this third poem, and indeed of salvation history itself. Now let me take a step back in the text, and try to enter more deeply into the intimate details, and their rich meaning. The Bridegroom has said:

You have ravished my heart, my sister, my bride,
you have ravished my heart with a glance of your eyes,
with one jewel upon your neck.
(Sg 4:9)

How deeply these words of the Bridegroom correspond with, and reveal, the profound experience of love! Is it not true that, when my heart has been captured in love for another person, I am moved by the slightest indications of their presence? Am I not touched, and, as it were, ravished anew by the smallest of reminders of them, which bring before my mind and heart the fullness of their unique beauty, causing my heart to leap anew with joy at the fact that they exist. It is like my heart spontaneously cries: "Here you are, my love, how beautiful you are!" Even if the beloved is not physically present, my heart goes out to them through these reminders, through these signs, and seeks, in a profound longing, to make living contact with them in intimate love.

Perhaps I once experienced a moment of deep intimacy with this person after a rainstorm. They came to see me after walking through the rain, and I could smell that sweetness, that freshness, that they carried with them. And then much later, perhaps years after seeing this person, my heart is still moved to the thought of them whenever I am granted that same smell once again. Or perhaps it is the very sound of their voice at a distance that immediately makes them fully present; perhaps I hear their laugh in a crowded room, or perhaps I hear them singing, and distinguish their voice among many other voices. Indeed, when I truly know another person, when I have let their image and their form be impressed upon my mind and heart, I can immediately recognize them even simply with the very edges of my peripheral vision. Further, spiritually speaking, I can even sense another person's presence without any indication through my external senses. I simply have a deep intuition of being spiritually, invisibly united to them—a sense of their closeness, of their heart throbbing together with mine. And then, while having this deep sense, perhaps they walk in the door!

In the Song we see this dynamic continually being played out: the bride is ever attentive (and becoming ever *more* attentive) to her Bridegroom's presence, to all the ways in which he is ceaselessly present to her. It becomes more and more the case, as she matures, that everything, simply everything, reminds her of her Beloved; indeed, everything in a profound way *communicates* him to her. All things become like a sacrament—a visible sign that mediates invisible grace—and she welcomes him in and through them, while her heart also reaches out ardently, wounded with love and longing, to make direct contact with the unmediated touch of the One whom her heart loves.

The Bridegroom and bride, therefore, are ceaselessly in loving communication—and yet they speak both through presence and through absence, through the contact of the senses which mediates the gift of the heart and the contact of the spirit without the use of the senses. They speak in the joy of togetherness and in the pain of longing; they speak with the interlocking of their eyes in a prolonged gaze and in the quick glance; they speak in the movement of a mutual dance, ever moving and ever active, and they speak in the stillness and repose of an abiding embrace.

In these words of the Song, it is the Bridegroom who is touched by the slightest signs of the bride's presence, by a single glimpse of her unspeakable beauty. But this is also true for the way that the bride beholds her Beloved, for the way in which her glimpse of his beauty ravishes her heart. How beautifully this sensitivity of the bride's heart is expressed in the accounts of Christ's appearances after his Resurrection! The Beloved, victorious over death, has entered into the realm of the Risen Life. He has passed beyond the boundary of sin and death—beyond that experience of the ultimate dissolution of relationships, beyond that mystery that causes the fear of annihilation or everlasting isolation. Rather, he has gone through death and, instead of entering into isolation, into the rupture of relationship, he has opened up in himself the very space of everlasting and unbreakable communion.

After all, sin, and its resulting suffering and death, is a state of isolation, the collapse of the heart upon itself in its turning away from true life—which is nothing but God himself. Christ has entered into the agonizing results of our sin; he has entered into solidarity with us in this place, yet in this very place he has broken open the shackles of fear, shame, and sin. He has stepped forth, beyond the abyss of death, into the realm of endless life. Yes, as Benedict XVI so beautifully said, he has opened up a "new dimension" of existence:

> Jesus' Resurrection was about breaking out into an entirely new form of life, into a life that is no longer subject to the law of dying and becoming, but lies beyond it—a life that opens up a new dimension of human existence. Therefore the Resurrection of Jesus is not an isolated event that we could set aside as something limited to the past, but it constitutes an "evolutionary leap" (to draw an analogy, albeit one that is easily misunderstood). In Jesus' Resurrection a new possibility of human existence is attained that affects everything and that opens up a future, a new kind of future, for mankind. ... Is not creation actually waiting for this...union of the finite with the infinite, for the union of man and God, for the conquest of death?[21]

What this means is that Christ can be seen, known, and experienced, not merely within the limitations of our normal experience of reality, within the dimensionality of the fallen creation. Rather, we know him insofar as we let him draw us into a living communication with this "fifth dimension,"[22] the dimension of the Risen Life, the dimension of eternal and Triune Love. Thus, to enter into living communion with the heavenly Bridegroom is a "stepping-out" beyond the enclosedness of the fallen self, beyond the very limitations of the fallen creation. It is an ecstasy of love into the realm of the eternal. And yet this ecstatic movement is first awakened by God's prior coming to me, and is ever complemented by the fact that, as I let myself be drawn out into union with him, the Risen One, I simultaneously find him pouring himself out anew into me and into the very concreteness of the world in which I live. These two movements will only come together fully whenever, at the end of time, the Risen Life finally permeates creation completely, and takes it up into itself, such that this dimension of eternal Love becomes the very atmosphere in which all is seen, known, and experienced. At that time, at the consummation of all things, the whole of creation will find itself cradled, palpably, in the embrace of the Trinity, and will find itself irradiated, in the light of total face-to-face vision, in the beauty of his loving gaze.

The bride, therefore, will see her Beloved as he is, and enter into living contact with him, to the degree that she lets herself be drawn into the same space he inhabits—the same space of pure Love, in which the person becomes pure relationship, pure openness in acceptance and reciprocal self-gift. This is why Mary Magdalene is the first person recorded as seeing the Risen Christ—because her heart is totally bridal, totally ravished by the beauty of the One whom she loves! The same is true for the beloved disciple, John, who comes to believe in the abiding presence of the Risen One even simply through a glance at the cloths laying in the empty tomb: "Then Simon Peter came, following him, and went into the tomb; he saw the linen cloths lying, and the napkin, which had been on his head, not lying with the linen cloths but rolled up in a place by itself. Then the other disciple, who reached the tomb first, also went in, and he saw and believed" (Jn 20:6-8). The same occurs when they are on the boat fishing, and Christ appears to them at a distance. He tells them to cast the net on the right side of the boat, even though they have been working all night and have caught nothing. Immediately, when they pull up a great catch of fish, the beloved disciple cries out: "It is the Lord!" These are the eyes of an ardent lover, who sees and discerns the presence of his Beloved in every thing and every moment, moved as he is by ardent longing to enter into, and remain in, profound and loving contact with the One whom his heart loves. And Peter too, even if he is burdened by the shame and guilt of his sin, comes to recognize his Beloved, through the words of the beloved disciple. "When Simon Peter heard that it was the Lord, he put on his clothes, for he was stripped for work, and sprang into the sea" (cf. Jn 21:1-14).

What does it matter, in the last analysis, if the bride has sinned and hidden from the face of her Beloved—if only she comes to the Cross and stands there, receiving the outpouring of the Bridegroom's love, which washes away all guilt and obliterates it, so that it should not even come to mind any longer! What does it matter if she has been like a Magdalene or a Peter, or like a John or like the Mother of the Lord? What matters is not where she has come from, what she has done in the past, but the intimacy into which she allows herself to be drawn by the Bridegroom's immense mercy, which makes all things new.

His love has been present to her from the beginning, even if she has hidden herself like a fearful dove in the clefts of the rock, even if she has delayed to rise and answer his call. He has never ceased to look lovingly upon her, never ceased to delight in her. Indeed, even her faults and foibles are knitted into the seamless fabric of his loving plan, as he gently coaxes her, in her unique beauty, to come forth from the isolation of fear and shame, and to let her heart's beauty breathe forth from within in trusting surrender to him.

Here in this most intimate place, cradled in the arms of the Trinity's mercy, in the tenderest embrace of the divine Bridegroom, all are brought together as one. All hearts come together, like lines that start out so far from one another, but which are all going in the same direction, meet at a single point: in the intersection of the reconciling Heart of Christ. As he said: "I, when I am lifted up from the earth, will draw all to myself" (cf. Jn 12:32). Yes, "he died to gather together into unity all the children of God who have been scattered abroad" (cf. Jn 11:51-52). And yet in this most intimate place, not only are hearts joined together as one, but the unrepeatable uniqueness of each heart is revealed in its deepest beauty, reverenced and held by Christ as he holds no other.

Here Mary Magdalene and Mary the Mother of Jesus meet and clasp hands. Here they are united as bride with the Crucified and Risen Heart of Jesus. If they have come from radically different places, this does not matter! They are each uniquely his bride, defined not by their sin or lack of sin, by the external contours of the journey they have taken to this place, but by their unique personal beauty in his eyes, touched and set free to blossom in radiant beauty under his healing and transforming gaze. Here John and Peter meet, cradled in the arms of Christ's merciful love; here they both welcome his love and cry out, "Lord, you know that I love you!" (cf. Jn 21:15-17). Yes, here they both lean back against the bosom of Jesus, listening to the throbbing of his heartbeat that ever pulses as one with the Father and the Holy Spirit.

ישוע

FAITH, HOPE, AND LOVE

In the last reflection I spoke about the new dimension of existence that Christ has opened up in his Resurrection, this dimension of pure and eternal Love that has permeated the entire humanity of Jesus, and in him has opened up this same newness for all of us. From this realm of eternal Love, Christ is able to come to us more intimately, more radically than he could in any other way, and yet he also comes in such a way that it is not immediately palpable. He communicates himself to me from another dimension, and unless I open my heart to this dimension through faith, hope, and love, I find myself incapable of hearing what he wants to say or feeling the outpouring of his love.

In the fallen state in which I find myself, in this world marred by original sin, the face of God seems veiled and hidden; but this is only because we have lost our ability to see and to perceive. Thus God has come to us and meets us where we are at, adjusting himself to our limitation and frailty, communicating himself in the humblest of ways: through living as a man among us, through dying and rising in our nature, through the witness of those who believe in him, through the Sacraments, teaching, and life of his Church, through the beauty of his creation, especially of the human person, whom he has inseparably joined to himself in the Incarnation and Resurrection. All of these are intimate places of contact between my heart and the Heart of Christ, and yet this contact occurs on a level of depth to which I am not accustomed.

Of course, this very dimension of Love cradles my life, in all its concreteness and limitation, within itself, and so Christ is able to communicate himself, to intimately work, even when I remain blind to what he is doing. After all, the very reality of his Love is unceasingly active permeating all of creation and transforming it from within, making all things new through the re-creating power of the Resurrection. Nonetheless, he tenderly invites me, like the fearful dove in the clefts of the rock, like the shy bride locked in her room, to arise and come to him. I do this by opening my heart in faith, hope, and love, and letting him introduce me ever deeper into the very space of the Trinity's life in which he exists. Yes, the intimate personal communication into which he invites me is rooted in my nature, in my natural human experience, while also infinitely surpassing it. In order to grow into communion with my divine Bridegroom, therefore, in order to live on the level of his self-communication and to let my life flow back freely to him in return—this requires a kind of "acclimatization," an "accustoming" of myself to the life of God.

This is precisely the work of the three theological virtues of faith, hope, and love, which themselves awaken and mature within me the "spiritual senses" and the capacity to make contact with the realm of the spirit and of God. Indeed, this very interior communication of the heart transfigures also my experience of the bodily senses, in that I come more and more to recognize the visibility of all creation as a kind of veil which both conceals and reveals God—which reveals him while concealing him, and, while concealing him, nonetheless reveals him to me. Thus the whole created order and all of my human relationships become like "sacraments" of God's presence to me, while also whetting my appetite ever more for the fullness, while enkindling my ardent thirst for the full, direct, and unmediated touch of God's own embrace which I will know fully only in heaven.

It is faith, hope, and love which bridge over the gap between my mortal existence and my eternal existence in God, between the intimacy that I glimpse through the veil of created reality and the direct union of eternity, face-to-face. For these three powers implanted within me are indeed nothing else than God's own life poured into me and active within me, grafted into the most intimate place of my heart and elevating my entire nature and the activity of all of my faculties. On the surface, perhaps it looks like I experience everything the way that I did before coming to faith. And yet, on a deeper inspection, everything has changed. It is like I have learned to look, not merely *at* created reality, or even *at* the longing of my own heart, but rather *along* them and *through* them, to the One who unceasingly communicates himself to me through them. Faith, hope, and love are like a hand touching another's Face in the darkness. I get to know and feel the contours of his beauty, the uniqueness of his countenance, not by direct sight, but mediated to me by a mysterious touch. Or indeed, even more fundamentally, faith, hope, and love are my willingness to let myself be touched, to let myself be loved by God. They are the way in which I allow myself to be looked upon by God, bathed in the light of his gaze. In this way my life becomes more and more sensitive to God's activity, to his guidance, to his tender and sheltering protection.

What are faith, hope, and love, as manifested in my concrete experience? *Faith* is above all the act of *trusting acceptance* by which I allow God to approach me, to communicate himself to me in love, to unveil before me his tenderness, his beauty, his truth. As Saint John writes: "We know and believe the love God has for us" (1 Jn 4:16). Faith is a matter of letting myself be embraced—like a child who lets herself be taken in the arms of her mother—and in this, I experience my entire life more and more being cradled in the arms of Love. The whole of the Church's life, teaching, and Sacraments find their place within this experience of being cradled in Love, and exist to serve it and to allow it to permeate our entire existence ever more deeply and intimately.

Hope is what is awakened in me by this trusting acceptance of faith; it is the *confident longing* which impels my heart toward the One in whom alone I can be at rest, and also assures me that he can and will bring this longing to full perfection in his eternal embrace. It is, indeed, a possession of this fullness already in seed, just as a seed already bears the tree, or a fetus is already fully the human person who will mature only over time. Hope is like a sure anchor cast into the Heart of God, and suspending me already in the life of heaven even as my feet remain fixed upon this earth. Or it is like God's anchor cast into the depths of my heart—somewhat like a fishing-hook in the mouth of a fish—drawing me gently yet powerfully toward my only true Home.

Love is the full flowering of faith and hope, the blossoming of the movement of *total surrender* into the arms of the One who calls me to himself. It is the mature expression of my acceptance of God's love for me, in which the vulnerability of need becomes the vulnerability of ardent desire, a radical response to the beauty of the One who has touched and ravished my heart. It is also the flowing forth of this love that I have received as a tender attentiveness to my brothers and sisters, in which I welcome them unreservedly into myself and give myself to them, as Christ has first done for me.

As Jesus said: "With the love with which the Father has loved me, so have I loved you; abide in my love… This is my commandment, that you love one another with the very love with which I have loved you" (cf. Jn 15:9, 12). This is not a matter of merely loving *like* God, but rather of *loving with the very love of God*, poured out into me and gripping my entire existence. Yes, faith, hope, and love together are the threefold dynamic by which God's love meets me in my need and pours itself out into me so totally that it possesses and transforms my entire being within itself. And in the last analysis these three are one. They are all elements of the single process of my *becoming love*, of my *living unceasingly as beloved, and therefore as lover.*

ישוע

THE PARADISE OF THE RESURRECTION

I have spoken about the new dimension of Love that is opened up within the Risen Body of Jesus, this space of perfect and eternal Love into which he draws all of humanity, so that we may share in the very intimacy of the Father, Son, and Holy Spirit. I have spoken about how this new dimension, while remaining "veiled" during this mortal life, is nonetheless fully present, even if it remains hidden from our eyes. We are already in communication with this dimension of the Risen Life, this newness of everlasting intimacy, even if we cannot experience it directly. And this contact is established through faith, hope, and love, which are God's own divine being and activity grafted into our being and operative within us. Through living a life of faith, hope, and love, we are truly in a direct and unmediated contact with our divine Beloved, with the Trinity who is the deepest longing of our hearts and in whom alone we will be fully at rest.

It is as though, in this way, we can reach out our hand beyond the veil that obscures our sight and can touch the face of the One whom our heart loves. In this way we get to know him, to "feel" his unspeakable Beauty even before we see it; and thus, when the veil is at last torn, we will immediately recognize him face to face, exclaiming, "Here you are, my Beloved; behold, you are beautiful!" recognizing in radiant contemplation the face of the One whose countenance was already impressed as a seal upon our inmost heart.

This recognition of the Beloved, and this intimate union with him, even through the shadows of this life and before the veil is torn, is a continual theme throughout the New Testament. One of my favorite passages comes from the First Letter of Saint Peter. He writes: "Without having seen him you love him; though you do not now see him you believe in him and rejoice with unutterable and exalted joy. As the outcome of your faith you obtain the salvation of your souls" (1 Pet 1:8). This is an amazing romance, in which the bride falls deeply in love with a Bridegroom whom she cannot see! But indeed the lack of sight is in no way an indication of a lack of presence, a lack of intimacy. Rather, the bride loves the One in whom she believes, and, believing, she rejoices already with an unspeakable and exalted joy. Is this not because she already touches him now, already experiences him in some way even as he remains veiled from her sight? And is this not because she has the confidence that one day the veil shall be removed, and she will at last behold him face to face in the joy of everlasting consummation? Saint Peter shortly continues:

"Through him you have confidence in God, who raised him from the dead and gave him glory, so that your faith and hope are in God," and this confidence radically transforms the heart of the bride: "Having purified your souls by your obedience to the truth for a sincere love of the brethren, love one another earnestly from the heart. You have been born anew, not of perishable seed but of imperishable, through the living and abiding word of God" (1 Pet 1:21-23).

The heart of the bride, the heart of the one who is beloved by Christ, is filled with an earnest love, with an ardent and tender affection, both for the Bridegroom himself and for all those in whom she discerns his image. In this love she truly learns to reach beyond the veil, to make contact with the throbbing heartbeat of the One who has ravished her heart. Is this not true already on the natural level also, in which the communication between two human hearts always occurs "through a veil," and yet love gives access beyond this? My heart goes out to another person who shares their heart with me, who expresses, vulnerably and trustingly, the deep movements of desire within them. I do not see their heart directly, I cannot make direct contact, from within, through their own experience, but my love draws me out and grants me an intuition, a sense, a "love without seeing" and a belief that gives confidence. Yes, it dilates my heart to be a tender and sheltering space for the other, so that I may spiritually cradle and hold them, their heart caressed and protected within my own. And then at the end of this conversation, we share a prolonged embrace in silence, in which two hearts beat together, sharing themselves with each other and receiving one another. No words can express this mutual throbbing of hearts, no words can express the love, the desire, the gratitude shared between two persons. But in this very embrace, in which the arms of each draw the other close and hold them there, two bodies as it were made one in the "we" of intimate communion —in this very embrace the veil is stretched thin and one "feels" what in this life cannot fully be seen.

This is the case, even more so, in my relationship with Christ, the divine Bridegroom, who shelters my heart within the tenderness of his own Heart, who truly draws me near and holds me gently in his arms, pouring forth the throbbing love of his own Heart into mine. Yes, I do not see it directly, I do not even feel it fully—and yet there is a sense, an intuition, an awareness that surpasses all words and thought. He is the One who *lives*, eternally, even in his very humanity, victorious over death in the Resurrection. And I too live in him, even while remaining externally in a world marked by death. The new dimension has been opened before me, indeed, it has been opened up within me, and I can remain always in contact with this realm of pure and perfect Life, this sphere of eternal Love. This is my hope, this is my joy, this is my confidence and my abiding gladness.

And this contact with the Risen Christ is not a merely spiritual or intellectual union—as if merely by "thinking" of him I was in communion with him. Of course, a single thought in my mind, a single sigh of prayer or longing, makes me present to him who is always fully present to me! But this contact of my being with the being of Christ is total, in that he is present to me, pressing upon me, not only in my mind or imagination, but in the fullness of my existence and in all that I am. After all, his very body has entered into the realm of the eternal, it has become pure Love. And thus, as Christ communicates himself to me, his very Body is joined to my body, and there is a kind of "one flesh" union that endures at every moment, that re-creates my very bodily existence here and now, as it prepares me for my own definitive resurrection at the end of time. As Pope Benedict XVI writes:

> [The Resurrection] is a historical event that nevertheless bursts open the dimensions of history and transcends it…in which a new dimension of life emerges, a new dimension of human existence. Indeed, matter itself is remolded into a new type of reality. The man Jesus, complete with his body, now belongs totally to the sphere of the divine and the eternal. From now on, as Tertullian once said, "spirit and blood" have a place within God (cf. De Resurrect. Mort. 51:3m CCSL II, 994). Even if man by his nature is created for immortality, it is only now that the place exists in which his immortal soul can find its "space," its "bodiliness," in which immortality takes on its meaning as communion with God and with the whole of reconciled mankind. This is what is meant by those passages in Saint Paul's prison letters (cf. Col 1:12-23 and Eph 1:3-23) that speak of the cosmic body of Christ, indicating thereby that Christ's transformed body is also the place where men enter into communion with God and with one another and are thus able to live definitively in the fullness of indestructible life. Since we ourselves have no experience of such a renewed and transformed type of matter, or such a renewed and transformed kind of life, it is not surprising that it oversteps the boundaries of what we are able to conceive.[23]

However, through the activity of the Risen Christ within us, through the very life of the Trinity grafted into our humanity, we can begin, in some way, already in this world to taste and make contact with this new kind of life, to glimpse the mystery of heaven while already on earth. But what does all of this have to do with the Song of Songs? It is precisely the deepest, most intimate meaning—the full flowering and the only consummation—of the words of the Song! If the Bridegroom is truly to call the earth "our land," and if the bride is truly to be his enclosed garden, his paradise, the he must renew and re-create her in the fullness of his Love. This precisely is what he has accomplished in his Passion and Resurrection!

Now she is truly his paradise, his garden that flows with the streams of living water. Therefore, she need not await paradise only at the end of a long and painful journey. Rather, even if the full consummation awaits her only at the end of time, the reality is already totally present under the veil of mortality, touched in faith, hope, and love. After all, she carries the new Jerusalem within her heart, for she carries the very Trinity within her, as "the river of the water of life flows from the throne of God and the Lamb" through the middle of her being, pouring forth from the most intimate space of her own heart, uniquely beautiful in his eyes (Rev 22:1-2). Yes, did not the Bridegroom himself say that this river of life was the Spirit whom those who believed in him would receive (Jn 7:37-39)? Therefore, the bride is truly his paradise, flowing with streams of living water just like Eden did in the beginning. And implanted within the core of her being is the Tree of Life, bearing fruit unceasingly from the self-giving of the divine Bridegroom who has definitively poured out his being as a gift to his bride, and who never ceases to give himself to her anew at every moment, until this union is at last consummated in their mutual self-donation at the end of time.

יׁשוע

LOVE AS A RESPONSE TO THE BEAUTY OF THE BELOVED

You have ravished my heart, my sister, my bride,
you have ravished my heart with a glance of your eyes,
with one jewel upon your neck.
(Sg 4:9)

The terms "ravished my heart" in this verse, when they were translated into Latin, were expressed as *vulnerasti cor meum*, that is, "you have wounded my heart." In this perspective, the Bridegroom is saying that he has been so deeply *touched* by the beauty and lovableness of his bride that his very Heart is wounded with love and desire. His Heart is wounded with longing for her—a twofold longing which is manifest in all authentic love, and in its highest, most perfect form, in this love of the divine Bridegroom for his precious spouse. This twofold longing is: 1) the longing for a deep and lasting intimacy with the one whose beauty has wounded and attracts his Heart; 2) the longing for the well-being and happiness of his beloved, which moves him to give himself totally to seek and foster this happiness. In Latin these two desires are traditionally termed the *intentio unionis* and the *intentio benevolentiae*, the "desire for union" and the "desire of benevolence."

In the history of Christian thought, there have been certain tendencies to reject the *intentio unionis* as something inherently selfish, as a mere human grasping for the pleasure that another can afford. This is often conceptualized as the choice of a pure *agape* love over and against the love of *eros*, that is, a pure and disinterested sacrificial love that excludes any possibility of the love of desire which seeks one's own happiness or longs for union with the beloved. I have spoken extensively of this elsewhere, and the Church is very clear—for example in Pope Benedict's encyclical *Deus Caritas Est*—that love in its fullness harmonizes these two movements together as one, even if *agape* has primacy over *eros*, and the *intentio benevolentiae* over the *intentio unionis*. In this reflection, I want to take a little different course, by trying to unveil the inner heart of love itself, in which these two desires are indeed unified, and from which they derive their authentic orientation.

First of all, it important to emphasize that love is not an *appetite* analogous to the appetite for food and drink, nor even for that matter a mere seeking of the human heart for the *good* that will bring it fulfillment. Yes, there is an "appetitive" element of our human desire *for* love (appetitive in the Thomistic sense), that is, we inherently yearn for loving relationships because these are essential to our well-being and happiness. However, if we were to relate to another merely on this level, on the level of "need," then perhaps there would be no real love at all, at least not in its mature and full sense.

What, then, is love, if it is not an appetite? It is a *response to the innate value and beauty of another person*. Yes, love is not some blind drive that wells up spontaneously within me and seeks to make contact with its object (and it doesn't matter who particularly that object is, I just need *someone!*). Rather, whatever innate longings there are in my heart for loving relationship, whatever desires to make contact with another and to enter into mutual sharing with them, have been implanted in me by God simply to "sensitize" me to the objective value of others, and to impel me to break beyond my isolation in order to enter into the joy of communion.

But love itself cannot be based merely on this innate longing; it must rather be founded on the rock-solid basis of a deep and heartfelt attentiveness to the unique beauty and dignity of the other person, which awakens within me a longing quite different from a mere appetite. In other words, the other person does not become a mere means to my own well-being or happiness. Rather, I love and affirm them—with my mind, my will, and my affectivity—in their own right and for their own sake. I am happy simply that they are, that they exist. This is where the definition of John Paul II comes in that love is "willing the good of the other." Love is definitively more than this, but this is an essential element of love. It springs from that exclamation, "Here you are, my beloved, behold, you are beautiful!" And this kind of exclamation, this kind of vision of the inner heart, spontaneously awakens my desire that the other is affirmed in their beauty and goodness, that they experience themselves as beautiful, and that their being flowers in authentic and enduring happiness.

But, in addition, this very disinterested affirmation of the beloved in their own right also overflows immediately as a source of great joy and gladness for me. I am simply enriched by the light that pours forth into me from my contemplation of their beauty and goodness. If, however, I were to cling to the other on the level of mere satisfaction, or even for their mere objective goodness for me, then the deepest enrichment, the deepest fecundation and flowering of my heart would not occur. This is because this kind of fecundation occurs directly as the result of the "ecstasy" of my heart out of itself toward the beloved, of the radical donation of my heart to the other for their own sake, and of the way that, in this very movement, the other comes to live inside of me, dilating my being and immeasurably enriching it.

In this context, some more ideas of Dietrich von Hildebrand can be very helpful. He makes a distinction between three different kinds of "interest," of "goodness," which have perhaps not been adequately distinguished in the tradition of human thought. For example, in the writings of Thomas Aquinas, or at least in some of the interpretation that followed him, love was reduced to a "sensitive appetite," a longing in the human person to make contact with the good that brings it fulfillment. In this perspective, love is the most basic and central "passion," in that all that we do we do out of love—out of the innate drive to enter into union with the good that fulfills us. In this understanding, I can say that I love food, or rest, or education, or another person. Even non-personal things "love" in this way by tending toward the end for which God made them. But this, clearly, is love only in an analogous sense, and I would prefer to call this "appetitive love" not love but *desire*.

True love itself occurs on an entirely deeper and more spiritual level, and is only possible for spiritual persons created for intimate communion. This is because it is not founded on the goodness of another person or thing *for me*, but rather on its goodness *in itself*. (This goodness-it-itself is what von Hildebrand calls a "value.") Therefore, let me now state his three "kinds" of interest or goodness, and then explain them. First, he says that things can awaken our interest and desire because they are *subjectively satisfying*; second, they can do so because they are *objectively beneficial* for us; third, they can do so because they are *valuable in themselves*.

Something that is *subjectively satisfying* is a created reality that in itself does not have an intrinsic value, but only becomes valuable because it provides some kind of pleasant experience for me. For example, a soft bed or a sofa is such a value, as well as a cigarette, a tasty meal, and things of this nature. These have a certain important role in human life, but it is clearly secondary. The next kind of goods are those which are *objectively beneficial*. These are higher and more noble goods that not only subjectively satisfy us (though they may do that as well), but truly enrich us and elevate us when we encounter them. They benefit us by helping our nature to grow toward its authentic good in the fullness of truth, beauty, and love. For example, education is one such value, and the relationship of friendship is another (though the *person* of the friend himself falls in the third category).

This third category, this highest level of goods are those that are *intrinsically valuable* (or *valuable-in-themselves*). These are things that are simply good, simply beautiful, simply worthy of admiration, regardless of their particular relationship to us. The greatest example is, of course, the human person. Each person bears in himself or herself an absolute value and dignity, such that they deserve to be respected and loved for their own sake. Indeed, the human person's value transcends the value of the whole visible creation, awakening in us an awe and reverence that can really only be compared with our value response to God himself or the angels. Other values of this kind are moral values. Moral values issue a special "word" to me, a special call, and seek to awaken in me a kind of absolute response, simply for the sake of the value that they bear within them. For example, when I am faced with an important moral decision, my heart senses, in deep awe, that I am standing before something that is inherently important, something that issues a call to me and seeks a heartfelt response simply because it is good (or inherently evil). Indeed, even a morally good act is in itself intrinsically valuable—for example, the act by which Saint Maximilian Kolbe asked to be "exchanged" with another Auschwitz prisoner condemned to die by starvation. Such an act should awaken my admiration, my reverence, simply because it is worthy of such a response—and not because of any "benefit" I receive from it. Nonetheless, in this very reverence I myself am enriched through contemplation of what Maximilian has done.

Also, things that are inherently beautiful are also valuable in themselves, and awaken my response to their value—simply because they manifest something of the goodness, the glory, and the radiance of God's own uncreated Beauty. For example, a piece of music, or a sunset, or the beauty of mountains or ocean—all of these speak a "word" from God, a message of his goodness which comes to me as a kind of "sacrament" of his own loving presence. I cannot, of course, try to grasp and possess the beauty of these realities, as if they could be appropriated to myself as my own. It is rather, in a way, that I enter into them and they enter into me; there is a kind of communication between the beholder and the beauty of what is beheld. There is a kind of communion, in which my heart is both dilated and enriched, lifted up out of its often petty preoccupation with the subjectively satisfying—with pleasure and ease—and even beyond a preoccupation with what is objectively beneficial for me. Rather, I am raised up into the sacred sphere of God's own absolute Goodness, Truth, and Beauty…into the realm of eternal Love pouring itself out, and here I pour myself out into the Love that ceaselessly pours itself out into me.

Precisely in this "ecstasy" of response to the objective value and beauty of the other, I am profoundly enriched, and indeed in a way I come "home" into the authentic truth of my own heart. In other words, I am truly unified within myself, not by forcibly "gathering myself together" through my own efforts at recollection. Rather, I am unified within myself precisely by letting beauty draw beyond me myself; I come home to my innermost being precisely in response to the beauty that touches me from the outside. This is because I am admitted again, through the grace of God's love that comes to me (either mediated through the beauty of created reality or directly from him), into the "garden" of my own inner being. I am drawn from the "exile" on the surface of my nature—lost as I am on the "periphery" of what is merely subjectively satisfying, or in a preoccupied concern about my own well-being—and *I get back in touch with that sacred space* where, *in my most authentic being, I am pure relationship with Another, united to the very Source of goodness.* This is the gift of "ecstasy," in which, by getting in touch with the word of God's Love that invites me, I am also simultaneously admitted into the sanctuary of my own heart where he unceasingly dwells. This is what Saint Augustine was referring to when he said that God is "more interior to me than my inmost self, and higher than my highest being."

What does all of this have to do with the way that I started this reflection—with saying that love is not a mere appetite for the good that fulfills me, but rather a pure response to the goodness and value of the beloved? It reveals that only this kind of disinterested love, this pure affirmation of the beloved for their own sake, can truly also be, in the fullest sense, "good for me." It alone can fulfill the deepest longings of my heart—the longing to know myself as I am in intimate relationship with another, and to enter into a deep and lasting intimacy with them. This intimacy is possible, not when I relate to another on the level of mere need, but rather when the two of us give ourselves to one another in radical self-donation, affirming and seeking each other's authentic good, while also wholeheartedly welcoming the enrichment and joy that comes in being loved by the other. Indeed, one of the greatest joys consists simply in seeing that the other is joyful, and also in welcoming their unique beauty, their unrepeatable personal mystery, into my inner heart, and cradling them there unceasingly in tender love, as I myself—and both of us together—are unceasingly cradled in the love of God himself.

ישוע

TRANSFORMED IN THE PLACE OF GREATEST NEED

In the light of what was said in the previous reflection, we can enter more deeply into understanding the words of the Bridegroom: "You have ravished my Heart, my sister, my bride." If love is not based merely on *need*, but rather is a radical *response to the beauty of the beloved*, then these words of the Bridegroom reveal in a particular way the authentic nature of love. Christ says to me: *vulnerasti cor meum*. "You have wounded my Heart." Yes, Christ is vulnerable before me, his Heart is truly moved and touched by me, by my beauty and goodness. Thus, my love or lack of love truly affects him. I can wound his Heart with the anguish of rejection, or I can wound his Heart by letting him gaze upon me in my beauty, in my own vulnerability, such that this beauty ravishes him in his contemplative gaze. Indeed, I can ravish his Heart with the beauty of my own reciprocal love, which allows his love for me to ever expand and deepen in me as it pours itself out into me and awakens my own surrender to him.

However, Christ is not vulnerable before me by necessity (except, of course, by the "necessity" of Love, for it is the essence of God to be utterly vulnerable in love!). Rather, he is in himself "invulnerable," that is, un-woundable, even in his radical openness of heart in love. He has no inherent need, as I have, for all "need" in him is already always perfectly fulfilled in the innermost heart of the Trinity's eternal embrace. And yet, out of the fullness of his love, he freely chooses to become woundable, to become vulnerable, before me. In other words, he does not need me, and yet he *chooses* to need me. He is perfect and complete in the life of the Trinity, in his endless bliss with the Father and the Holy Spirit; and yet, out of his goodness he creates unique beauty in me, and then is touched, ravished, and drawn by this very beauty to unveil his Heart to me in tender desire. Yes, he makes himself vulnerable, he makes himself needy, through the depths of his longing for the unique beauty that he sees in me, and which attracts his Heart.

He yearns, more than for anything else in our relationship, to see me truly happy. He yearns for my happiness and well-being with the profound longing of his Heart. And yet his Heart, in its response to my beauty, in its yearning for my good, also welcomes me as his own good, as his own happiness, such that he yearns to be united intimately to me, now and forever, to welcome me into his embrace, such that my happiness becomes his own and his happiness becomes mine. Indeed, here the *intentio benevolentiae* and the *intentio unionis* become inseparably one. This is because my happiness consists precisely in union with God, and God's deep desire is precisely my happiness, which comes about only when he intimately unites me to himself as he so ardently desires!

When Christ calls out, therefore, "You have wounded my Heart, my sister, my bride," he is emphasizing that his love for me is utterly intimate, utterly unique, a true response to the particular person that I am, fashioned unrepeatably by the creative hand of God. He is expressing the way that his whole being is moved by me, such that he intensely desires both to seek my true happiness as well as to experience himself the happiness of being intimately united to me in my unique beauty.

And this ardent love of Christ, the eternal Son of the Father, moves him from his very throne in heaven in order to make his throne upon earth. This is precisely why he calls me "my sister, my bride." For he becomes my Brother in the Incarnation, bearing the same nature, the same flesh. And only as a Brother can he truly also be a Bridegroom in the fullest sense—giving his very Body and Blood as a gift to me, and receiving my own gift in return, so that we are united, through mutual self-giving, in a communion of being and life that truly makes us one flesh and one spirit!

In this blessed encounter between the Bridegroom-Christ and my own bridal heart, the fullness of eternal Love, abundant and overflowing, meets the poverty and neediness of my own heart. Yes, for even if love is not based on need, it is nonetheless true that I deeply need—I deeply need love, I deeply need another, I deeply need above all the One who is himself perfect Love! And this need is in no way something bad, to be rejected or repressed. Rather, Christ wants me to get in touch with this deep need, this deep poverty of longing in my heart, and to open it before him so that he may touch and fulfill it with his own love! My very innate longing for happiness and intimacy, therefore, is a "sacrament" of God's own love for me, the very space in which he comes to me.

It is precisely in this place that my weakness is transformed into a space of grace, and my need is transformed into the vulnerability of loving and liberating encounter. He draws near, the One who lacks nothing, sheltered as he is in the enduring embrace of the most perfect Father. He draws near and makes himself vulnerable before me, needing me and yearning for me out of the fullness of his love. And thus the vulnerability of perfect Love in his Heart encounters the vulnerability of need and longing in my heart.

As these two encounter, as these two communicate with one another, gradually my need is changed; it is healed, transformed, dilated. Yes, if before I related to God (and others) primarily on the basis of need, moved by my deep insecurity of being lovable and beautiful, now things have changed. My heart is now deeply sensitive to the beauty of the Christ himself, and in Christ to all persons, such that I am moved, wounded, and drawn by the ravishing beauty that I encounter in them. This is the primary, greatest gift: I have discovered true and enduring security in the loving gaze of Christ, in his tender embrace and that of the Father.

And in this place of belovedness I spontaneously begin to love as I have been loved! For this security in love does not close off my heart, but rather opens it ever more beautifully and radically! My wound of need is transformed into a wound of love, and my vulnerability of lack is transformed into a vulnerability of fullness! Now my heart, cradled always in the glorious wound of the Heart of Christ, reflects and shares in his own love, loving as he loves, since I have first been loved so beautifully by him.

ישוע

A WELL OF LIVING WATER

I have tried to show how the bride, in her unique beauty, is a kind of paradise for the Bridegroom. She is his delight and his place of rest, "a garden enclosed, a fountain sealed" (Sg 4:12), in which, in an exclusive and unrepeatable way, he unites himself to her in marital union. And yet, at the same time, she is also a "garden fountain, a well of living water, and flowing streams from Lebanon" (Sg 4:15). There seems to be a deliberate paradox here, in that the bride is sealed and enclosed, a place for the Bridegroom alone, and yet also a fountain flowing forth with great abundance.

First of all, she is utterly virginal, exclusively given to her one divine Beloved. She lives, and she welcomes him, in the "cloister of the heart," pronouncing her "yes" to his ardent love and the gift of himself. This "yes" is indeed the very core of her existence, her virginal and bridal receptivity to the gift of the Bridegroom's love. In this place she experiences who she truly is in the loving eyes of her Bridegroom, and she surrenders her entire being to him in order to welcome the outpouring of his love and to shelter it within herself, as she is first sheltered within him. This is indeed the most personal, the most intimate union between two hearts, where no other heart has direct access.

And yet, not only is the bride a garden enclosed or a sealed fountain, but, in the very act of being enclosed for her Beloved, she is also open with him to pour forth the living streams of his love for others. In other words, her intimate and spousal union with Christ her Bridegroom spontaneously impregnates her with the very fullness of the divine life—the "rivers of living water" of which Jesus spoke in John's Gospel—which then pour forth in a tender love for all those around her.

Here we see the deep union between the personal and the communal, in that the most intimate and unique bond of love between Bridegroom and bride also flows out beyond the embrace that they share in order to touch, ravish, and draw other hearts too. There is an immense fecundation that happens here, flowing forth from the mutual self-giving of Lover and beloved, a kind of mutual enrichment that is uncontainable in its fullness. It is the very outflow of the way that each person lives in the heart of the other and the way that they share a single life as one. This union of Bridegroom and bride (itself enfolded in the embrace of Father and child) is the fundamental communion, the foundational relationship of love in which the human person knows her true identity. She is beloved; she is seen, known, and loved; she is cherished by the heavenly Father and by his Son, the divine Bridegroom; and she is called by the Spirit into a profound union, to share in the very innermost life of the Blessed Trinity.

And yet from this very constitutive relationship with God, her heart dilates to see, know, and love others as she has first been seen, known, and loved, and to welcome them as she has been welcomed by God. Indeed, in this place there is no competition between one heart and another, since God's love for each person is utterly unique, indeed exclusive, founded as it is in the unrepeatable identity of the person, born uniquely from the loving heart of the Trinity.

The beloved bride comes to see in every human person—reflected in their eyes, in their countenance, in their very flesh, and in their words, gestures, and silence, and indeed in the whole of their existence—the unique beauty that God has created in them. And she yearns for this beauty to make contact again with its Source. She yearns for the human heart to return into the embrace of the perfect Lover, and in this way to become also his paradise, wholly surrendered to him.

She sees in each heart already this mystery of the garden, even if they themselves live caught up on the surface, in exile from their own authentic identity. Thus she yearns that they may let themselves be drawn back into this sacred place, this sanctuary at the core of their being where they are alone and defenseless before God. Here, in a radical receptivity and confident trust, they can allow themselves to be gazed upon, to be known; and they can welcome the gift that alone brings true fulfillment and perfect happiness: "If only you knew the gift of God!"

ישוע

I COME TO MY GARDEN

The bride, knowing herself to be infinitely loved by Christ, welcomes him into the innermost sanctuary of her being, into this "cloister of the heart," which is her "garden enclosed," her "fountain sealed." She offers to him the pure flower of her virginal love, which blossoms for him alone in purity and ardent love. She lives in this place with him who lives in her, letting him make her very spirit, her very body, a sacred temple of his divine presence. Yes, he is closer to her than her very heartbeat; he fills her more surely than the air that fills her lungs; he pervades her more entirely than the blood that surges through her veins.

A garden enclosed: she is a paradise protected from disturbance from the outside, in which the sweetness of her perfume and the beauty of her flowering can yield itself up freely to the One who has first breathed forth his perfume and his beauty into her, loving her freely. A fountain sealed: she shelters in her inmost heart a deep well of living water, which is the love of God for her, and which she does not indiscriminately spill out before any passer-by. No, she is not merely a channel, a flowing river through which the water of God's love quickly passes on its way to somewhere else. Rather, she is a reservoir, a still and peaceful lake reflecting the beauty of the sky, reflecting the beautiful gaze of the Beautiful One in the stillness of her own being, which is immeasurably beautiful in his eyes.

It is precisely in knowing herself to be loved and cherished in this way, reflecting forth the beauty that he first sees in her, that her whole being can spontaneously surrender into his welcoming arms. Yes, she calls out for the breath of his Spirit to fill and pervade her, bringing fully into the welcoming Heart of her Bridegroom the total self-surrender of her heart and her life:

Awake, O north wind,
and come, O south wind!
Breathe upon my garden,
let its fragrance be wafted abroad.
Let my Beloved come to his garden,
and eat its choicest fruits.
(Sg 4:16)

The beloved heart offers herself as a dwelling-place for the One whom she loves, inviting the Spirit to prepare her heart, to breathe through her and to awaken all the beauty and goodness and desire that slumbers within her. It is as if, when her Beloved comes, she wants him to find her whole being astir with pollen and fragrance, with the sweetness of all plants and flowers, carried on the gentle wind of the Spirit. It is this Spirit who, cradling and caressing her, draws forth her inmost being and makes it an unreserved gift for the One whose gaze she yearns to encounter, and into whose arms she yearns to abandon herself entirely. And the Beloved comes:

I come to my garden,
my sister, my bride,
I gather my myrrh with my spice,
I eat my honeycomb with my honey,
I drink my wine with my milk.
(Sg 5:1a)

Yes, here, at the conclusion of this third poem, the Bridegroom comes fully into the garden of his bride and unites himself to her. He gently whispers, in the very breath of the Spirit who is already breathing in her: "I come... I gather... I eat... I drink..." Here the breath of the Bridegroom and the breath of the bride mingle together as one in the single breath of the Spirit whom they share. As he gives his Body and Blood for her to eat, for her to drink, and lets her gather him close to her bosom, so he in turn rejoices to take her to himself in a deep and lasting union.

And unable to contain his enthusiasm for the beauty of his precious bride, he wants all to see and experience her beauty, her goodness, her lovableness:

Eat, O friends, and drink:
drink deeply, O friends!
(Sg 5:1b)

Is this not a trait of deep love, that it yearns that all will see the beloved as he sees her, that all will love her as he loves her? For his Heart is ravished with the profound awareness of her beauty, and he knows that she deserves precisely such a loving and cherishing gaze from each and from all. And yet, at the same time, this love embraces her, her alone, in a sacred space where no other can gain access. This is that sacred space opened up in the communication of two hearts, where a third cannot enter. That is, unless, of course, they let the love shared between the two flow forth to touch and draw them also.

In other words, here the enclosed garden of the bride becomes a garden for all. At the heart of her own unique beauty as his beloved, her friends can come, in order to see and experience the love of the Bridegroom himself, reflected in her. This love reaches out, through her, also to make contact with the garden of their own hearts, yearning for the One who is the only true rest of every longing heart and the fulfillment of every desire.

ישוע

THE ONTOLOGY OF GIFT,
THE METAPHYSICS OF LOVE

In all that we have seen in the third poem, we touch on the very heart of the wounds of our contemporary culture, as well as the true remedy for these wounds. How many people in our world really feel that they are a gift, that their very existence is a gift ever flowing from the loving hands of God? How many people feel that this material world is a "home," a true dwelling-place in which God's own beauty is sacramentally made present? Rather, do not hearts so often feel a sense of profound existential homelessness in this world, like they just do not belong, because they have never been loved, affirmed, and welcomed as they are, experiencing the sheltering love of others that really mediates to them the love of God himself?

Of course, it is true that this world is not our true and definitive home. We will only experience this definitive home in the resurrection of the body at the end of time, when God will re-create the heavens and the earth, utterly permeated by his own presence and his Trinitarian Love. Nonetheless, this reality is already present now and profoundly at work in the limitations of this created existence. Through the Paschal Mystery at work renewing creation from within, all of reality can again be experienced as God's pure and loving gift, revealing him even as it conceals him, and drawing our hearts ever deeper into the welcoming embrace of the Trinity.

But above all there is a fundamental gift that makes our receptivity to all other gifts possible, even the gift of eternal life with God: *the gift of my own self, my own existence as a person*. Here, indeed, we touch on perhaps the deepest wound of our current society. After the distorted individualism of the Enlightenment—after the radical rupture of human thought and experience away from the objective beauty, goodness, and truth of reality—we have not found ourselves liberated to be what we want to be. Rather, we find ourselves alone and isolated, grasping out for meaning and security in the beauty and love of another which we cannot give to ourselves. Whenever the beauty and goodness of objective reality is dismissed, whenever the very structure of existence as a constitutive relationship with God and with other persons is abandoned, then the individual human person finds his or her life isolated, unsheltered, and terribly alone.

What David L. Schindler calls the loss of the "ontology of gift," and therefore of the metaphysics of love (i.e. seeing all of being as a pure expression of God's own Being-as-Love), lies at the root of the painful disorders that plague our culture. As he writes (forgive the technical philosophical language):

> What the constitutive relatedness among human beings implies, in sum, is that I am in my original and deepest meaning as such a *substantial individual* who is *ordered at once from and toward* God and others. My being thus bears the character of gift: of a "what" that is given and received. Indeed, my reception is a response to the gift, a response that, in its very character as receptive-responsive, already participates in the generosity proper to gift-giving. I bear a constitutive order *toward* generosity that always anteriorly participates in the generosity I *have received* and am *always already receiving*—from God and other creatures in God. ... [I]t is the very relation to God, which relation always already includes relation to all other creatures, that establishes each person in his *individual substantiality*. ...
>
> The logic of gift characteristic of creaturely being is best described as *filial*. My being in its substantial unity is constitutively dependent on God and on others in God. It is for this reason that Cardinal Ratzinger [Benedict XVI] has stated that the child in the womb provides the basic figure for what it means to be a human being. And indeed it is important to recall in this connection what is perhaps the central emphasis in his Christology, summed up in the claim that "Son" is the highest title of Jesus Christ [his Name which is oil poured out!]. Thus the basic logic of our being as creatures is disclosed in the child: the obedience, humility, and dependence characteristic of the child disclose creaturely being's deepest and most proper symbolic nature.[24]

Often people say that the root problem of our contemporary Western society is *individualism*, a selfish narcissism that cuts the person off from the surrounding community, and from any indebtedness to or responsibility for this community, so that he or she can pursue their way autonomously and independently. There is profound truth in this, but this disorder itself is rooted in something even more fundamental: *the loss of the awareness of gift, of the fact that my very existence has come to me as a gift from the creative generosity of God, mediated also through other human persons*. Thus, the crisis of our culture is not fundamentally a crisis of *irresponsibility* as much it is a crisis of *ingratitude*. Yet this ingratitude is simply, in a way, a natural response to the deep fracture that we experience in our culture, in which the sacred space of the family home is often so broken, and in which we are taught from an early age that our identity comes, not as a pure gift mediated through the loving gaze of another, but through our own efforts, achievements, or activity. We are told that we can find security, in other words, not through who we are—our pure *being* in love—but rather only through what we do. And this *doing* itself, we are told, must spring from within ourselves, not dependent in any way on a prior gift that we receive from another; otherwise, after all, it would not be ours.

The radical rift, therefore, between the individual and the community is a result of the rift between humanity and God, this "forgetfulness of God" that Benedict XVI has lamented. When God is not seen and experienced as the very Origin of our existence, the Love from which our whole being springs forth in an act of pure creative generosity, then all of our other relationships—with one another and with the whole creation—become fractured and wrought with misunderstanding and alienation. The individual no longer feels safe within the love of others, within the bosom of a community, but feels the need to forge his or her own way—since no one can be trusted except the self. There is a deep terror of vulnerability throughout our culture, since we no longer glimpse the face, and the tender embrace, of Love, both in and beyond all created things. The image of God in us, therefore, is struggling to find full expression, even as it unceasingly pushes forth from deep within us to make contact with its Source. What is this Source to which we seek to return as our true End, as our only place of abiding rest? Pope Benedict says:

> The Trinity is absolute unity insofar as the three divine Persons are pure relationality. The reciprocal transparency among the divine Persons is total and the bond between each of them is complete, since they constitute a unique and absolute unity. God desires to incorporate us into this reality of communion as well: "that they might be one even as we are one" (Jn 17:22). The Church is a sign and instrument of this unity. Relationships between human beings throughout history cannot but be enriched by reference to this divine model. In particular, *in the light of the revealed mystery of the Trinity*, we understand that true openness does not mean loss of individual identity but profound interpenetration.[25]

This profound interpenetration in love, in which Lover and beloved live in one another in a secure and everlasting embrace, is the reality for which our hearts long. We thirst for this loving interpenetration both on the divine level, in our relationship with God, as well as on the human level, in our relationships with other human persons. But our culture militates precisely against this, as any vulnerability before another—any "transparency," to use Benedict's word—is seen as a threat to our individuality. But the opposite is actually the truth! If I have been created in a pure constitutive relationship with God, if this constitutive relationship is the very foundation of my being, and is also inherently ordered to relationship with other persons, then to refuse these relationships is to directly contradict the truth of my being.

To get back in touch with the Love that lies at the foundation of my being, and at the ground of all created reality, therefore, is the only adequate answer to the woundedness of our culture. As the pope again says:

> We receive our life not only at the moment of birth but every day from without—from others who are not ourselves but who nonetheless somehow pertain to us. ... Human beings are relational, and they possess their lives—themselves—only by way of relationship. ... To be a truly human being means to be related in love, to be *of* and *for*.

The widespread occurrence of anxiety, depression, and suicide in our Western world is a sign, an awful symptom, of this profound loss of our sense of Love, of the "ontology of gift" that lies at the very origin, ground, and consummation of our existence. This fundamental experience of love, received first through our mother and father, and meant to grow and mature in an ever deepening receptivity and reciprocal generosity to the gift that we have first so generously received, has now degenerated for so many into a fearful grasping for security apart from others, and from God, who are perceived as a threat. But the promise of this Love still stands, even in our fractured existence, for the light of goodness can never be extinguished. Let us look back at the foundational experience that stands at the earliest moments of our life: the communion between parent and child.

> For what is at stake here? The being of another person is so closely interwoven with the being of this person, the mother, that for the present it can survive only by physically being with the mother, in a physical unity with her. Such unity, however, does not eliminate the otherness of this being or authorize us to dispute its distinct selfhood. However, to be oneself in this way is to be radically from and through another. Conversely, this

being-with compels the being of the other—that is, the mother —to become a being-for… We must now add that even once the child is born and the outer form of its being-from and -with changes, it remains just as dependent on, and at the mercy of, a being-for. … If we open our eyes, we see that…the child in the mother's womb is simply a very graphic depiction of the essence of human existence in general.[26]

Yes, this vivid relationship between mother and child reveals to our eyes the truth of the *whole* of reality. The world is a kind of womb, in which my existence and the existence of every person is sheltered; all of reality has been born from the creative love of God, and in order to manifest and extend this love into the lives and hearts of those whom he has made for himself. But now we very little experience this reality of the womb; we feel very unsheltered, unloved, and unsafe. We feel anonymous in the midst of an impersonal world, lost in a faceless crowd, and threatened with absurdity. But the "womb" of God's own Love still enfolds us, even if we have become blind to it! His tenderness still envelops us and seeks us out!

And the divine Bridegroom himself has come to us! He who is the eternally beloved Son of the Father, who receives his very being unceasingly as a gift of the Father's Love, has come in order to reveal to us anew this Love that stands at the foundation of our being as well. He has come to draw us into his own filial relationship with the Father, into the joy and gratitude of childhood. And in this space he also seeks to restore our whole being to the mature and generous self-surrender of spousal love, which blossoms forth in spontaneous fruitfulness. In this way he heals and fulfills our deep and innate longing for a filial, spousal, and fruitful love, a love of complete receptivity, of total reciprocal self-gift, and of enduring belonging, which radiates out freely to spread the goodness and beauty of this love with all. Is this not what we have seen in this third poem, powerfully and deeply present, even if veiled under the allegory of the Song?

ישוע

BEAUTY ENCOUNTERS BEAUTY

The last reflection, based in philosophical and theological thought, reconfirms what I already said earlier about the foundational importance of affirmation in human existence. Unless I truly receive the "originary experience" of another lovingly affirming my goodness, then I will find a fundamental insecurity at the very root of my being and my identity (of my relationships with myself, with other persons, with the whole of creation, and with God himself). It is precisely the experience of this affirming love—this generous gift of self from another—that gives me to myself, and opens up my heart to live in a reciprocal generosity. When I experience generous and affirming love pouring forth upon me from God, mediated through the love of another person, then I, from the fullness of love I have received, become a generous affirmer in turn.

If, however, I do not have this foundation, then I find myself spontaneously tempted to compensate for my insecurity through what can be termed "self-affirmation." Rather than tenderly receiving and resonating with others, lovingly affirming them in their unique beauty and dignity, I struggle instead with trying to elicit the love and affirmation that I have never received, and which I rightly feel that I deeply need. Self-affirmation does not mean that I affirm myself by telling myself how good I am, etc., which obviously does not work. It is rather a way of living my life that seeks to elicit the affirmation of others, or to make myself feel good and worthwhile through what I do, achieve, or possess. Nonetheless, part of the gift of affirming love is precisely that it cannot be forced or coerced, but is always given freely and gratuitously. Precisely its gratuitousness is what makes it a true sacrament of the abundant love of God that constitutes me in my identity as his beloved, and which indeed lies at the very foundation of the whole created order as its never-ceasing and ever-present wellspring.

This all leads anew to what I mentioned in the previous reflection. We live in a culture that fosters individualism and selfishness, but this is really to say that we live in a world that fosters *self-affirmation*, because it fails to create a space in which individuals are authentically affirmed. Of course, this is not universally true, as there are also significant numbers of affirmed persons; but a lack of affirmation, a lack of the experience of one's own goodness and of the goodness of reality, is most definitely an epidemic in our society. And this causes such great pain precisely because this wound lies at the very core of our existence: our innate need to be seen, known, and loved as we are.

In other words, it frustrates our inherent need to experience life as a gift, as a beautiful gift flowing from the hands of Love and drawing us into intimacy with this Love. Only in this way, in the confidence born from the experience of affirmation, can I live my existence in true childlike liberty and playfulness, and also, in this very playfulness, give it back in an uncalculating generosity to the One who has first loved me, and also to my brothers and sisters.

As a side note, let me mention here that, in the perspective of these reflections, the difference between *training* and *education* becomes clear. Training is aimed simply at changing actions, at developing habits, and therefore is something that can be effected even in animals. Authentic education, on the other hand, is something much more profound. It is the way of fostering living contact with the richness and beauty of reality in oneself or in another person. But here in education, two realities meet that must exist in a deep interrelationship: the first is a reverence for the unique person of the other, and the second is the gift of truth to this person. At different times in history, there have been extremes in both directions, which ultimately break down and lose the very thing that has been overemphasized.

For example, in our current culture, there is a tendency for parents to "over-affirm" their child's unique identity in such a way that they fail to *educate* the child. (But this couldn't really be called over-affirmation, which is actually impossible as long as the affirmation remains authentic.) Rather, it is a *failure of affirmation*, since—imagining that freedom consists merely in the avoidance of any external influence or coercion, and that identity is prior to relationship rather than flowing from relationship—they choose to keep their distance from the child for fear of being overbearing or imposing on the child's freedom or identity. They want the child to establish his or her own identity *first*, apart from the love of the parent, and then, after this identity is established, to open themselves to being loved.

Paradoxically, this tendency of "keeping one's distance" often coincides with the other extreme: falling into mere training rather than authentic education. Because the child does not feel himself or herself to be intimately and tenderly loved, they begin to interpret their identity and their freedom precisely the way their parents did: as autonomy and mere independence. But then the only way of making a child responsible for his or her existence, the only way of making them give a semblance of deep and living contact with reality, is to force or coerce their actions through discipline or training!

For completeness, let me mention another tendency, which was very prevalent in the nineteenth and the first half of the twentieth century, but which is also very much present today as well (as least in some quarters). This tendency is the direct opposite of that false affirmation which keeps a distance from the child for fear of imposing on them. It is the tendency to be overbearing on the child, not with tender love, but *with rules and regulations, expectations and guidelines*. This creates a repressive and suffocating atmosphere, in which the individual feels hemmed in by "obligations" and "burdens" and is not allowed to be himself or herself. (Notice the breakdown in true *education*, which can flourish only on the basis of *desire*, and not of *fear*.) In this case, the person stuffs down their inherent desires for happiness, enjoyment, and well-being, and lives instead an obligation-oriented life that consists almost exclusively in training themselves (by mere force of the will) to do what they "ought" or "must." They think that this is the only way of "measuring up," of being "good enough," or of living a "moral life." They do not realize that morality is ultimately nothing but the expression of God's own loving and creative hand impressed upon our existence, marking out for us the path of authentic happiness and personal flourishing in his Love.

Obviously, the truth lies in the middle—or rather, beyond both extremes in the space of a deep, intimate, and sheltering love. Love alone can reveal, communicate, and protect the child's identity. True love is not imposing upon the child the parent's wishes or expectations, but rather listening deeply to the heartbeat, the desires, and the experiences of the child, and helping them to expand in safety into a deep and enduring contact with reality as it truly is. In other words, true education first of all means creating a safe space in which the child (or the adult for that matter), can experience the goodness of his or her own existence, and thus can become curious, hopeful, and desirous of discovering reality surrounding them. It is in this context of sheltering love, in which I feel myself to be interesting, beautiful, and delightful because of the interest that another takes in me, that I can take ever deeper interest in others, and in the beauty, goodness, and truth of creation as God himself has made it. In this context, education in the narrower sense—of teaching, explaining, correcting, guiding—can unfold freely, for it will find receptive soil in the heart of the one who, affirmed in his or her unique beauty, yearns to make contact with the truth of reality itself.

In the light of these words, let me now conclude by going deeper into this experience of affirming love, and how it is experienced as "beauty encountering beauty." This will bring us right back to the intimate nature of love, to the "romantic" context of the Song of Songs. Not only do I experience my own goodness, my own inherent beauty, through the loving gaze of another, but *I also experience the beauty of the other in turn*. In my mother's eyes I not only see that I am beautiful and precious, but I also see, and am grasped by, her own personal beauty. Yes, my mother is the first person that I ever "fall in love" with, in that her beauty truly breaks down the limitations of my self and draws me out in a kind of ecstasy toward another, giving me access into the realm of Love itself. It is precisely in this dynamic relationship of "I" and "You" that I find myself getting in touch with the mystery of "We," and indeed with the divine "Thou" who alone can truly bind us together as the space of enduring Love in which we meet and are united.

Since this reality is so central, so important, we can truly say that *the experience of love lies at the very heart of the Gospel*. We have been created precisely for this—namely, intimacy with God and with one another—and also because this experience is the "good news" that heals and liberates us. "In this is love, not that we loved God but that he loved us and sent his Son. ... So we know and believe the love God has for us" (1 Jn 4:10, 16). "Father, may they be one even as we are one, I in them and you in me, that they may become perfectly one, so that the world may know that you have sent me and have loved them even as you have loved me" (cf. Jn 17:22-23). Even as the Father has loved the Son, so he also loves us! And in the Heart of this very Son he unveils for us the fullness of this Love! It is thus precisely in standing before Christ and experiencing his loving gaze—in letting him fall in love with my beauty as I simultaneously fall in love with his—that I am truly healed and transformed. He is the great Affirmer of the human heart, who shelters each one of us in the tenderness and abiding delight of his love. He is thus the true Educator, who by creating this space of security in his own Heart, freely communicates to us the living contact with Goodness, Beauty, and Truth for which our hearts inherently thirst. Yes…he is himself also the Beautiful One who ravishes and draws us all to himself, in order to immerse us in the endless joy of the Trinity.

Only when I experience this tender gaze of Christ can I let go of my need to be "adequate," to act and do and perform perfectly, and in this way to safeguard my own "identity." Instead, I can sink back into the place of my poverty and weakness, the space of my littleness and need for gratuitous love, *in which my life ceaselessly flows as a gift from the generous love of the Trinity*. And here, surprisingly, I find myself lifted up in the very surging of God's love which is true strength! By having my own beauty and goodness affirmed by God himself, I find my heart liberated from fear and shame, and my being dilates spontaneously according to the very gift of love that I have first received. Further, in this very experience of being loved I also get to know and feel the immense beauty of the One who loves me. His Beauty touches, ravishes, and draws my heart, and this very Beauty, as it draws me, also sustains me with a strength that, on my own, I could never have.

Yes, in letting myself be loved in my littleness, my authentic beauty is set free by the Beauty of the One who loves me—and the grace of God, pouring forth generously into me, carries me unceasingly in generous love back into the embrace of God, and into authentic love and relationship with all of those whom he has so lovingly created.

ישוע

THE PARADISE OF CREATION RENEWED

What does all that I have said about the importance of affirmation, and about the restoration of an "ontology of gift," mean concretely for our lives? It means many things, but, in the context of these reflections on the Song of Songs, I can affirm that it means in a special way *the fostering of communities that are founded, not primarily on a shared mission or apostolate, but on a unique yet communal pursuit of the face of the Bridegroom and of intimacy with him.* In other words, in the light of the crisis of our contemporary culture (both outside of and within the Church), there is a pressing need for spaces, for "homes," in which the true heartbeat of love is again felt. I have spoken of this in great detail elsewhere: in my words about the Church as the "Home of Communion," about the Marian dimension of the Church, and about the importance of having small communities that can "incarnate" this great mystery in such a way that persons experience themselves truly seen, known, and loved in their unrepeatable beauty, and sheltered in the safety of love's intimate and abiding embrace.

As a perhaps unexpected and surprising result of our reflections on the Song of Songs, we can see that this reality of "home" indeed stands at the heart of Biblical revelation. How is this so? Because the intimate nuptial union of the bridal heart with her heavenly Bridegroom stands at the very heart of the Church. It is the intimate space from which all else flows and to which it returns. Mary, first of all, has experienced this reality; she is the paradise of God, the garden enclosed and fountain sealed that is nonetheless, precisely in this way, also a garden open for all to come and dwell and a well of living water pouring forth God's Love for all of his children. As the *Catechism* says:

> In the Church this communion of men with God, in the "love

[that] never ends," is the purpose which governs everything in her that is a sacramental means, tied to this passing world (1 Cor 13:18). "[The Church's] structure is totally ordered to the holiness of Christ's members. And holiness is measured according to the 'great mystery' in which the Bride responds with the gift of love to the gift of the Bridegroom." Mary goes before us all in the holiness that is the Church's mystery as "the bride without spot or wrinkle" (Eph 5:27). This is why the "Marian" dimension of the Church precedes the "Petrine." (par. 773)

Indeed, in God's original intention, the entire universe is meant to be a garden, a paradise in which humanity walks in communion with the Trinity. But this garden is also a temple, a place of ceaseless worship of God. Yet if this creation is a temple, then what is worship? Worship, in its deepest truth, simply means the disposition in which God is free to pour out the fullness of his Love without reserve into the receptive human heart and life, and in which his beloved pours herself out, in loving adoration and joyful wonder, to him in return. Indeed, in Eden, Adam and Eve were created as "priests," mediating between God himself and the whole created world. Through their filial relationship with God, and also through their relationship with one another, they were to draw the whole of the world together into unity in themselves and to bind it inseparably—in their childlike obedience and their playful surrender (and liturgy should always be both reverent and playful!)—to the Trinity from whom it came and to whom it was meant to return.

Thus the whole of creation was, and is, meant to be both a paradise and a temple, a garden of intimacy and a space of true adoration and worship. But it can be so only when the human person—upon whom the whole of creation is "hinged" for its own authentic well-being—abides in true intimacy with God. When this is the case, when the person remains open in a "Marian" trust and confidence before the Love of the Trinity, then the whole created order itself reveals its authentic meaning as a "sacrament" of his presence. As Alexander Schmemann writes:

> We *need* water and oil, bread and wine in order to be in communion with God and to know Him. Yet conversely—and such is the teaching, if not of our modern theological manuals, at least of the liturgy itself—it is this communion with God by means of "matter" that reveals the true meaning of "matter," i.e., of the world itself. We can only worship in time, yet it is worship that ultimately not only reveals the meaning of time, but truly "renews" time itself. There is no worship without the participa-

tion of the body, without words and silence, light and darkness, movement and stillness—yet it is in and through worship that all these essential expressions of man in his relation to the world are given their ultimate "term" of reference, revealed in their highest and deepest meaning.

Thus the term "sacramental" means that for the world to be means of worship and means of grace is not accidental, but the revelation of its meaning, the restoration of its essence, the fulfillment of its destiny. It is the "natural sacramentality" of the world that finds expression in worship and makes the latter the essential ἔργον [work] of man, the foundation and the spring of his life and activities as man. Being the epiphany [manifestation] of God, worship is thus the epiphany of the world; being communion with God, it is the only true communion with the world; being knowledge of God, it is the ultimate fulfillment of all human knowledge.[27]

In other words, the whole world becomes a garden precisely when the bride allows her own heart to become a garden. This is true, first of all, in the spirit and the flesh of the Virgin Mary, in whom the whole of creation is in a way contained and is espoused again to God in intimate love. This is true, universally, in the Catholic Church, the Bride of Christ, who is the garden of God's paradise, his living Body in this world. It is in her that the world is truly lifted up from its state of estrangement in sin, purified and healed, and set free to be what God has always intended it to be. This is true, also, in the unique life of each one of us, seen, known, and loved by God, and called into an intimate nuptial union with him in the bosom of his Church.

When this happens, then this threefold bride—Mary, the Church, and the individual human heart—becomes the garden in which God works his greatest marvels of healing and reconciliation, marriage and consummation. He unites her lovingly to himself in a bond of unspeakable intimacy in the enclosed garden of her being, in the rich fabric of her personal existence in intimate contact with himself. But this most intimate touch also pours forth in spontaneous and expansive fruitfulness. The sacredness of God's touch in her inmost being pours forth, not only throughout her entire body (a virginal garden precious in his eyes), but also spreads to touch and transform the whole creation into a garden of the Trinity's glorious presence. It is precisely in this way, through the loving eyes and heart of the bride, that the "ontology of gift" and the metaphysics of love can again reveal itself in full splendor. It is in her and through her that creation can again be opened to its authentic meaning throughout the passage of time, and can also be carried toward its full consummation at the end of time in the eternal marriage of the Lamb.

FOURTH POEM

THE STORM OF SUMMER

THE HEALING OF MEMORIES

The third poem, through which we have just journeyed in great detail, is the high point of the Song—with the exception of the last verses of poem five and the words of the epilogue. It is the celebration of the marriage of the Bridegroom and his beloved, his entry into the garden of his paradise in which he promises to renew, not only her, but the whole of creation. We have seen him exclaim with joy how he comes to "gather my myrrh with my spice," to "eat my honeycomb with my honey," to "drink my wine with my milk." Then the poem ends with the exuberant call of the Bridegroom: "Eat, O friends, and drink: drink deeply, O friends!" (Sg 5:1). The bride, unspeakably beautiful and precious in his eyes, and reflecting his own beauty like a still and placid lake, also pours forth this beauty throughout all of creation. In other words, by the beauty that the Bridegroom has bestowed upon her, she attracts others to him who is all-beautiful, and whose beauty is so radiantly manifested in and through her. Is this not what God has said in the book of Ezekiel? "And your renown went forth among the nations because of your beauty, for it was perfect through the splendor which I had bestowed upon you, says the Lord GOD" (Ez 15:14).

After this crescendo of love and delight, we are perhaps surprised by the way in which the fourth poem begins. Poems one and two both ended with the Bridegroom's gentle refrain: "Stir not up nor awaken my love until she please" (Sg 2:7; 3:5). But the third poem ended with a loud cry of joy in the profound union of Lover and beloved. Therefore, it can be startling to find the bride, as the fourth poem commences, saying:

I sleep, but my heart is awake.
Hark! my Beloved is knocking.
"Open to me, my sister,
my love, my dove, my perfect one;
for my head is wet with dew,
my locks with the drops of the night."
I had put off my garment,
how could I put it on?
I had bathed my feet,
how could I soil them?
My Beloved put his hand to the latch,
and my heart was thrilled within me.
I arose to open to my Beloved,
and my hands dripped with myrrh,

> *my fingers with liquid myrrh,*
> *upon the handles of the bolt.*
> *I opened to my Beloved,*
> *but my Beloved had turned and gone.*
> *My soul failed me when he spoke.*
> *I sought him, but found him not;*
> *I called him, but he gave no answer.*
> *The watchmen found me,*
> *as they went about in the city;*
> *they beat me, they wounded me,*
> *they took away my mantle,*
> *those watchmen of the walls.*
> (Sg 5:2-7)

What is this? Hasn't she already slept and awakened, arising to seek him out and to find him during the night? This was the theme of poem two. And now it is being repeated again, almost exactly the same! Has she therefore fallen asleep again? And indeed, is she still so slow to answer his call, even after the experiences of poem three, such that he leaves her and she must go out anew to seek him? Of course, in one sense, is it not true that a bridal soul, as long as this mortal life lasts, will be continually seeking the face of her Bridegroom whom she can never definitively grasp—not until she is definitively grasped by him in the endless consummation of eternity? However many times she awakens, seeks him, and finds him, she will always awaken more deeply yet and find him more intimately still…until the final discovery, until the face to face encounter, for which her heart longs and in which alone she will be fully at rest. I have also mentioned, however, that this very dynamic of seeking-and-finding unfolds within the peace of *already-having-been-found*, such that even in the most anguishing experience of the absence of the Bridegroom, he is already always present, gently sheltering and upholding her in her very search for him.

There are two ways of understanding this passage, depending on the way in which the tenses of the words in the verses are interpreted. For indeed, there is an unexpected shift in the bride's words which indicate that perhaps she is not talking about the present, but rather recounting something that is already past. She begins in the present tense: "I sleep, but my heart is awake." But after recounting the call of the Bridegroom, the bride's words are all in the past tense: "I had put off… I had bathed… My heart was thrilled… I arose…" Yes, she once slept, but now, from her present awakeness, she looks back on her previous sleep and recounts the way in which her Bridegroom has lovingly awakened her.

Therefore, perhaps in this fourth poem she is indeed in a deep union with her Beloved, and from this place she is looking back on the journey that she has walked to this state. She does this in order to recognize, on the one hand, her own frailty and even the infidelity of the past, but in doing so only to thank her Beloved for the way he has loved her even here. Indeed, her own frailty has been victoriously overcome by the enduring fidelity of the Bridegroom, and her very slowness taken up in the gentle patience of God. Indeed, he has infused into her very hardened heart the burning fires of love which enkindle in her an ardent thirst, drawing her out in love to the One whom her heart loves, dilating and liquefying her heart in the process.

In this case, this fourth poem would be a revisiting of the experience expressed more summarily in poem two—a deeper revisiting of this experience from a place of greater light and thus of deeper perspective. In my opinion, this is a very good approach (even if it is not the literal meaning of the Song), as it explains the radical likeness between these two poems, and it also illustrates how important is the *healing of memories*. In other words, a part of the bride's experience of the Bridegroom's love, and of union with him, is letting his light radiate back into those places of darkness in her past, in order to illumine, heal, and transform them. In this way, what before was ugly and black can become beautiful, because transfigured in the light of mercy and made to shine with the radiant love of God who works all things for good.

The other way of reading this passage is to see it as explaining the present. The bride's slow rising is a matter of the fourth poem itself, a recurrence of her slothfulness and fear in responding to the ardent call of the Bridegroom. Even if now her heart is vigilant—awake even as she sleeps!—nonetheless she is not yet fully and definitively awake. And therefore the Bridegroom must call her out anew; he must draw her, and, appearing to hide his face, dilate her heart to love him and receive him more deeply still. As Saint Gregory the Great so beautifully writes: "The Bridegroom hides when he is sought, so that, not finding him, the Bride may seek him with a renewed ardor; and the Bride is hampered in her search so that this delay may increase the capacity for God, and that she may find one day more fully what she was seeking." Saint Augustine says in the same vein: "God, by making us wait, stretches desire. Stretching desire, he stretches the soul. Stretching the soul, he makes is capable of receiving. ... Such is our life: we must endeavor to desire."

Whether the bride is recounting her past struggles from the light of a definitive union, or is experiencing anew her frailty and infidelity and searching anew for the Bridegroom, it ultimately makes no significant difference. In both cases, the bride's frailty is still conquered by the unconquerable love of God. Yes, in either case, we can make contact with God's love as it touches and attracts the frail and broken human heart, and can understand the path on the which the heart walks —cradled mysteriously by Love—into the experience of Love's enduring and life-giving embrace. Let us therefore look deeply at the dispositions of the bride, even in her selfishness and sin, in order to see how she is granted to let herself be drawn gradually out from herself and into ever deeper union with her Beloved. Yes, it is love alone, however frail it may be in her at first, which pulls her out of her preoccupation with herself, and into the radical surrender that allows intimacy between her and her Bridegroom to flower. Yet we will also see that, as she goes out of herself to her Beloved, she discovers that she is indeed simply descending into the inmost depths of her own heart, this holy sanctuary in which he already dwells, this garden which is his enduring delight.

ישוע

WEAKNESS TRANSFORMED INTO STRENGTH

I sleep, but my heart is awake.
Hark! my Beloved is knocking.
"Open to me, my sister,
my love, my dove, my perfect one;
for my head is wet with dew,
my locks with the drops of the night."
(Sg 5:2)

Who is this Bridegroom who always seems to come in the middle of the night? Just when the bride has retired to her bed, he draws close and asks her to arise. Again, like in the second poem, he is standing outside, gently knocking on the door of her heart and asking for entrance. Yes, he is the same One who would later say in the book of Revelation: "Behold, I stand at the door and knock; if any one hears my voice and opens the door, I will come in to him and eat with him, and he with me" (Rev 3:20). The divine Bridegroom desires to renew the nuptial banquet with his precious bride, and he draws near in order to seek her willingness, her loving and trust-filled consent.

And he comes in the night, knocking and asking for admittance, like a poor beggar who cannot force his way in, and would not wish to do so. His only power is the power of gentle persuasion, the touch of tender love. And so he seeks to awaken the bride's sensitivity by telling her of his pitiful state: "for my head is wet with dew, and my locks with the drops of night." But in this very complaint we can read the sacred anointing that covers the head of the Bridegroom. For is not dew used throughout Scripture to indicate the presence of God, the descent of his Holy Spirit upon creation? Even in the liturgy this is present, when the priest prays that God the Father may "send your Holy Spirit like the dewfall" upon the gifts that, through the very action of this Spirit, are to be transformed into the Body and Blood of Christ. Therefore, at every Holy Communion, the Bridegroom comes to us with his head wet with dew! He comes to us to renew the marriage-covenant, bathed as he is with the full presence of the Spirit whom he also pours out upon us:

> I will be as the dew to Israel; he shall blossom as the lily, he shall strike root as the poplar; his shoots shall spread out; his beauty shall be like the olive, and his fragrance like Lebanon. They shall return and dwell beneath my shadow, they shall flourish as a garden; they shall blossom as the vine, their fragrance shall be like the wine of Lebanon. (Hos 14:5-7)

And does not this this intimate touch of the anointed Bridegroom also spread out to make all of us one within his love? As the beautiful verses of the Psalm express: "Behold, how good and pleasant it is when brothers dwell in unity! It is like the precious oil upon the head, running down upon the beard, upon the beard of Aaron, running down on the collar of his robes! It is like the dew of Hermon, which falls on the mountains of Zion!" (Ps 133:1-3a). This is the hair and beard of the true Aaron, the true Priest, Jesus Christ, who has made us one with himself as his mystical Body. And so these wet locks, bedewed with the Spirit, also directly effect us. If Jesus is locked outside in the dew and the rain, in the chill of the night, knocking on the door, and we do not let him in, we find that we are actually the one who is standing outside! This is because his very asking for admittance is his invitation for us to take refuge in the shelter of his own Sacred Heart!

This beautifully explains the following verses of this poem. The Bridegroom seeks to enter, but in truth he wants the bride to enter into herself to discover him there. Thus his call for her to arise, and her mad search through the city, really occurs nowhere else than in her own interior being, where the Bridegroom is present, though hidden. Nonetheless, we see that she is loath to rise, caught up on the periphery of her being and unwilling to exert the effort to make contact with him in the place to which he invites her:

I had put off my garment,

> *how could I put it on?*
> *I had bathed my feet,*
> *how could I soil them?*
>
> (Sg 5:3)

Why are you preoccupied with such things, lovely bride? Have you forgotten how beautiful and lovable your Bridegroom is? Have you forgotten your own beauty, which ravishes and attracts his Heart? Ah, in the very excuses of the bride we discover the true nature of sin. Yes, she has turned away from the Bridegroom and is refusing his loving invitation. He invites her to step out, in vulnerability and trust, before his loving gaze, but she prefers to remain where she is, in the false security provided by her own efforts. This is the core of every sin—this deliberate refusal of Love, of the invitation to step out into intimate communion with the Love who is already near, enveloping and sheltering me. Rather, I grasp for my own security; I create my own "safe space" out of the materials that surround me; I become preoccupied with my own self, divorced from the authentic truth of this self as God's precious beloved.

Can we not hear an echo, in the words of the bride, of the excuse of Adam, "I was afraid, because I was naked; and I hid myself" (Gn 3:10)? Yes, the bride complains that she had put off her garment—how could she rise to meet him in this vulnerable state? She says, "how could I put it on again?" Is she really just too lazy to throw a robe around her shoulders? Or is something else being referred to here? Perhaps she has already begun to experience this vulnerability and spiritual nakedness before—for example, in the seeking and finding of the second poem, in which she was called like a fearful dove out of the clefts of the rock. And she knows that she cannot enter into hiding again; after her life-changing encounter with God, she cannot clothe herself anew with the "fig leaves" that now she knows do not offer any authentic protection.

But, as the Bridegroom calls her deeper into his healing love, deeper into intimacy, to have cast off the fig leaves of formal sin alone is not enough. Rather, he wants her to step out even more radically into complete dependence upon him, with nothing to cover over or protect her except his own Love. "How could I rise and come to you in this state, pitiable and naked as I am?" the bride complains. And we can hear the Bridegroom's answer echoing from the book of Revelation again. He acknowledges her nakedness, her need, and, sheltering this in his own Love, he says to her: "Therefore I counsel you to buy from me gold refined by fire, that you may be rich, and white garments to clothe you and to keep the shame of your nakedness from being seen, and salve to anoint your eyes, that you may see" (Rev 3:18). The garment that will truly protect her is the Bridegroom's own Love. He will shield and clothe her; he will anoint her that she may see; he will make her rich with the abundance of his own love and goodness.

Here, in these three gifts that the Bridegroom offers to his bride, we can discern the three inner dispositions of love: poverty, obedience, and chastity. The garment covering her nakedness is chastity; the salve that anoints her that she may see is obedience; the gold given to her is poverty. How paradoxical is this! It is precisely her poverty which is wealth, her virginity which is intimacy, her trusting obedience which is true sight! Yes, he is teaching her that her authentic security lies only in his Love, in the shelter of his perfect and enduring embrace. In this way, he is leading her to get in touch with one of the central dynamics of the spiritual life: her deepest poverty, weakness, and need is transformed into the place of deepest encounter and intimacy with him! Yes, it is precisely when she consents to be no more than his "little one," to stop comparing herself with others or seeking for sources of meaning that lie within her own control, that she finds the enduring meaning of his tender love pouring freely into her. As Saint Paul says, "I will all the more gladly boast of my weaknesses, that the power of Christ may rest upon me" (2 Cor 12:9).

This paradox of weakness transformed into strength lies at the core of authentic humility, as well as of authentic strength and fortitude. Humility does not consist in looking into oneself and counting all the things that are wrong and broken within oneself. Of course, it is important to be aware of these things, to have one's eyes open to the reality of one's condition, one's brokenness—if only to cast oneself unceasingly in the arms of mercy and to rely entirely on the One in whom alone is hope for constancy and fidelity. But humility in its deepest truth is born when I descend down into the inmost depths of my heart and discover, not merely my brokenness, but also *how unspeakably beautiful I am in the eyes of God*. This experience of my own beauty, revealed in the loving eyes of the Bridegroom, frees me from the need to compensate for my insecurity through pride. Rather, I can simply be myself as he sees me, knowing that all that I have is his gift, and that the unfolding of my life in beauty depends, not on my own perfect performance or on the ability to somehow be more than I am, but on his own activity within me, to which I need only pronounce the trusting "yes" of my heart in moment by moment cooperation with grace.

ישוע

A HOMELESS CULTURE

In the last reflection, I mentioned that the nature of sin is to be a refusal of the love of God, a turning away from his invitation and toward a false and self-fashioned security. There are many ways in which we may seek this security, many ways in which we may seek to fashion our own life, our own meaning, apart from the true meaning that comes only as God's free and generous gift. Sadly, the conception of freedom as something created spontaneously and merely from within myself is one of the foundational presuppositions of our liberal culture. And it is deeply destructive. Perhaps it is not too much to say that the primary aspiration of our contemporary world is a kind of "idol"—founded as it is so deeply in the perspective of the Enlightenment and indebted to the thinking of the atheistic existentialists. In other words, it is the same desire that tugged on Adam and Eve through the seduction of the tempter: the fruit of the tree of knowledge of good and evil. This is the "fruit of independence," the fruit of false "adulthood" divorced from its ceaselessly foundation in the trusting receptivity of childhood. Rather than letting our lives be born in gratitude and wonder, pouring forth as God's pure and loving gift, we seek instead to grasp, possess, and control, because our culture tells us that in this way alone can we truly be safe, and truly create our own identity.

But, after all, is not independence a virtue, a good quality to have? Is it not something that defines human beings as rational and self-determining creatures who are not merely subject to uncontrollable and irrational forces from without, but can take personal responsibility for their own lives? Of course, this is true. A large part of our nobility consists precisely in this, in the ability to rise above external circumstances, which may blind us either through pain or through seductive pleasure and ease, and to choose something transcendent, something lasting, something that gives a meaning deeper than the peripheral moment. Let me pause right here, and note that a part of that sentence is the key, the part which our world has forgotten: to choose something *transcendent*.

In other words, my freedom is not oriented toward itself. I am not free just so that I can be free, such that the apex of my freedom would be simply having the ability to say: "I am free to be free! I am free to choose what I want without anybody else forcing me otherwise!" Rather, my freedom is inherently oriented toward the good—

indeed, toward the true, good, and beautiful, which are but the irradiation of Being-as-Love enveloping me and unveiling itself before me. It is only in a deep and lasting contact with this great mystery, with the reality of Being, that I am authentically liberated into freedom.

Nothing else can make up for this lack of contact with the *real*—no efforts at self-affirmation or self-care, no discipline or activity in the world or in my own nature (like rising to the top of the business or political ladder, etc.), nor even my philosophizing and trying to "create" reality as the product of my own thought (*qua* Nietzsche, Sartre, and Camus). Rather, my contact with reality is something that is always already *given* in my very existence and as the foundation of my existence. Whatever truth there is in the words of the existentialist philosophers about creating the meaning of our own lives finds its authentic place only within the *already given meaning* which I can only gratefully receive and to which I am invited to conform myself.

In other words, in order to be truly free, to experience a meaningful and rich life, I am to rely before all and in all on *receiving*. My whole existence bears the fundamental character of *gratitude*, of *indebtedness*, of *humility and childlikeness*. My own authentic maturity and adult activity, to be truly fruitful (as opposed to merely "productive"), must spring from and remain enfolded within a prior and abiding *receptivity*, a contemplative dependence on and a filial trust in the truth, goodness, and beauty which are greater than myself, and in which I find myself ceaselessly enfolded.

But is this not what our culture finds so difficult to do? With the fundamental presuppositions of our contemporary Western culture, we are able to see why this is the case. With the breakdown of the family, the fundamental unit of society in which the individual himself is sheltered and allowed to grow in security, and thus in authentic freedom; with the divorce between individual choice and the innate inclinations implanted in us by God for the truth, goodness, and beauty that exist outside of us; with the terror of vulnerability that so many experience in the face of a world that is felt, not as a home, but as a threatening place that offers only danger of being wounded or even destroyed, or into which one must infuse meaning from within their own "will-to-power;" with the emphasis on the individual over relationship, as if relationship were something totally accidental to being a human person, something entered into at will by someone who is already fully constituted as an isolated and "atomic" individual; with all of this, we see the root causes of the profound *existential homelessness* that plagues our world.

But do we not see these roots going even further back in history?

Of course, these roots go the whole way back to the roots of the tree of knowledge of good and evil. Bearing the inheritance of sin within ourselves, there is the tragic possibility of rejecting the awesome gift of the love of God, and the beauty of existence that flows forth within his love, grasping instead for our own way. But nowadays so many just make excuses. It is as if, in making an isolated freedom of choice our idol, we also claim that any of our choices that may bear guilt are "not our fault," but are rather due to our cultural conditioning, etc. Therefore, we are free insofar as we want to be free; but we refuse to acknowledge the deep unfreedom of sin, of which Jesus said: "He who commits sin is a slave of sin" (Jn 8:34).

Saint John Paul II noted this deep problem of contemporary society when he spoke of the *loss of the sense of sin* which makes it very difficult for contemporary men and women to experience the Gospel as it truly is: as the Good News of God's mercy for sinners! (cf. Catechism, 1846). Our culture teaches people—each of whom is God's precious bride!—to delay to answer the Bridegroom's call, or to refuse it entirely. Even though our hearts have been made for him, and can truly rest only in his embrace, our culture seeks to condition us to say: "No...don't call me to rise out of my bed of comfort and security. What you ask is too much!" The bride, then, is not in touch, not with her own deep longing for love and intimacy, nor with her own innate beauty as beloved, nor with the beauty and attractiveness of the One who invites her and how much her refusal hurts both him and herself. And all of this is due to the fact that she no longer understands his word, his law, his invitation, and the very reality of her existence in this world, as his pure gift poured out upon her in order to draw her into the happiness of his own life!

Only in the light of God himself can we understand fully the longings of the human heart, and the nature of a truly happy society, and the destiny for which we have been made. And when we turn our gaze to God, we realize immediately that he is not an isolated individual who finds his freedom in doing whatever he pleases. Rather, he is a Communion, a Family intimately united in love: *he is the Father, Son, and Holy Spirit in an endless interchange of mutual acceptance, self-giving, and shared delight!* This is the Being from which our own being flows at every moment; this is the Being, the Love, from which the whole of creation pours forth, bursting forth from the floodgates of the divine generosity! This is our true Origin and our only ultimate Home! Each one of us, and the whole of our creation itself, has been born from the loving heart of the eternal Father, in the Son and through the Holy Spirit. And this birth is modeled on the very eternal begetting of the divine Son himself in the bosom of the Trinity's life. This is what it means to be created in the image and likeness of God: to be created from the innermost life of the Trinity (a life of love and intimacy) and in order to share in this very life, now and for all eternity.

יְשׁוּעִי

HOLY UNSELFCONSCIOUSNESS

I would like to make an important caveat to what I mentioned in the last reflection on the "loss of the sense of sin" pointed out by John Paul II. This attitude that pervades our culture actually has two radically different effects in the human heart. The most obvious one is that a person simply dismisses the possibility of sin, viewing all guilt feelings as something pathological (for how could there be guilt if there is no standard, no "blueprint" of authentic happiness, i.e. sharing in the life and love of the Trinity)? On the other hand, however, this loss of the sense of sin has been replaced by something truly pathological: a deep and irrational feeling of *inadequacy*. This is because, in place of authentic holiness—which is really a matter of living in childlike dependence on God's love and sustaining grace, and letting the very life of God gradually permeate all of our existence and acts—our culture has placed the idol of *self-perfection*. Instead of yearning for the loving relationship for which our hearts were made, we are told instead to strive to be "the best version of yourself," to achieve, create, and fashion a perfect existence for ourselves.

And, of course, even if it is said that there is no standard but our own interior freedom ("don't let anyone tell you who you should be") the human heart inherently needs the gaze of another to mediate one's identity from God, and to reveal the goal to be pursued. Therefore, what takes the place of the gaping void of longing for intimacy —or rather what falsely tries to fill it—is the dream of a worldly success, happiness, or achievement. What this usually looks like is a very unrealistic striving for money, earthly security, and a well-being in which no one interferes on us living life as we want to, but also on having people in our lives insofar as we want them and in the way that we want them. Firstly, this is impossible, and, secondly, even if it were possible, it would not make us happy.

What does all of this mean for those who still believe in guilt and sin within a culture that denies them? What kind of effect do the presuppositions of our culture have on those who are striving to live a Christian life? Often, these persons tend to fall into viewing sin, not as a *deliberate* offense against God and a willful harming of our being or another's as his gift (which is what sin really is). Instead, we view sin simply as any "shortcoming," as if we incurred guilt simply by being imperfect and needy, broken or wounded. Thus, a true awareness of sin *as a refusal of Love, a betrayal of Love,* and a reverent awe before God and the goodness of his creation which aches at the effects of sin which threaten to obscure it, is replaced by *the irrational striving that pervades our culture to be "perfect," to somehow do everything right, to avoid all weakness, neediness, or dependence.* And this striving is not a striving of love, of ecstasy beyond the enclosed and fearful state of the broken bride and towards the Bridegroom, but rather a self-focused and self-protective attitude that seeks to fashion security (however subtly) apart from God. And in this attitude, when we experience our failure to live up to our own "ideals," we end up feeling guilty, not for having hurt the one whom we love, for having wounded our being given as his gift, but rather for being less than we idealize ourselves to be, or even, indeed, *for simply being at all.*

This is because we all inherently feel deeply inadequate (because we *are* inadequate, and deeply need God and one another!), and thus experience the pain of never being able to live up to the world's idea of "perfect," or the idea that we ourselves have fashoined. In other words, we are no longer able to experience that the admission of our very "inadequacy" is the condition for being adequate—that, in our very need and dependency, indeed, in our very woundedness, we are invited to open ourselves up unreservedly to the gratuitous gift of Love. This feeling of "never-measuring-up" is transposed, not only from our relationship with ourselves or the world, but directly into our relationship with God. He is no longer experienced as an intimately loving Father who invites us to turn away from sin, to reconcile us to himself in Christ, and who wants to cradle us in his embrace and draw us into an ever deeper communion with himself through the healing and transformation of our being. Rather, he is experienced as a distant and inaccessible standard that we must attain through our own efforts before we can feel safe and secure. Here the joy of repentance and forgiveness is replaced by the feverish pursuit of self-fabricated perfection, and the peace of filial dependence upon God's sustaining generosity by the agitation and restlessness of prideful self-reliance.

Our relationship with ourselves and with all things, therefore, becomes one, not of gratitude for our existence, in which a healthy guilt plays an important but secondary role in recognizing what we have done and chosen again true love and communion—a guilt, also, which is more and more irradiated and even obliterated in the mercy pouring forth from the Heart of Christ, and is transfigured into the grateful joy of redemption. Rather, we become ashamed of simply being the inadequate and broken selves that we are in the first place, and are perpetually at war with ourselves in a sense very different than that desired by Christ. We can therefore be tempted to beat ourselves up for, and to continually confess, things which are not sinful at all, or to confess in a way which is not truly a surrender to *another*, but a safeguarding of self. We lose sight of the distinction between willful guilt and simple human brokenness and limitation, or between the forgiveness and reconciliation that comes from the outside and the merely psychology security of feeling in control or relieved of a burden. And in the midst of all of this, we become terrified of weakness, of neediness, of dependency. These traits are seen as mere lacks, as voids that make us less than we ought to be, when in fact they are allowed and even willed by God as *places of profound grace*. Indeed, the very reality of holiness, in its authentic truth, consists most especially, not in some kind of autonomous ability to overcome our limitation and weakness, but in a radical receptivity and dependence, within our very weakness, which root us unceasingly in the sustaining grace of Christ, and from which alone all of our thoughts, choices, and actions can spring in integrity and truth.

Indeed, both sin and scrupulosity (two apparently very different extremes) are ways of fleeing from the experience of one's human weakness and limitation. The only authentic answer, however, to such an experience is to open it and surrender it to God. Here, in the touch of his mercy upon the heart, is found true freedom, the humility of being ardently and unconditionally loved, and called forth, by the very sustaining presence of love, to grow into love oneself, in all of one's being. Only by his gift, which elicits my humble and persevering cooperation in each day, can true love springs up spontaneously in my heart for the One who has first loved me. This is how authentic holiness is unleashed in me, not through the rigidity of my own isolated efforts, through the heavy burden of responsibility, but through the joy and playfulness of childlike gratitude and wonder-filled responsiveness, which holds responsibility within itself and truly makes it possible in the deepest sense. As G.K. Chesterton said: "The angels can fly because they take themselves lightly." The same can be true of me. This lightness of heart can be mine, this "holy unselfconsciousness," as I gradually fall ever more deeply in love with the unspeakable beauty of Christ, such that my preoccupation with myself and my own "perfection" gives way to a wonder and awe that grips me and draws me into a profound and ceaseless occupation with my one Beloved, and with all of those whom I love in him.

Yes, dependence and receptivity therefore are not things to be avoided in the name of "maturity" or "independence." Rather, they lie at the very foundation of the Christian life, and of authentic maturity, activity, and ability, as their true wellspring and authentic form. They are in themselves virtues, indeed, the central virtues of the Christian life. This is because they are *filial* virtues—the virtues of a son or daughter, of a bride, who relies confidently upon another for everything, and whose very strength and constancy are but the result of their unceasing contact with the Love that upholds and shelters them at every moment. Thus, holiness is not a matter of casting off our weakness or neediness—our creaturely condition as oriented-toward and needing the gift of Another for our fulfillment. Rather, it is precisely at the heart of this weakness of need that we encounter the space in which we can be conformed to the sonship of Jesus Christ, in his existence both as a man and as the Son of God. In other words, our creaturely dependence is but the flip-side of our vocation to share in the filial intimacy of the Son with his Father, in the intimate embrace of complete mutual belonging at the heart of the Trinity!

ישוע

TO SAY "FOREVER":
THE MEANING OF VOCATION

Whenever I get in touch with the foundation of my existence through experiencing the love of another, I realize that I am a gift flowing from the generosity of God. I realize, not only intellectually but with the spontaneous awareness of my heart, that the innermost nature of my being and my life is *filial*. In other words, it is an existence of belovedness—of being seen, known, loved, desired, and ceaselessly cherished by the One who is himself perfect Love.

And what is the result of such an awareness of being loved? First of all, of course, it is simply joy and peace, the abiding security of knowing my self to be sheltered by absolute Love. Further, in this very space in which I experience my being as a gift of God's generosity, the desire matures in me to give my life totally back to him in response. Touched by his love and cradled in his embrace, my heart falls deeply in love with him and I yearn, I thirst, I ardently desire to give myself to him without reserve. This yearning is manifest, specifically, in the desire to say "forever" to the love and the union that is flowering between myself and God. It is the desire to set the seal of my wholehearted "yes" on the gift of intimacy which lies at the very origin of my life, which is its abiding foundation, and which is also my ultimate and eternal destiny.

Here is where the reality of vocation finds it place. Love bears in itself the seal of eternity, the seal of endless and everlasting union, the seal of constant fidelity and devotion. This longing for eternity is inscribed into our very nature and is manifest wherever authentic love begins to flower between human hearts or between a human heart and God. Is not this the meaning of marriage? It is a way of giving radical expression to the innate desire of love to say "forever" to the beloved. God, in creating the world, instituted marriage as the *primordial sacrament* in which this lasting "yes" would be pronounced between two persons, binding them indissolubly together throughout life. In this way, such a union manifests, and in a mysterious way even incarnates, the love and intimacy of the Trinity in the very concreteness of human life—in the communion of man and woman and in the family that is created by their becoming one flesh and one soul. In their mutual self-giving and their loving, lifelong devotion, the very relationship of the Father and the Son is reflected. Indeed, this Trinitarian relationship is at work within the hearts of both persons and draws them together as one, so that, growing together in this love, their hearts may be knitted together on the basis of the very love of God that comes to them and draws them into the embrace of the perfect Family of the Father, Son, and Holy Spirit. We can say, therefore, that marriage is a way, designed by God himself, of *incarnating eternity within time*, truly if imperfectly. It is a marvelous design of God in which man and woman—created for a deep union of mutual love and understanding with one another—join their lives together in the most intimate form of community, which is also the foundation of all community within creation, the bed-rock of society.

In marriage, the "forever" of love between man and woman is rooted in the bosom of the Trinity, inherently ordered to participation in the divine life. Indeed, the lofty vocation of marriage, in its full beauty, is impossible without this explicit orientation toward and sharing in the intimate love and enduring fidelity of the Persons of the Trinity. In other words, the relationship between two human persons —the bond between "I" and "You"—gives what Martin Buber calls an "intimation of eternity." And this occurs with such depth, such radiance, precisely through the "forever" that I and You pronounce to one another in the presence of God who unites them together. As Buber writes: "Only the being whose otherness, accepted by my being, lives and faces me *in the whole compression of existence*, brings the radiance of eternity to me. Only when two say to one another with all that they are, 'it is Thou', is the indwelling of the Present Being [God] between them" (italics added). Do we not experience this in all forms of deep love, and particularly in mature friendship (of which marriage, indeed, is but a particular form)? We are granted a glimpse of the uniquely profound and unspeakably beautiful "You" of another person, and we are drawn to pronounce a pure and loving affirmation of their dignity, to set the seal of our "yes" to the goodness of their existence.

Indeed, both on the natural level, in the relation between two human persons, and in relation to God, this process of falling in love is essentially the same. There is, on the one hand, my deep experience of my own beauty, revealed to me in the tender gaze of the other. On the other hand, there is the breathtaking unveiling before my eyes of the beloved's beauty, which ravishes my heart and evokes within me a word of profound reverence and affirmation before their unique identity and mystery. The spontaneous desire awakened by this encounter, as it matures, is to say "forever" to this twofold beholding, indeed, to join these two beauties together in a single beauty of enduring love. And this "yes" always already bears the mark of eternity, or rather of the longing for eternity, which the presence of the Eternal One, God, alone can safeguard. In love, therefore, my heart says to the loved one, in the words of Gabriel Marcel: "Because I love you, because I affirm you as being, there is something in you which can bridge the abyss that I vaguely call 'Death.'" And yet the mystery of the Trinity—Eternity gripping time and present mysteriously at the heart of human love—alone can fulfill the promise which love so spontaneously desires to make, the promise of *forever*.

In addition to the path of marriage, however, since the coming of Christ another way of making this "forever" present within human life has become possible. Another way has also been opened up for the human heart, another vocation: the way of *consecrated virginity or celibacy*. If marriage is the natural, primordial sacrament of God's love incarnate in human flesh and life—manifesting eternity within the limits of time—then virginity is *the anticipation of eternity already within time, the lifting-up of time to be immersed in the timelessness of eternal love*. This is because the consecrated vocation, rather than being a rejection or repression of the human desire for intimate communion—or even a rejection of the full richness of human sexuality—is instead a super-affirmation of precisely this reality, on the basis of Eternity itself. As John Paul II says, it is a renunciation which is but a deeper affirmation. And how is this? Because it is a yet more radical expression of the desire of love to say "forever," for now the "You" to whom I pronounce this word is not a human other, but *the Thou of God himself.*

Therefore, virginity is the most radical way of saying "forever" to the reality of Eternal Love, not in the light of "time-looking-forward-to-eternity," but in the reality of "eternity-already-transfiguring-time." It is a vocation in which this "yes" to forever is placed directly in the hands of Christ, who is taken as one's unique and only Spouse. And yet in this very place, intimate human communion is not left behind and forgotten. Rather, this particular spousal union with Christ simply dilates the heart to see, receive, and be united to others in a new way. This is a way of loving intimacy and virginal communion that anticipates the virginal form of love as it will exist in the new creation, when the whole of created being will be re-made and consummated within the perfect love of the Trinity. Here marriage will have passed away as an institution, while all the depth of love and relationship fashioned between human hearts in this life will be consummated forever in the fullness of the everlasting marriage between Christ and his Church, in which each one of us finds ourselves intimately espoused to God in eternal and unbreakable love.

ישוע

MY HEART WAS THRILLED WITHIN ME

In the light of the words on vocation in the previous reflection, we can look back at the text of the Song and see a new avenue of interpretation opening before our eyes. As I said before, there are two very similar scenes in which the bride is tenderly called out by her Bridegroom into intimacy with himself, two scenes in which she at first delays to answer his call, only then to arise in ardent longing to seek for him until he is found. Perhaps these two scenes are representing two fundamental experiences of the human heart: identity and vocation.

The first scene, which we saw at the climax of the second poem, is the bride's *fundamental experience of God's love*, drawing her out of the exile in which she does not know who she is, lost among lies, wounds, and fears. Here *she steps into the light of his loving gaze and discovers her authentic identity as his beloved.* She descends into the authentic truth of her being as it flows unceasingly from his creative hand and is cradled always in the arms of his perfect love. This indeed is the experience and the reality that lies at the very foundation of her existence, which is the abiding wellspring of her entire life. This is the place of simple *being* in the shelter of his love, the place of *pure intimacy for its own sake*, which transcends all the external circumstances of her life while giving them meaning. In other words, this is the original and all-encompassing "forever" which is pronounced at every moment within her by God himself, and into which she inserts the "forever" of her own heart in response.

It is only from within this place, indeed, that she can find the freedom to open her heart also to hear and to welcome the Bridegroom's call to walk a particular path, to say "forever" in a particular vocation. Her identity, while deeper than any path, any vocation, is precisely what allows her to walk this path in freedom—in the playfulness and lightheartedness of knowing herself to be unconditionally loved for her own sake, and cradled always in the arms of this perfect Love. And yet here she yearns spontaneously to manifest this "forever" in the deepest way she can, to give her heart away in a radical "yes" that will anticipate the unchanging and unbreakable love of eternity. She wants to unite the generous self-offering of her own heart to the generosity of God's outpouring love which lies at the very origin of her existence and of the existence of the whole creation. She wants to live what Saint Francis of Assisi so beautifully described: "Hold back nothing of yourself for yourself, so that He who gave Himself totally to you may receive you totally."

How beautiful all of this is! We see in the Song of Songs, however, that the bride, despite all that she has experience of God's love, is still slow to answer this call. He ardently beckons her out, and yet she delays. Has she forgotten how much he loves her? Has she forgotten her true identity as his uniquely beloved? Yes...there can be no other adequate explanation for her delay. She has, if only for a moment, lost sight of this radiant and all-enfolding Mystery at the foundation of her existence, in which and from which her life can unfold in freedom, joy, and ardent generosity. Is this not shown in what she says to the Bridegroom? "I have taken off my garment, how could I put it on again? I have bathed my feet, how could I dirty them?" Do you not know, lovely bride, that he alone can be your garment, and he alone your true purification and transformation? Yes, you have experienced his love at the foundation of your identity, and yet you are not yet solidly established in this...not yet. Though you will be! You must still experience more deeply that truth about which Saint Paul wrote: "Christ loved the Church and gave himself up for her, that he might sanctify her, having cleansed her by the washing of water with the word, that he might present the Church to himself in splendor, without spot or wrinkle or any such thing, that she might be holy and without blemish" (Eph 5:25-27).

This is why, as the Bridegroom approaches his bride during the night, he calls her and says to her: "Open to me, my sister, my love, my dove, my perfect one" (Sg 5:2). In the Hebrew text, there is a beautiful poetry to these words: "*Pit-hi li, ahoti, rayati, yownati, tammati.*" We can hear the gentle insistence of the Bridegroom in these titles he gives to the bride, his tender reassurance of how lovely she is to him: *ahoti*—my sister; *rayati*—my love; *yownati*—my dove; *tammati*—my perfect one. Indeed, there is a kind of progression here between the titles: she is his sister, since she bears the same flesh and belongs to the same Father; and because she is sister he can make her his bride; as bride she is filled with the breath of the Spirit whom they share, his true and lovely dove; and, holding her close in his arms, filling her with the Triune presence, she is truly his perfect one.

How gently and sweetly, therefore, he calls his bride forth from the bed of her comfort, in order to draw her out, not into insecurity, but into the enduring security that can be given only by his own embrace! Yes, the desire for comfort is something very different from the encounter with beauty, as pleasure is centered on the self and beauty is centered on the other, while beauty also takes up the self and immeasurably enriches it, by gripping it and drawing it into the sacred realm of Being that is unveiled by the touch of beauty upon the heart. Indeed, in the light of the Beloved's beauty that pours out upon me, I am simply reaffirmed in my own beauty—for in his Beauty I see my own reflected, cradled secure in his embrace, as, indeed, my eyes are opened to see and receive the beauty of all that he has made.

Nonetheless, since the bride does not respond to his words of invitation, his words of tender love and affirmation, he reaches out yet more intimately to unveil himself to her, to touch her heart:

My Beloved put his hand to the latch,
and my heart was thrilled within me.
(Sg 5:4)

In the Song of Songs, we encounter a progressively deeper and more intimate approach of the Bridegroom—from his bounding over the mountains to his bride, through his standing behind the wall, his peering through the lattice, to his speaking to her in invitation, to his gentle yet impatient trying of the handle of the door, as if to see if it might perhaps be unlocked! And this latch does not belong to any external, material door; rather, it is to the door of her own heart. Ah, how beautiful an image is this! The Bridegroom touches the latch of the door, seeking entrance. And what is the door of the heart? Is it not the bride's very faculty of perception—her mind and affectivity, her physical and spiritual senses? He is gently touching her, not in an intrusive way that would force her will, but nonetheless with a strong and sweet persuasion. He is communicating himself mysteriously to her: perhaps through the mind, touched by his beauty through contemplation of Scripture; perhaps through the affectivity, mediated by the beauty of creation or of another person, or through an insight into his own uncreated loveliness; perhaps through the sense of hearing or the sense of sight. He is touching her, loving her, calling her—with words from without that echo in her spirit, with a touch from without that nonetheless reverberates within. Indeed, with a touch that is simultaneously without and within, since his gentle touch upon the latch of the door causes her very heart to thrill and vibrate with his presence!

And therefore, touched in this way, at last she arises from her bed and goes to the door:

I arose to open to my Beloved,
and my hands dripped with myrrh,
my fingers with liquid myrrh,
upon the handles of the bolt.
(Sg 5:5)

She goes to open the door which he would not force, but which can only be opened of her own volition. She arises to pronounce her "yes" to his love and to his tender invitation. Myrrh, the very symbol of the Bridegroom's presence poured out upon her, drips from her hands and her fingers, as she opens the door to him. It is as if she is already drenched in her Beloved even as she opens to welcome him! Why then, when the door swings open, does she exclaim his absence?

I opened to my Beloved,
but my Beloved had turned and gone.
My soul failed me when he spoke.
I sought him, but found him not;
I called him, but he gave no answer.
(Sg 5:6)

How deeply does this correspond to our own spiritual experience! It is as if, every time that God touches our hearts more deeply with his love—every time that he puts his hand to the latch—our heart is dilated to love him and seek him more ardently. And this very dilation of the heart increases our capacity for him, such that we feel his absence more keenly, even in his presence (while also sensing his presence more deeply, even in his "absence"!). Ravished by his beauty and by the touch of his goodness, we cannot but go out to seek him anew and more deeply—progressing from love to love, drawn, carried, and sustained by the very Love that has preceded, accompanies, and awaits us as our Origin and Consummation.

ישוע

THEY WOUNDED ME

The bride, after experiencing her inmost heart thrilled by the touch of her divine Beloved, and arising to him, goes out through the streets and the squares of the city to seek for him. But at first she encounters, not the One whom her heart loves, but the watchmen of the city:

The watchmen found me,
as they went about in the city;
they beat me, they wounded me,
they took away my mantle,
those watchmen of the walls.
(Sg 5:7)

Ah, how painful this is to see! Now the bride is wounded, not only by the ravishing touch of her Bridegroom, by the ardent longing for his enduring embrace, but also by the irreverent and violent touch of fallen mankind! The first wound, as I have said, is truly healing, even if it causes pain—the wound of love received through the Bridegroom's gentle touch which awakens her heart to life and gives her a foretaste of the intimacy for which she was made. The other wound, however, truly deserves the name of a wound—for it injures her heart. It seems to confirm her previous fear of vulnerability, her fear of being hurt in her nakedness and cast away as unlovable and unimportant. No, lovely bride! Do not turn away and hide in the rocks again; do not return to your room to nurse your wounds in isolation! Trust in the One who calls you. Turn not back, but rather forge ahead, drawn by ardent longing for him…drawn by his own voice echoing in your heart and his own beauty impressed upon your soul!

Even if it seems that he is far away, he has not forsaken you. He is intimately near, even if you do not have the eyes to see. Call out to him. Lay before him the vulnerability which has just been hurt by others, that he may touch and heal you here, that he may shelter and cherish you where you need him the most. Whether you have been hurt by the betrayal of a friend, by the misunderstanding of an acquaintance, a spouse, a companion, by the abuse or disrespect of a stranger, or even by the "watchmen" whom God has appointed to care for his Church—lovely bride, he is deeper than the faults and imperfections of men! He is deeper than even the gravest of sins, the deepest of hurts! Turn your gaze beyond the darkness that surrounds you. Flee from this situation of pain, not into isolation, not building up walls to protect yourself. Rather, flee, even in your nakedness, flee into the sanctuary of your heart where he awaits!

He is here, suffering in you, suffering with you, suffering for you. Only lean back, in your exhaustion and pain, and you will find yourself buoyed up in the gentleness of his embrace. This is how close he is, holding you even here, even now. The compassion of his Heart is aching with the pain of your heart, and he wants to bind up and heal all of your wounds. Lean back, therefore, lean back into his embrace, so that his left hand may uphold your head and his right arm may embrace you, as he holds you intimately to himself and pours forth, from one Heart into another, the healing torrent of love and mercy.

ישוע

WHERE IS HE?

After experiencing the abuse of the watchmen of the city, rather than closing in upon herself and nursing her own wounds in isolation, the bride turns to seek the only One in whom she can find true healing and enduring rest. But she still does not yet know where he resides; and so she cries out, not to the watchmen, but to others who might know a little better where to find him:

I adjure you, daughters of Jerusalem,
if you find my Beloved,
that you tell him
I am wounded by love.
(Sg 5:8)

Yes, her heart is in love, and so even if she laments the wounds she has received from men, she knows that the wound that above all needs to be healed is the wound of love, in which she is satisfied only with the Bridegroom's presence. And so she cries out, she cries out to her maiden companions for help. She tells them that, if they happen to find her Beloved, they relay a simple message: that his precious one is wounded with love for him! They could not say any more than this, could they? They do not love him as she does, and so they could say no more. Further, she alone can express to him, in the silence of her heart, those true words of love which convey the depth of her longing, the depth of her profound need for him who is her only hope and security.

It is quite upsetting then, to see that these maiden companions

don't understand. They say to her:
> *What is your Beloved more than another beloved,*
> *O loveliest among women?*
> *What is your Beloved more than another beloved,*
> *that you thus adjure us?*
> *(Sg 5:9)*

Ah…but their uncomprehending response stirs up in the bride anew her longing, and directs her gaze immediately upon the One whom her heart loves. And it is precisely in turning to look upon him, in gazing upon and describing his beauty, that she will find him anew! This is the very nature of such a Bridegroom: that to simply think of him is to make him present. Or rather, to simply turn the mind and heart toward him, to long for him with a holy nostalgia, is immediately to make contact with the ever-present One, who can never withdraw for a moment from the one whom he loves. He does not take refuge in the past or in the future, but presses upon her with the fullness of his Eternal Being at every moment, enfolding her gently in the depths of his divine embrace. When she turns the interior gaze of her heart upon him, therefore, this moment of time intersects directly with eternity, and the Heart of God and the human heart intimately communicate. But we are getting ahead of ourselves! She hasn't even begun to describe him yet, and I'm already talking about her finding him! And so she says:

> *My Beloved is all radiant and ruddy,*
> *distinguished among ten thousand.*
> *His head is the finest gold;*
> *his locks are wavy,*
> *black as a raven.*
> *His eyes are like doves*
> *beside springs of water,*
> *bathed in milk, fitly set.*
> *His cheeks are like beds of spices,*
> *yielding fragrance.*
> *His lips are lilies,*
> *distilling liquid myrrh.*
> *His arms are rounded gold,*
> *set with jewels.*
> *His body is ivory work,*
> *encrusted with sapphires.*
> *His legs are alabaster columns,*
> *set upon bases of gold.*
> *His appearance is like Lebanon,*

choice as the cedars.
His speech is most sweet,
and he is altogether desirable.
his is my Beloved and this is my Friend,
O daughters of Jerusalem.
(Sg 5:10-16)

So speaks the bride to her maiden companions. She has been quite carried away by enthusiasm for the One who has ravished and thrilled her heart! And it is beautiful to see that they have understood. The daughters of Jerusalem have let themselves be moved by her explanation; they have let themselves be "evangelized" by her ardent and loving description of the Bridegroom! And so they exclaim in response:

Where has your Beloved gone,
O loveliest among women?
Where has your Beloved turned,
that we may seek him with you?
(Sg 6:1)

Now what is this? The bride first asked these maidens if they had seen the Beloved, since she could not find him. And yet now, after hearing her description, they are the ones begging her to show the way to him! And the amazing thing is that *she knows!*

My Beloved has gone down to his garden,
to the beds of spices,
to pasture his flock in the gardens,
and to gather lilies.
I am my Beloved's and my Beloved is mine;
he pastures his flock among the lilies.
(Sg 6:2-3)

Now we know where the Bridegroom is! He is in the very garden sanctuary of the bride's heart! He has never left, but rather has gone deeper into her in order to pasture his flock in the garden, to gather the lilies of her beauty. After recounting to her maiden companions the beauty of her Beloved, therefore, the bride is immediately directed back to him and discovers his radiant presence deep within her. And what is her experience? All sense of loss is forgotten, all the feelings of abandonment, all the fear of being unable to find him. Rather, she is touched more intimately than ever before by the One who is always present, and so she simply exclaims: "I am my Beloved's and my Beloved is mine." This seeking and finding, this yearning search for the One who is never absent, has only renewed even more deeply and intimately the covenant of love sealed in the very sanctuary of her heart!

ישוע

CRADLING YOU IN SILENCE

The description that the bride gives of her heavenly Bridegroom is very "non-descriptive," in that, after she has finished, we really have no idea what he looks like! But that's precisely the point! His Beauty surpasses all that the mind can grasp and anything that words can say. The heart alone, spontaneously touched and moved by him, can receive some glimpse, some taste of his ravishing Beauty. But even then he surpasses, even then he is deeper, even then he is both more transcendent and also more intimately close! It is only faith, hope, and love which give an adequate and direct contact with him, the All-Beautiful One. As I have said, it is only this radical surrender of the heart, this poverty of laying my being open to his unforeseen and uncontrollable gift, that can allow me in some way to reach beyond the veil and to touch the face of the One whom my heart loves. And yet this very surrender on my part, this radical abandonment of myself into his care, is simply a response to his prior gift, an acquiescence to his calming and reassuring touch.

Yes, my surrender to Christ is well likened to a child falling asleep in her mother's arms, in which cares, worries, and fears fade away through the touch of his tenderness received through feeling his arms wrapped around me. It is like what the beloved disciple must have felt as he reclined against the bosom of Jesus at the Last Supper, listening to the throbbing of his most tender Heart. But how can I come to feel this if I do not? Ah, what a question! God, why don't you make yourself more immediately felt, more directly visible? If our broken hearts struggle to trust in you, struggle to rest in your embrace in our suffering, in the busyness of life, in the wounds that trap us in ourselves—why do you not come and open us to feel and know you? I have said "yes," even if my "yes" is frail and afraid. I have given permission. Why then do you not immediately answer? Indeed, why do you come at night and beckon me out, only to have me search for you through the streets and squares of the city, where I am lonely, lost, and wounded, only to find you after a painful process of searching and purification?

It is not that he does not answer…it is only that we have not yet learned how to perceive his presence and his activity. But again another objection immediately arises: if that is the case, then why doesn't he just "change tactics" and do something that works better? The only way of stepping beyond the frustration that these questions express is first to step back. It is to step back and see that they all arise from a deep insecurity in the heart, even from a kind of "grudge" against the goodness of God. In this attitude, God himself is being put "on trial" by the human heart, as if he had to justify himself and his activity before us. As if we knew better than he did what is best for us, as if we knew better how to control the course of the world. But the beautiful thing is that God receives even this from us without reserve—he receives our anger, our pain, our frustration, our anguish, and makes it all his own in the Heart of his Crucified Son. In the noble silence of Christ hanging upon the Cross, God says to us:

"I understand your pain; I hold your wounds as my own; I shelter you in this loneliest place... And, my dear child, my precious spouse, I want you to see and to know—in a radical trust that draws you out beyond your ordinary way of seeing into something new—I want you to know that I am ever present loving you and sheltering you. Though you may not understand, the way in which I love you, the way in which I communicate myself to you, is indeed the best. I am like the air that surrounds you, like the breath that fills your lungs. I am like the light that surrounds you and, while itself not being seen, enables you to see all things. I am like the warmth without which you could not live, move, or have your being. Yes, I am like the heartbeat within your breast, like the blood pulsating through your veins. I am like the very matter of which your body is composed, like the very consciousness of your every thought, feeling, and desire.

"In other words, I am so near to you that you are always experiencing me, always touching me, always encountering me—even if the fullness of my radiant presence will only be known when the veil of mortality is torn and you encounter me, in the fullness of who I am in myself, in the definitive face-to-face meeting. But even now, I permeate your consciousness, I pervade your being—hidden though true. The only difference, when the consummation at last comes, is that I will openly, visibly, palpably pervade and permeate you and all things, bathed as they will be in the light of my glory which itself is seen, and in which all things reveal their truest meaning and beauty. Patience, beloved, patience... When you trust in me, you will come to dwell already now in the sacramental meaning of each unique moment, in which I silently yet deeply communicate myself to you without ceasing. And I myself will awaken this trust and bring it to maturity. I am already doing so! Only try to keep your eyes fixed on me, on this invisible but true Figure who comes to you in all things and through all things, touching and cradling your heart in silence."

ישוע

TRANSFORMED AND UNITED
IN HIS LOVE

> I do not believe we can truly enter into our own inner pain and wounds and open our hearts to others unless we have had an experience of God, unless we have been touched by God. We must be touched by the Father in order to experience, as the prodigal son did, that no matter how wounded we may be, we are loved. And not only are we loved, but we too are called to heal and to liberate. This healing power in us will not come from our capacities and our riches, but in and through our poverty. We are called to discover that God can bring peace, compassion and love through our wounds. (Jean Vanier)

Is this not the blessed experience that the bride has now had? She has encountered God's intimate love in the very place of her greatest woundedness. She has felt his presence in the place of her greatest loneliness, his light in her deepest darkness, his consolation in her most intense anguish and pain. She has been wounded, yes, but she has found God—perhaps unexpectedly!—in this very place of woundedness. She has encountered him at the heart of her vulnerability, sheltering and holding her with his inexpressible love. Indeed, she has found him not only sheltering her, but delighting in her and cherishing her in the unique beauty that is deeper even than her wounds and her pain.

Her very poverty, therefore, her very abiding need for him, is but the space in which she unceasingly receives true strength. It is in her poverty that she is a gift for him, in her poverty that he can unite her to himself and make her one with him in the radiant fullness of the divine poverty of the Trinity. Yes, it is in her poverty that his love pours out, and pours through her into the thirsting hearts of her poor brothers and sisters, yearning, every one of them, for the rest, happiness, and fulfillment that only the Bridegroom can give.

We have therefore seen something very beautiful in this fourth poem. There is a profound growth, a kind of "dilation" of the bride's heart into a deeper and more radical love and intimacy, both with God and with others. Having passed through the night of loss and longing, she has discovered a more lasting communion with the One whom her heart loves, a communion which also reaches deeper into the inmost spaces of her heart. And this deep intimacy and interiority is also more expansive, more open, radiating out to touch and draw other hearts too.

Knowing herself to be uniquely and unrepeatably loved by the divine Bridegroom, she feels no need to keep him to herself, as if his love for others were in competition with his love for her. Rather, his love for her is always unique, always special, always exclusive and unrepeatable. And yet from this very place of belovedness, her heart is freed from insecurity, and she ardently desires for all to love him as she does. She yearns for them to experience, in their own right and in the intimate space of their own hearts, his unique love for each one of them.

Indeed, she herself draws and attracts them to her Beloved. And this primarily occurs simply by her own longing for him, and by the way in which she makes his beauty visible! She cannot help singing the praises of the One who is "the fairest of the sons of men" (Ps 45:2), and her words tug on the heart-strings of her companions, causing them to long also to get to know him directly, to feel the gentleness of his touch and the shelter of his embrace.

She has become, therefore, a healer of souls, a mediator of God's own loving gaze and his healing embrace. Yes, and she has become this precisely from the heart of her own woundedness, irradiated with the healing and transfiguring grace of Christ!

My Beloved has gone down to his garden,
to the beds of spices,
to pasture his flock in the gardens,
and to gather lilies.
I am my Beloved's and my Beloved is mine;
he pastures his flock among the lilies.
(Sg 6:2-3)

There is a great joy present in these words, which operates on two levels inseparably. The first level is the intimate personal level of the one-to-one union of the bride and her Bridegroom, of the unique human heart and her God. Her heart is his garden, and he has come to pasture his flock within her and to gather the lilies of her unique and unrepeatable beauty, her own identity, unspeakably precious in his eyes. The second level is the level of interpersonal human love, of communion that flowers between human hearts that encounter within this sacred space of the Bridegroom's own love. In other words, the bride's deep union with her Bridegroom does not separate her off from the rest of humanity, enclosing her in herself. Rather, it opens wide her heart to be a garden for all, a sheltering space in which others can encounter the Bridegroom who longs for them.

Indeed, as human hearts grow together in love for the one divine Beloved, and in the perfect security of his unique love for each one of them, they experience the unity of being his single flock, pasturing together in deep interpersonal intimacy among the lilies of his own all-enfolding Love and his sheltering Tenderness. This is how there shall truly "be one flock and one Shepherd" (Jn 10:16), as human hearts are knitted together in the enfolding arms of the single Bridegroom's embrace, sharing, at the heart of their own intimacy with one another, in the breathtaking beauty of the life of the Father, Son, and Holy Spirit! As the Bridegroom has so ardently prayed: "that they may all be one; even as you, Father, are in me, and I in you, that they also may be in us, so that the world may believe that you have sent me. The glory which you have given me I have given to them, that they may be one even as we are one, I in them and you in me, that they may become perfectly one, so that the world may know that you have sent me and have loved them even as you have loved me" (Jn 17:21-23).

FIFTH POEM:

THE AUTUMN OF THE FRUITS

BEAUTIFUL AS TIRZAH AND JERUSALEM

The bride has passed through quite a journey! At the beginning of the Song of Songs, she was enslaved to the "chariots of Egypt," dark but beautiful, yearning and calling out for her Beloved. And he came to her; he gazed upon her in her astounding beauty, radiating even through the bonds of her slavery, and he drew her to himself. The Bridegroom and the bride shared a prolonged look of mutual love, exclaiming one another's beauty, a gaze which was but the preface to a deep embrace in which their hearts beat together as one, emitting the fragrance of shared surrender. But even after this first embrace, the bride was called out more deeply still into a more radical love and a more total surrender. She awoke at the beginning of the second poem as the Bridegroom bounded across the hills and called her forth like a fearful dove from the clefts of the rock. When she did arise, she pursued her Beloved through the streets of the city at night, encountering him and holding onto him in an ardent love. But both of these embraces were preparations for the definitive embrace of marriage which unfolds in poem three. Here the Bridegroom comes up from the desert like a column of fire and receives the crown of his wedding day: the bride herself. And after exclaiming in great detail her beauty, he draws near and enters into the garden of her being in order to consummate his marriage with her.

But we have just seen that in this fourth poem, the bride is still seeking for the Bridegroom, still feeling the pain of his absence. Perhaps she is just looking back and remembering the events of poem two, or perhaps this is yet another deepening of the drama in which the Bridegroom enters more intimately into the depths of her heart and draws her to be united to himself there. For after she pursues him, at the climax of the fourth poem, we witness an astounding intimacy between Bridegroom and bride, in which the bride has become a pure garden in which her Beloved ceaselessly dwells, and in whom and through whom other hearts are drawn together into intimacy, into the intimacy of the Bridegroom's love, as his flock pasturing together among the lilies.

This astounding union at the end of poem four, however, is surpassed by the exaltation of poem five. The fourth poem concluded with a deep intimacy, but an intimacy taking place hidden in the sacred space of the bride's heart, which, purified and transfigured, offered itself freely and totally to her Beloved even in the darkness of this mortal life. In the fifth poem, we will see, the mutual belonging becomes even deeper and more total, or perhaps better, the marriage-bond forged in the shadows of this life is drawn toward its final consummation, beyond the veil of mortality, in the eternal wedding of heaven.

Perhaps this is what immediately strikes us at the beginning of the fifth poem: the bride is no long weak and frail, crying out in pain and longing. Rather, she is exalted in radiant glory and beauty, to the admiration of all! And the imagery shifts now from earthly to heavenly, from the soil of virginal creation to the exaltation of the divine Bridegroom's glory in the bosom of the Father, where the bride herself is now transfigured in the fullness of the divine light.

> *You are beautiful as Tirzah, my love,*
> *lovely as Jerusalem,*
> *terrible as an army with banners.*
> *Turn away your eyes from me,*
> *for they assault me—*
> *Your hair is like a flock of goats,*
> *moving down the slopes of Gilead.*
> *Your teeth are like a flock of ewes,*
> *that have come up from the washing,*
> *all of them bear twins,*
> *not one among them is bereaved.*
> *Your cheeks are like halves of a pomegranate*
> *behind your veil.*
> *There are sixty queens and eighty concubines,*
> *and maidens without number.*
> *My dove, my perfect one, is only one,*
> *the darling of her mother,*
> *flawless to her that bore her.*
> *The maidens saw her and called her happy;*
> *the queens and concubines also,*
> *and they praised her:*
> *"Who is this that looks forth like the dawn,*
> *fair as the moon, bright as the sun,*
> *terrible as an army with banners?"*
> *(Sg 6:4-10)*

The Bridegroom begins by comparing his bride to Tirzah and Jerusalem, the two capital cities of the Jewish people, of the northern and southern kingdom, respectively. On the literal level of the text, therefore, this bride is the restored and reconciled Israel, drawn back from her exile and united within the love of the single Bridegroom-God. She is the reconciliation of the two "camps" that are mentioned in verse 13: "Why should you look upon the Shulammite, as upon a dance between two camps?" In this consists her strength, which is so palpable in these verses of the Song: in her unity. Weakened before because of division and enmity, she is now the strong bride, the bride who is like an army with banners, assaulting the very Bridegroom with her ravishing beauty.

If this is true of Israel, how much more true is it of the Church, who is in herself nothing but the seed and the first realization of the reconciled creation! All the nations of the world should call Israel blessed, because of the One who had chosen her for himself, and indeed should let themselves be drawn through her to him: "Many peoples and strong nations shall come to seek the LORD of hosts in Jerusalem, and to entreat the favor of the LORD. Thus says the LORD of hosts: In those days ten men from the nations of every tongue shall take hold of the robe of a Jew, saying, 'Let us go with you, for we have heard that God is with you'" (Zech 8:22-23). Yes, this unique choice of Israel was ordained for the incorporation of all people into a single family of God, a single Church, the Bride and Mother who encompasses in her embrace, in her mystical womb, the whole of humanity! Therefore, rising from the heart of the Old Testament, from the heart of the nuptial love that is woven as a thread through the whole of Scripture, we see the contours of the Catholic Church appearing before our eyes. And not only does she unite the divided camps of estranged and scattered humanity. Not only does she astound all people (the queens, concubines, and maidens) with her beauty and with the attractiveness of the intimacy and unity to be found within her. Not only does Christ perpetuate within her his work of universal reconciliation and cosmic restoration—until this occurs perfectly at the end of time—but she herself is the very locus in which this unity flowers. She is the mystical Bride, both visible and invisible, both hierarchical and mystical, both Petrine and Marian, in whom all the persons who are being saved are already incorporated, whether they know it or not.

Yes, and this universal Church is not a mere political society, not a mere "corporation" in which the unique individual becomes anonymous in the mass of the crowd. The Church is rather the exact opposite: *she is the maternal womb in which each unique child of God is sheltered, cherished, and cared for on his or her unrepeatable journey into the definitive Home of heaven, of the Trinity's embrace.* Indeed, she is the very embrace of the Trinity already extended into this world and taking root deep in the human heart, drawing us together as one within the very unity of the Father, Son, and Holy Spirit. This is why the Marian dimension of the Church—the dimension of Mary—is the central reality of the

Church, her true *heart*, which pumps the blood of divine love throughout the whole of the Body and toward which all of the Church's life and activity is directed. Yes, the heart of the Church, the very essence of the Church, which gives meaning to everything else within her, is *intimacy*. It is deep personal communion, not on the level of mere roles, vocations, or ministries, but *on the sacred level of the heart-to-heart communion that flowers within the Heart of the One who unites us together within himself.*

In this intimacy, in this sacred family of the Church, each human heart can find the home for which it is longing—the shelter and security of being seen, known, and loved, of being cradled always in the arms of a Love that will never let go. Ah yes...the Bride has truly taken the Name of her Bridegroom! She is the Beloved! She is indeed Love, incarnate within this world! And it is therefore in her and through her that the Bridegroom himself conceives and brings new children to life; it is in her and through her that he shelters and cares for us; it is in her and through her that he teaches us, feeds us, fosters and protects us. She is the Woman who, held unceasingly by the protective embrace of the Man, is able to hold as she has first been held. She is the Bride who becomes a Virgin-Mother through the impregnating power of the Spirit of her Bridegroom.

But who am I talking about? Who is this beloved daughter, this immaculate bride, this virgin-mother? Mary, or the Church? Both, as one and indivisibly... Mary is the Church-in-person, the Church as a unique individual before she became a community. The whole of the universal Church was born from the unique heart of Mary in her unrepeatable intimacy with the Trinity. And therefore it is Mary, above all, who helps to preserve, safeguard, and foster the *personal* reality of the Church, the heart of the Church, not as a mere institution, but as *interpersonal intimacy*, uniquely sheltering and holding every unrepeatable human heart.

In the chamber at Nazareth where the angel Gabriel appeared to her, Mary was the Church, fully and completely: the beloved child, precious bride, and fruitful mother. At the foot of the Cross she was the Church, receiving the Bridegroom's gift and reciprocating it, bringing forth from the unity between them the children of God, of whom the beloved disciple is the first. At Pentecost, the heart of Mary, dilated to universal proportions through her closeness to Christ, through the mystery of his Passion and Resurrection, now enfolds all of the disciples of Jesus. They are all together with her in the upper room, praying, when the Holy Spirit descends upon them—as it had upon her alone in Nazareth so many years ago—and from this place the fullness of the Church's mystery bursts forth into the world. Yes, Mary stands forever at the very heart of the Church; we are all together with her in prayer; we are all enfolded within her maternal embrace, children sheltered by this beloved Daughter, spouses sheltered by this Bride of Christ, mothers or fathers within this Virgin-Mother who conceived the very Son of God in her womb, and through her union with this same Son cooperated in bringing forth each one of us into the very family of the Trinity.

ישוע

THE VICTORIOUS BRIDE

The Church is the Home of Communion, the space of true reconciliation and communion among human hearts. She is the Bride that astounds all the nations with her beauty, and especially reveals the beauty of the One to whom she belongs, the One who by his presence transfigures her: "We all, with unveiled face, beholding the glory of the Lord, are being transformed from glory unto glory, into the very image of the One whom we reflect" (cf. 2 Cor 3:18). Yes, Mary-Church is not only limited to the confines of this world, but she bridges over the distance between the earthly creation and the splendor of heaven—by the very power of the Resurrection of her Bridegroom, which she has also been granted to share in through the gift of the Assumption.

This is how she truly "looks forth like the dawn, fair as the moon, bright as the sun, terrible as an army with banners" (Sg 6:10). She rises above the earth, drawn by her heavenly Bridegroom, like the dawn rising above the earth. She is fair as the moon, gentle in her radiance which is but a pure reflection of the light of the One who loves her. Yet even in her gentle light, she is also a burning conflagration of love and heat, like the Son whom she conceived and whom she still bears within her forever, this Son who "comes forth like a bridegroom leaving his chamber, and like a strong man runs his course with joy. His rising is from the end of the heavens, and his circuit to the end of them; and there is nothing hidden from his heat" (cf. Ps 19:5-6). How beautiful is the bride of such a beautiful Bridegroom! How radiant is the beloved of such a brilliant Lover!

And this beauty, this glory of the divine Bridegroom pouring forth through the transparency of the bride, works like a magnet to draw all together into unity within her—within his own embrace manifest in and through her. Truly, lifted up from the earth in the Resurrection and the Ascension—and in every Mass in the Eucharist!—this Bridegroom draws all of humanity to himself, in order to "gather together into unity all the children of God who have been scattered abroad" (cf. Jn 11:51-52; 12:32). In this way the rupture caused by sin is overcome; in this way the wounds of division and misunderstanding, of estrangement and isolation, are healed by the indestructible power of Love:

> But now in Christ Jesus you who once were far off have been brought near in the blood of Christ. For he is our peace, who has made us both one, and has broken down the dividing wall of hostility, by abolishing in his flesh the law of commandments and ordinances, that he might create in himself one new man in place of the two, so making peace, and might reconcile us both to God in one body through the cross, thereby bringing the hostility to an end. And he came and preached peace to you who were far off and peace to those who were near; for through him we both have access in one Spirit to the Father. (Eph 2:13-18)

Yes, this is the work of the true Prince of Peace, the true Solomon —the Peaceful-One! He reconciles us all within himself so that we may be one, all enmity done away with in the unity of a single Body, his own Body sheltering and holding us. And this Body is also his Bride; and each one of us is also body and bride! This bride has taken her Beloved's Name; she is now, just as he is, the Peaceful-One. Is this not what we see in the Song, in these verses about the bride being the place of reconciliation between the two camps that were estranged before?

Return, return, O Shulammite,
return, return, that we may look upon you.
Why should you look upon the Shulammite,
as upon a dance between two camps?
(Sg 6:13)

She is called the Shulammite, the Maid of Shulam. In Hebrew there are no vowels, so this would really be a way of calling her the maid of Solomon—and *Shlm* means both Solomon and Peace (shalom). Yes, she belongs to the true Solomon who is the King of perfect and enduring peace. Yet how does she overcome the warfare that wages on this earth? How does she overcome the warfare that wages between earth and heaven, as Saint Paul writes: "For we are not contending against flesh and blood, but against the principalities, against the powers, against the world rulers of this present darkness, against the spiritual hosts of wickedness in the heavenly places"? (Eph 6:12). She does it only through her love and her beauty! For she is "terrible as an army with banners" precisely because of the intensity of her ravishing beauty! She is the woman of whom God prophesied to the serpent in Genesis: "I will put enmity between you and the woman, between your seed and her seed. You shall strike at her heel and she shall crush your head" (cf. Gen 3:15). Indeed, she casts away the forces of the enemy by a single glance of her eyes! How is this possible? Because her eyes have gazed so long and so deeply into the eyes of her Bridegroom that now she sees as he sees, now she loves as he loves. And now in her own eyes one can see the ravishing beauty of God himself, pouring forth from within her as a radiant and inextinguishable light!

ישוע

A DANCE BETWEEN TWO CAMPS

I went down to the nut orchard,
to look at the blossoms in the valley,
to see whether the vines had budded,
whether the pomegranates were in bloom.
Before I knew it, my desire had hurled me
on the chariot of my people, as their prince.
(Sg 6:11-12)

The Bridegroom, after listening to the chorus exclaim the beauty of the bride as she rises above the earth like the sun or moon, lifts his voice again. He speaks of his going down into his garden (obviously a recurring theme by now!). But he goes, not this time to gather fruits and flowers, at least not yet. Rather, he goes to see, to look... And what he looks at is expressed under four different images: the nuts, the blossoms, the vines, and the pomegranates. It seems that he wants to confirm for himself, by direct touch and vision, that the spring has fully and definitively come, and that the bride will not fall back into winter. And he is—what beautiful wonder!—he is now completely satisfied!

Yes, the hard shell that once surrounded the bride has broken and the tenderness and nourishing sweetness of her heart is now freely accessible to him. The blossoms of her flowering love and trustful surrender have fully burst forth, like petals opening in the sun and drinking in the light and warmth of the Bridegroom's own love. Her vines have stretched forth and are bearing abundant fruit, because she has become, deeply and enduringly, rooted in him who is her Life.

She experiences the reality of which Jesus spoke: "I am the true vine, and my Father is the vinedresser. Abide in me, and I in you. As the branch cannot bear fruit by itself, unless it abides in the vine, neither can you, unless you abide in me. I am the vine, you are the branches. He who abides in me, and I in him, he it is that bears much fruit, for apart from me you can do nothing. As the Father has loved me, so have I loved you; abide in my love" (Jn 15:1, 4-5, 9). Finally, the pomegranates are in bloom, these sweet fruits which are so often associated, precisely because of their appearance in the Song, with love!

But then…what is this that follows? He comes. He sees. He is satisfied with what he sees. And then he cries out: "My desire hurled me on the chariot of my people, as their prince!" Here is the Bridegroom whose Heart is so tender, so sensitive, that he cannot see the beauty of his bride without immediately giving everything to her and for her! And simply to run toward the one whom he loves is not enough; not even bounding across the mountains like a stag is enough. Now he must ride into her heart, into her presence, on a chariot, flaming with the fire of the Spirit like the chariot that carried Elijah away.

In the Hebrew, this verse on the chariot is almost incomprehensible, and its original meaning seems difficult or impossible to decipher. Here I am following the reading of Arminjon, who in his turn relies upon André Robert. Let me quote some of Arminjon's words here:

> The image of his Bride has kept all its charms in the eyes of the Bridegroom; it has been praised before him magnificently by the chorus of the nations; he has seen for himself in his garden that the irreversible spring has come; this image acts so powerfully on his heart that he hurls himself, irresistibly as it were, in his extreme impatience on the chariot that will draw him victoriously into the heart of his people, into the heart of his Bride, to settle there forever. "When love carries you away," says Saint John of the Cross, "don't ask where it is taking you." And so it is with the Bridegroom. The "before I knew" introducing the stanza does express the kind of sudden and uncontrollable impulse against which he cannot struggle anymore, having already said twice to his Bride: "You ravish my heart" (4:9).[28]

Immediately after the Bridegroom's exclamation of his ardent haste in coming into the heart of his bride, the chorus cries out again:

Return, return, O Shulammite,
return, return, that we may look upon you.
(Sg 6:13a)

Where has the bride gone that the chorus calls her back that they may gaze upon her? Surely they are not calling her to repent, to turn back to the Bridegroom? No, this is not a call to repentance and conversion. Rather, it is the cry of the thirsting hearts of her brothers and sisters that she may turn back, her face radiant from her encounter with God, in order to convey to them something of what she has seen and felt. This brings to mind what Saint Paul wrote, suspended as he was between heaven and earth, between ecstasy in God and ardent service of his brethren: "For if we are beside ourselves, it is for God; if we are in our right mind, it is for you" (2 Cor 5:13). So the bride is immersed in her Bridegroom, transfigured by this face-to-face encounter, after the veil has been removed; and her companions simply ask that they may be allowed a glance upon her loveliness, manifesting as it does the very loveliness of the Bridegroom himself. It is as if they are crying out: "Turn back and love us as you have been loved by him! Turn back and reveal to us his face, for we are thirsting for the One whom we glimpse in you, and we need you to lead us to him!"

This also brings to my mind Jesus' words to Saint Teresa of Calcutta: "They do not know me, so they do not want me. Who will bring them to me? Will you refuse to do this for me? Come, be my light…" And yet then comes the rest of the verse, which seems to come from the Bridegroom himself. He does not want his precious bride, however generously she loves her brethren and lays down her life for them, to be squandered and lost, fractured away from the sacred intimacy that she has with him:

Why should you look upon the Shulammite,
as upon a dance between two camps?
(6:13b)

What does he mean by these words? Yes, it seems that he is, as it were, drawing the veil again over the secrecy of the bride, sheltering her in reverence and awe, so that her inner beauty may not be scattered like pearls before swine. Of course, the people should desire to see her, and they should also be allowed to see her, in the right way and at the proper time. And above all to see him alive in her! But at this moment, as the bride takes flight into the embrace of her Bridegroom—arising to him like the moon as he descends to her like the fiery sun riding a chariot!—he wants an encounter between the two of them alone. She is not merely an instrument for the good of others…no, she is his uniquely beloved, ardently desired for her own sake! And so he comes…and so he draws her to himself. Yes, they meet in the marriage union that takes place in the intimacy of the secret bridal chamber, a chamber, however, which is the expanse of the glorious heavens!

Indeed, at the heart of her vulnerability before the Bridegroom, the bride is veiled and clothed anew now, not with earthly protection, but with the very light and love of her Beloved. She is perfectly radiant and beautiful, her inner truth set free through the loving and cherishing gaze of the One who first came to her in her slavery, and has now drawn her out into the most intimate meeting place of Lover and beloved. Now she is no longer a dove hiding in the clefts of the rock, but a woman radiant and pure, dancing with her Bridegroom to the eternal melody of heaven: in the ever surging movement of self-giving between the Father, Son, and Holy Spirit!

How beautiful… She has allowed herself to be caught up into the very dance of the Trinity, finding her full flowering precisely in this blessed space. And here she unites heaven and earth within her own heart, immersed as she is in the reconciling Heart of Christ. Here the truest and most enduring fruit blossoms spontaneously for the good of all, as she magnifies the light of her Beloved into the hearts of her brothers and sisters—precisely by the depth of her union with the One whom her heart loves! These two hearts, of Bridegroom and bride, dance together in the lightness and joy of love; they throb together a single hymn of delight, wonder, and mutual understanding; they sing, they dance, they play in the eternal playfulness, in the everlasting ecstasy of the Trinity, who is perfect Love, and therefore utter Happiness.

ישוע

THE UNIVERSAL DANCE

The Jerusalem Bible translates the second half of verse 13 as follows: "Why do you gaze upon the Maid of Shulam dancing as though between two rows of dancers?" What does this add to our previous reflection? It reveals that these "two camps" are not static, just standing with mouths wide open as they watch the Bridegroom dance with his bride (of course, at this point, there are certain things that they cannot watch anyway, but which occur hidden in the sacred space between the two lovers). Rather, these two camps are themselves dancing! If we understand these two camps as being those of heaven and earth, respectively, as I have tried to show, then we can see how these words are a beautiful exposition of what happens when the central petition of the Lord's Prayer is fulfilled: "Thy will be done on earth as it is in heaven."

What does it mean for God's will to pour forth from heaven to permeate even the earth? It means that earth, flooded with the torrents of Divine Love, will come to dance in harmony with the eternal dance ever occurring in the depths of heaven, in the bosom of the Trinity's own eternal life of love and intimacy! To pray "Thy will be done," therefore, is really to say: "May your Love pour forth, Father, into me and into all of your precious children—yes, into all of creation—and take us up into the joy and happiness of your own life of perfect intimacy and joy!" To live this prayer is therefore to correspond with the deepest desire of God (Thy will!) to pour himself forth in ardent generosity into all that he has made, into every heart, and to draw all back, gently yet powerfully, into the shelter of his own eternal embrace!

> For the Lord himself will descend from heaven with a cry of command, with the archangel's call, and with the sound of the trumpet of God. And the dead in Christ will rise first; then we who are alive, who are left, shall be caught up together with them in the clouds to meet the Lord in the air; and so we shall always be with the Lord. (1 Thes 4:16-17)

Ah, the meeting of heaven and earth within the Sacred Heart of Jesus Christ! This is the beautiful mystery, the radiant restoration, which we so ardently await, and toward which are hearts are ceaselessly being drawn! To be always with the Lord! Surely this is why Saint Paul concludes this passage by saying, "Therefore comfort one another with these words" (1 Thes 4:18). The distance between Bridegroom and bride will then be definitively overcome, the veil of estrangement at last utterly removed, and we will encounter him, face-to-face, knowing even as we are known by him, perfectly and forever!

Here at last will be the definitive consummation of the universal marriage, the intimate union of Bridegroom and bride in an embrace that will never end. And this will occur, not in the night of this life, hidden and obscure, but in the radiance of heavenly glory in which the whole universe itself will be renewed and restored to its full beauty. Indeed, all things will then be made new in an unheard-of way, perfecting all that we glimpsed and knew in this present life, carrying it to a fullness that allows God himself to be seen in all things, and all things to be seen in God. This is because all things will reveal their true nature as *love*, as the Love of God himself poured out in a creative act, and sustained unceasingly by his tender and sheltering embrace. This will be the eternal dance of heaven penetrating and permeating the whole of creation, transfiguring and renewing it.

This will be the intimate self-giving and mutual indwelling of the

Father, Son, and Holy Spirit pouring forth into my heart and into the heart of each person, taking us up, by awakening our total freedom in reciprocal surrender, into their own embrace and their own ceaseless dance of love. Here I shall be definitively and totally united with the One whom my heart loves! And in him I shall be intimately united with every one of my brothers and sisters. Within his own Love we will fully taste the intimacy for which our hearts have longed, as this Love shelters us all together as one and affirms each of us uniquely and unrepeatably—protected, cherished, and fully known and loved precisely in this true Home of his own Heart, which has itself made the entire universe a Home, transparent to his own gaze and to his own sheltering embrace.

How beautiful all of this is! Let us not fail to rest, to contemplate, to rejoice in this great promise and hope! But how can we "descend" from these heights back to the apparent ordinariness of our daily life? And how can we bring this hope and joy with us? In the light of such a radiant vision of consummation, will not our existence in this world look drab and boring? I hope not! The exact opposite should really be the case. Every moment of our life, here and now, is preparing us for that final and eternal destiny. Every moment of our life, indeed, is already in some way anticipating that reality, glimpsing it, tasting it, reaching out to touch it beyond the veil. Yes, the heartbeat of eternity is already secretly present in every moment of temporal time. The heartbeat of our Beloved is already pressed up against my own heart, throbbing unceasingly its hymn of tenderness and love, and inviting me to enter ever deeper into intimacy with him, already in this life, and perfectly forever in the next.

ישוע

HELD CAPTIVE IN THE TRESSES

André Chouraqui has some beautiful words explaining the name that the bride is given at this point in the Song, "the maid of Shulam." He says:

> Up until now, the Bride was black, beautiful, veiled and, more, the lily of Sharon, the rose of the depths, the dove, the immaculate, the closed garden, the sealed fountain, the source of gardens, the well of living water, the promised Bride, the sister, the perfect, the wonderful, the terrible, identical to dawn, to the moon and to the sun; more than twenty images describe her in her fiery beauty, in the torments of her love. And here she finds

at last, after the drama of exile is over, her true name. In her new wedding, in the eternity of her mystical wedding, she is the maid of Shulam. ... Love transforms the Bride into a living figure of plenitude and peace. ... She is the image of triumphant peace.[29]

Yes, the bride has been so beautifully transformed in the image of her Beloved that she herself has become a living fount of peace for all, a perfect image of total and enduring peace. At this point in the Song, we discover that beautiful gift that Christ breathed forth upon his disciples after his Resurrection: "'Peace be with you...' and when we had said this, he breathed on them" (cf. Jn 20:20-22). Indeed, we come to grasp how he was able to impart this peace, even on the verge of his Passion, assuring them that even as he walks a path of suffering, he remains totally at peace in the sheltering love of his Father, and therefore is also a rock of peace and security for those whom he loves: "Peace I leave with you; my peace I give to you; not as the world gives do I give to you. Let not your hearts be troubled, neither let them be afraid. ... I am not alone, for the Father is with me. I have said this to you that in me you may have peace. In the world you have tribulation; but be of good cheer, I have overcome the world" (Jn 14:27; 16:32-33).

Is not peace the greatest gift, the inestimable grace that God offers to us in his love? This peace is not due merely to the absence of conflict, as it can exist even when there is external conflict within this world. It is a deeper and abiding restfulness of the heart. But it is also a peace that draws us beyond conflict, beyond confusion and fear and anxiety, even in this life and perfectly forever in the next: into the sheltering embrace of the One who is himself perfect Peace. Yes, peace, *shalom*, is not a mere external lack of conflict or disagreement, nor even a mere agreement and concord. It is, as the Hebrew word implies, a state of total wholeness, a state of completeness.

It is what Jesus referred to when he invited us to be *perfect* as our heavenly Father is perfect. To be perfect in the Gospel sense is not to be free of all weakness, all neediness, even all faults; rather, true perfection consists in the restoration of the spirit of childhood. It is the knitting together of my heart to the Heart of God, the joy of a shared gaze of love and understanding which is but the preface to a silent embrace in which we hold each other in a togetherness that will never be torn asunder, our hearts beating together as one in a perfect symphony of intimacy and joy.

Yes, the bride is the woman of peace, the virginal creation who has opened herself to the outpouring and fecundating love of the heavenly Bridegroom. She is now an icon of the peace of God, radiating with the serenity of his love, with the confidence of being ceaselessly held and cradled by him, cared for by his infinite goodness. And this bride is beautiful, not only with the beauty of her Bridegroom, but also with a beauty that never ceases to ravish and attract the Heart of the Bridegroom himself! And so he lets himself be touched anew by the contemplation of the beauty of the one whom he loves, and he cries out to her:

> *How graceful are your feet in sandals,*
> *O queenly maiden!*
> *Your rounded thighs are like jewels,*
> *the work of a master hand.*
> *Your navel is a rounded bowl*
> *that never lacks mixed wine.*
> *Your belly is a heap of wheat,*
> *encircled with lilies.*
> *Your two breasts are like two fawns,*
> *twins of a gazelle.*
> *Your neck is like an ivory tower.*
> *Your eyes are pools in Heshbon,*
> *by the gate of Bath-rabbim.*
> *Your nose is like a tower of Lebanon,*
> *overlooking Damascus.*
> *Your head crowns you like Carmel,*
> *and your flowing locks are like purple;*
> *a King is held captive in the tresses.*
> (Sg 7:1-5)

The Bridegroom, though he has described the beauty of his bride before, now enumerates her beauty from her feet to her head. The third-person ending to this description has made some think that these words come, not from the Bridegroom, but from the chorus. But who could really describe the precious bride in this way but the Bridegroom himself? He alone has the eyes to see her this deeply, to reverence and shelter and cherish her with such ardor and yet such tenderness. For indeed, love alone truly gives eyes to see the beloved as they really are! And he is the perfect Lover!

Of all the things that could be said about this description, let me mention only one: the captivity of the King in the tresses (the long locks) of the bride's hair. For me, this is a very moving verse of the Song. After enumerating the "global" beauty of his beloved, the Bridegroom concludes with a simple statement that the locks of her hair are enough to hold him captive with love! A simple glance, a simple part, and he is able to intuit the whole of her beauty, radiant in his eyes. Indeed, is this not the nature of love, to be able to see the whole of the beloved even in only a small gesture or reminder of them? I know I have mentioned this before in these reflections, but it bears repeating. A simple hearing of their voice at a distance, a simple glance upon their figure in passing, perhaps only through the corner of my eye…and my heart is ravished, captured, drawn!

Truly the King, with such a sensitive Heart, lets himself be conquered by the beauty of his bride. Her glance has ravished his Heart, such that he even found himself asking her to turn her eyes away from him, if only for a moment, because he was overcome by her beauty. But this weakness of the Bridegroom is his true strength! It is but the vulnerability of his perfect and all-powerfully Love, which lets itself be conquered by the beauty of the creature whom he has made, and whom he has taken to himself as his very bride.

יׁשוע

MAY YOUR BREASTS BE LIKE CLUSTERS

The Bridegroom, after at first requesting the bride to turn away her gaze because it ravished and assaulted his Heart, then calls her back and sings a hymn of ardent love to her. He enumerates her beauty in its totality, from head to toe, with a description which is incredibly intimate. But that is not all. As the Bridegroom turns his gaze back to the bride, unafraid now to gaze upon her beauty, he not only sings. No, he himself draws near in order to unite himself to her, saying:

How fair and pleasant you are,
O loved one, delectable maiden!
You are stately as a palm tree,
and your breasts are like its clusters.
I say I will climb the palm tree
and lay hold of its branches.
Oh, may your breasts be like clusters of the vine,
and the scent of your breath like apples,
and your kiss like the best wine
that goes down smoothly,
gliding over the lips of those who sleep.
(Sg 7:6-9)

Now the Bridegroom is asking his bride for a kiss! Yes, if the Song of Songs opened with the bride's ardent request for her Beloved to kiss her with the kiss of his mouth, then at the climax of this final poem, we find the Bridegroom himself coming to his bride and asking her to kiss him, to let herself to kissed. And here again the image of the tree reappears, as it has so often throughout the Song. But now the tree is not the Bridegroom, but the bride.

What is this reversal? It is like the whole movement of the drama has now been turned on its head! We thought all along that the bride was the one who was primarily seeking. She was the one longing for her absent Beloved, the one yearning and crying out with desire and expectation. She was the one refreshed and sustained by her Bridegroom's love, the one who ate of the fruit of his tree. But now we see that the Bridegroom has even more been the One seeking, the one passionately longing for his precious bride. He has been the One ardently drawn by love and asking for a kiss, an embrace. And now, after drawing the bride through this path of love and transformation—bringing her from the slavery of sin and shame into his intimate embrace, and making her into the peaceful one who shares in his own perfect peace—now, after this, the Bridegroom himself is able to draw near and kiss her as he has always desired!

And clearly, in the text something more is implied. This is the true, virginal consummation of the marriage between the divine Bridegroom and his bride, whom he has redeemed with his Cross and Resurrection. This is the nuptial union that surpasses all the unions of this earthly creation, a foretaste and anticipation of the eternal marriage feast of the Lamb in the heavenly Jerusalem! This is the "spiritual marriage" of which the mystics of the Church have spoken, the fulfillment of the deepest longings of the human heart made for intimacy with God. This is the fulfillment of the desire that has been burning like a flame, throbbing like a heartbeat, at the core of the Song of Songs. And it occurs as a result of the Bridegroom's initiative, to which the bride is asked simply to consent, to pronounce her own "Let it be to me according to your word" (Lk 1:38).

When the Bridegroom seeks to climb up into the arms of the bride and to lay hold of her breasts, it is hard not to think of the infant Jesus reaching up to his Mother in the desire for her to lift him up and nurse him at her breast! And we can ask: what do the breasts of the woman signify, what "language" do they speak about her as a person? John Paul II said that our bodies speak a language, that they reveal our own personal mystery as oriented toward love and communion. What, then, do the breasts signify? Do not the breasts of the woman represent *the gift of her heart,* over which they rest? Do they not represent the outpouring of her very being into the child whom she loves —the gift of her very essence, as it were, in the form of milk fashioned in her own body?

Yes, is not the experience of nursing at a woman's breast one of the most primal experiences of every human being—this unspeakable intimacy in which two persons are joined together so intimately that one is entirely dependent for his being upon the nourishment and care he receives from another? The reality of nursing, therefore, is as it were a "primordial sacrament," an image of the gift that each one of us is meant to become for another—and also of the fact that we first come as a gift from another, and depend entirely upon their prior gift in order to give ourselves in return!

But there is much more to say here, too. For if the breasts of the woman, resting as they do against her very heart, manifest visibly that her heart is made to be a gift—just as her womb reveals that in her inmost core she is meant to receive, in radical receptivity, the prior gift of Another!—then is there not a corresponding reality in the man? Here is where one of my favorite quotes from the early Church Fathers comes in. It comes from a Catechesis of Saint John Chrysostom, and is read by the Church on Good Friday as the second reading for the Office of Readings:

> If you desire further proof of the power of this blood, remember where it came from, how it ran down from the cross, flowing from the Master's side. The gospel records that when Christ was dead, but still hung on the cross, a soldier came and pierced his side with a lance and immediately there poured out water and blood. Now the water was a symbol of baptism and the blood of the holy eucharist. The soldier pierced the Lord's side, he breached the wall of the sacred temple, and I have found the treasure and made it my own. So also with the lamb: the Jews sacrificed the victim and I have been saved by it.
>
> *There flowed from his side water and blood.* Beloved, do not pass over this mystery without thought; it has yet another hidden meaning, which I will explain to you. I said that water and blood symbolized baptism and the holy eucharist. From these two sacraments the Church is born: from baptism, *the cleansing water that gives rebirth and renewal through the Holy Spirit*, and from the holy eucharist. Since the symbols of baptism and the eucharist flowed from his side, it was from his side that Christ fashioned the Church, as he had fashioned Eve from the side of Adam. Moses gives a hint of this when he tells the story of the first man and makes him exclaim: *Bone from my bones and flesh from my flesh!* As God then took a rib from Adam's side to fashion a woman, so Christ has given us blood and water from his side to

fashion the Church. God took the rib when Adam was in a deep sleep, and in the same way Christ gave us the blood and water after his own death.

Do you understand, then, how Christ has united his bride to himself and what food he gives us all to eat? By one and the same food we are both brought into being and nourished. As a woman nourishes her child with her own blood and milk, so does Christ unceasingly nourish with his own blood those to whom he himself has given life.[30]

This beautiful text speaks, among other things, of how the gift of Christ upon the Cross—the opening of his side from which Blood and water pour out—is a paradoxical way of giving his very Heart to us just as a woman gives her heart by nursing a child at her breast! But it is also much more than this too, as, in this sacred place of Christ's Paschal Mystery, all of the beautiful though imperfect images of love within this world are both surpassed and consummated in the most radical and perfect way.

Christ's gift of himself is, therefore, simultaneously an act of *paternal begetting*—as the new life of the children of God is implanted in the receptive "womb" of Mary's own virginal receptivity—and an act of *maternal sheltering*, as Christ's own Heart becomes a "womb" to receive and hold us all in the presence of his Father! Indeed, the Blood and water pouring forth from his side, from his Heart, are both the source of the Church's life, as the first woman was fashioned from the side of the first man, and also the very space in which he nourishes us, allowing us to drink from his breast the fullness of life and love that pours forth from the bosom of the Holy Trinity!

ישוע

THE BEAUTY AND MEANING OF THE BODY

In the last reflection I spoke about the breast as the place of the gift of one's heart, as the symbol of the outpouring of one's being as a gift to another. But I also hinted that there is another reality that the breast, both of the woman and of the man, symbolizes. Not only is it a place through which love is poured—revealed especially in the milk with which the woman nurses a child—but it is also *a space of sheltering tenderness, a place where one holds and cradles another.*

A number of passages of Scripture come immediately to mind,

since this image of the breast or bosom is such a rich theme in the Bible. But before I plunge into a few of these, let me pause in this reflection to look at the "sacramentality" of the human body itself. The importance of the body in our existence is due not to its being some "vessel" or "means" external to us (however necessary), but rather in its being an essential dimension of the person, and, in a true way, as being *the person* in his or her full incarnate nature. As Gabriel Marcel said, it is not accurate to say "I have a body," as this makes it seem to be a thing extrinsic to us; but neither is it accurate to say, "I am a body," even if this is technically correct, for I am not *just* a body, but a spiritual body in which the living flame of personal spirit lives. In order to bring together these mysterious dimensions of the human person, Marcel recommended the helpful phrase: *"I am bodily."* This expresses well the essential identity between ourselves and our body while also keeping intact the equally essential dimension of spirit and inner person that alone makes this body a living and personal body.

And if my body is truly *me*, then this body is precisely the living "locus" of my relationships both with God and with other human persons, and indeed of my relationships with the whole of creation. John Paul II understood and expressed this well in his basic premise of the *Theology of the Body*, saying: "The body, in fact, and only the body, is capable of making visible what is invisible: the spiritual and the divine. It has been created to transfer into the visible reality of the world the mystery hidden from eternity in God, and thus to be a sign of it" (TOB 19.4). Yes, every human body is never merely a "thing" within this world, an object, but always a *person*. It is never a "something" but a "someone," not a "what" but a "who"! And therefore every human body—or better said, every single embodied-person—is deserving of immense reverence and love.

In order to understand the meaning of the human body—the body of woman as oriented towards man and the body of man as oriented towards woman, as well as the wider orientation of the body to relationship, with children, friends, parents, and creation itself—it is necessary to understand why the body is beautiful, why it is good. It is important to try to hear and respond to the "word" that the human body speaks, a word of precisely vulnerable relationship between mutual self-giving. So we can ask, in the context of the current verses of the Song of Songs: Why does the body speak a particular "word," such that the breasts of the woman, for example, truly and inherently symbolize something (not to mention the "global" beauty of the male and female body)? And why is this very meaning, this very symbolism, beautiful? Let us try to look at this "primordial sacrament" of love that God has impressed upon our very bodies, beautiful in themselves and beautiful in the way that we relate to one another.

The first thing to say is this: is it not true that, in the human body, *meaning* and *beauty* are inseparably united together? I don't mean that the body is beautiful only because it is "well-fitted" to perform certain functions—e.g. eating, procreation, the nursing of children, work, athletic performance. Rather, I intend to say that the very meaningfulness of the human body is inherently beautiful, precisely because its meaning cannot be divorced from its beauty, and vice versa. It is not merely useful, in other words, perfect in a utilitarian way; rather, it is radiant, glorious, ravishing, because the very operation of the human body, indeed its very existence, is a manifestation of something of the beauty of God himself.

The rupture between meaning and beauty is often one reason that persons who do not have a healthily integrated sexuality struggle so much with chastity and even fall into sexual addictions. It is because, on one level of their being, they fear that sexuality is something bad, something forbidden, or at least something dangerous. But on a deeper and more spontaneous level of their being, they sense that it is indeed one of the deepest and most sacred of all created realities. They cannot but see and be attracted by its beauty. I would also add that, even beyond a developed disorder in one's sexuality, because of original sin itself, the pure beauty of sexuality (in the broadest sense) has become fractured from the realm of the person, from the realm of the spirit, and can incline towards the level of the flesh in its possessiveness and lust. What this means is that both the *beauty* and the *meaning* are obscured. And obscured by what? By a mere lust for pleasure and sexual gratification, by the "concupiscence of the flesh," which is ultimately blind to what really makes the reality beautiful and sacred at all.

The "virginal word" that the body speaks has been muffled, and sexuality has come for many persons to carry connotations of impurity and possessiveness. It calls for a deep healing and transfiguration of the human heart to "rediscover" the virginal beauty of the human body, even and especially in its gender and sexuality. And here the chaste beauty of sexuality itself, even in its concrete physical manifestations, becomes something sober and transparent to the light of God. And this rediscovery, this super-affirmation of the beauty and meaning of our bodies as the incarnation of our person and of our call to intimacy, is so necessary for our wholeness and holiness, as well as well as to respond more deeply to that "value not sufficiently appreciated" (TOB 45.4-5). And we can truly experience this gift, this healing, this renewal—through the amazing activity of grace flowing from the Redemption of Jesus Christ, pouring from his own sacred Body, Crucified and Risen and permeated with the very life and love of the Trinity. We can anticipate in some way already now, what will find full consummation at the end of time, when Christ comes again to re-create the heavens and the earth, where the meaning of sexuality will again be wholly virginal, wholly personal, penetrated and permeated by the life of the Trinity. In this way, meaning and beauty will be restored and perfected. And they will be perfected in a union that is no longer sexual (as we experience it in this life), but virginal, yet which precisely in this way super-fulfills sexuality in its fullness, even in the very body. And they will be virginal because they will be wholly Trinitarian, a pure participation in the mutual self-giving and everlasting intimacy of the Father, Son, and Holy Spirit.

This union will be the fruit of the pure donation of persons to one another through the medium of the body—fulfilling the partial word spoken by sexual union in this life, while fulfilled in an immeasurably deeper measure on the model of the Passion and Resurrection of Christ, and indeed on the basis of our participation in the very innermost life of the Trinity. In other words, the body will be so permeated by love, and by the loving desire of my heart to give itself to another in the love of God, that my whole bodiliness will be harnessed into a gift for the other. It will not be a part of me, but the whole of my being, which pours forth in tender love as a gift for the one whom I love, and which also becomes a sheltering space to receive and gently cradle them. And this gift and receptivity between persons is a living share, a transparent participation, in the innermost life of the Father, Son, and Holy Spirit, who live precisely this mystery for all eternity: mutual acceptance and self-giving in which they are so deeply united that they interpenetrate and mutually indwell, each living in the other in the sweetest embrace.

We obviously cannot adequately imagine what this virginal union will be like, but we can glimpse it by looking at the deep desires of our hearts and at the way that love is most deeply manifested in this world. We can recognize that the sexual union between man and woman, as paradigmatic as it is in the life of history, and as beautifully as it distills the whole nature of reality, is really but a particular expression, a symbol and an incarnation, of the mutual self-donation of persons to one another in the whole of their life and existence. It is a way of saying to the other: "I give myself to you completely and forever, and I also welcome you entirely to myself." And in pronouncing this word, I am also saying: "I desire to be united together with you so intimately, so totally, that while we remain two, we become one." This is the nature of the sexual embrace, but it is also the inner essence of all love, born from and expressing the love of the Trinity. And insofar as we allow ourselves to be permeated by God's light and love, and begin to live already now "in the light of eternity," we can taste, can feel in some way in anticipation, the virginal super-fulfillment that awaits us. And thus we come to the profound experiential conviction that heaven and the life of eternity are not actually far away, but intimately close, pressing upon us in each singular moment.

What is the point in saying all of this? Essentially, what I am trying to say is that all of the natural expressions of love within this earthly life (sexual union, nursing a child, a physical embrace, a kiss), while truly expressing and incarnating the beauty of love, also point towards realities that surpass them and which will find consummation only in eternal life. This is what I was referring to in speaking of the *virginal union* that awaits us at the consummation, and indeed about the *virginal word* that the body already speaks. No sexual embrace, however total, can give enduring rest to the human heart, or truly unite two persons together so deeply that they are inseparably bound to one another in love. No nursing mother can truly pour forth into her child the fullness of her love and the whole of her being. No kiss can truly breathe forth into another person my very life-breath and receive their life-breath in return. But are not these precisely the things that we long for? Is it not precisely this *totality* of communion, this *totality* of gift, and this *everlasting* intimacy for which our hearts thirst?

In conclusion, let me say this: at the end of time, not only will Christ fully reunite the *meaning* and the *beauty* of the body, yes, of the whole human person and indeed of the whole creation. Rather, he will restore them so totally that beauty and meaning shall be *one*. The very pouring forth of God's uncreated Beauty into us—rapt as we will be in ceaseless, face to face contemplation of the Trinity—will enable us to pour forth the fullness of our own beauty as a total gift, both to God and to one another. Yes, the very Being of God, pervading our entire being, will enable us both to give and to receive that complete gift for which our hearts long, and to experience that "forever" of perfect intimacy in which alone our hearts will find enduring rest.

ישוע

SHELTERED IN YOUR BOSOM

In the previous reflection I spoke about the meaning and the beauty of the human body, and about how these two are inseparably joined together in the single reality of love. All the things that are beautiful about the human person, and about creation as a whole, can be traced back in one way or another to the very uncreated Love of God, which is both their Origin and the very sustaining Ground of their existence. Especially, the whole of our humanity, body and spirit, person and nature, is beautiful. It is beautiful precisely because we have been made in the image and likeness of God, and thus we manifest the Trinity, not merely in an impersonal way, but by being called to reflect and to participate in the very relationships of love that the Father, Son, and Holy Spirit live for all eternity.

After seeing all of this, hopefully we can return to our earlier reflections with a deeper awareness, a deeper sensitivity to the sacramental meaning of creation. And through this, hopefully it will be easier to trace our way back unhindered into the very Reality that this sacrament communicates and toward which it directs our hearts. For as we will soon seen, in Christ alone, making all things new by his Incarnation, Passion, and Resurrection, is the very "promise" of our nature fulfilled. This is because, in our very flesh, in our very humanity, God has already placed the seed of longing, the irresistible orientation, toward a full participation in the life of the Trinity, and toward the perfect human communion that flowers only in this place.

So let us turn our gaze back to the earlier theme: the symbolism of the breast. I said that the sacramental "word" that the breast speaks is twofold: first, it is the place through which I give my heart to another, through which I pour out my being as a gift to them; second, it is the space in which I welcome them tenderly, holding and cradling them in the shelter of my love. Who has not been moved by the beautiful reality of a woman nursing her child at her breast? Who has not been touched by the way in which a woman holds a sleeping child close to her breast, against her bosom, sheltering him in the most gentle way? This is, indeed, one of the most beautiful things that we can see in this world. It speaks a profound "word" of love and tenderness to any heart that is open to see and receive.

Yes, in the bond of intimate love between mother and child, we are granted a glimpse of the very mystery of God. How is this? Because the heavenly Father, while transcending the distinctions between the sexes, carries the perfection of both within himself. He is truly our *maternal Father* who manifests—who is—all the fullness of beauty that we glimpse in the woman and the mother, as well as in the man and the father. And what does this Father do for all eternity? *He cradles his beloved Son against his bosom! He pours himself out as a gift into him, without holding anything back, and welcomes the Son entirely into his sheltering embrace in return!*

"No one has ever seen God; the only-begotten Son, who is *in the bosom of the Father*, he has made him know" (Jn 1:18). Yes, Jesus Christ is the eternal Child, the Son of the eternal Father, who has become incarnate within our world. Even in his full manhood, he never leaves behind the truth of his childhood, his sonship before the One who has begotten him and who always cares for him. In other words, Jesus never departs for a single moment from the bosom of his Father, but lets himself be sheltered and cradled there at every moment! His every feeling, thought, word, and action never departs from here, and indeed flows forth from this deep intimacy between the Father and the Son, revealing it to us and drawing us to share in it. Even in the anguish of his Passion, Christ is, and knows that he is, cradled in the bosom of the Father from whom nothing can separate him.

And yet by descending into our darkness, he does something incredible: *he offers his own bosom as a sheltering space in which we can rest; he gives us his breast on which we can repose and from which we can drink the very throbbing heartbeat of the Trinity*. Is this not the significance of that beautiful verse concerning the position of the beloved disciple at the Last Supper? "One of his disciples, whom Jesus loved, was *reposing against the bosom of Jesus*" (cf. Jn 13:23). Yes, the disciple of Jesus is invited to rest against his bosom just as Jesus rests in the bosom of the Father. The word in Greek is the same in both verses, even if it is usually translated differently. Κόλπον: *Kolpon* literally means bosom, that place upon the breast where the garment would be folded over, making a kind of pocket. It is here that Jesus unceasingly rests, in the bosom of his Father; and he welcomes us to rest against his bosom in the same way. What this does, however, is communicate to us the very shelter of the Father's bosom, since Jesus has said: "Whoever has seen me has seen the Father" and "I am in the Father and the Father is in me" (Jn 14:9-10). It is impossible to rest against the breast of Christ without also feeling the tender heartbeat of the heavenly Father, indeed, the very surging of the life and love of the entire Trinity!

This is what we see so beautifully now, at the climax of this final poem of the Song of Songs. The Bridegroom is now resting his head against the breast of his bride, listening to her own heartbeat and delighting in her. Did she not say earlier that her Beloved is "a sachet of myrrh that lies between my breasts?" (Sg 1:13). Now this is supremely true. She is offering herself totally and without reserve to the One whom her heart loves, so deeply that he is able to press himself directly against her heart and receive the outpouring of her being into himself. But this very resting of the Bridegroom against her heart is even more his taking her to rest against his own Heart! Yes, for however much he rests in her, even more she is resting in him. And so the bride truly finds herself wrapped within the Bridegroom's arms, gently held by him, her head pressed up against his breast as she listens to the hymn of love that his Heart ever sings in unison with the Father and the Holy Spirit, and which her own heart itself now sings too!

ישוע

THE FINAL BREATH

How can we proceed from such a breathtaking intimacy, from such a beautiful vision—this mutual embrace of the Bridegroom and the bride, as they hold one another and rest against one another's heart? But we haven't finished the poem yet! The bride, experiencing such a profound love, such a deep intimacy, cannot but exclaim:

I am my Beloved's,
and his desire is for me.
(Sg 7:10)

Yes, lovely bride, you have at last come to understand how deeply desired you are, how passionately your Bridegroom has longed to draw you to himself and to unite you to him forever. And, in response to this realization, what does the bride say? Ah, we see the same reversal that we noticed earlier playing out in yet another way. For now it is not the Bridegroom who is inviting the bride to "arise" and "come." Rather, the bride herself, in the impetuosity of her love, is almost dragging the Bridegroom after her:

Come, my Beloved,
let us go forth into the fields,
and lodge in the villages;
let us go out early to the vineyards,
and see whether the vines have budded,
whether the grape blossoms have opened
and the pomegranates are in bloom.
There I will give you my love.
(Sg 7:10-12)

Why do they need to go out to see if the vines have budded and the pomegranates are in bloom? Have they not reached full flowering by now? Yes, they have. This request is of another kind. Now the bride is ardently asking for something deeper yet—and we can hear the request of the Bridegroom himself silently present in her words, for surely he desires it too! What is she asking for? She is asking for the definitive consummation, the final flowering, which will occur only when the veil of this life is at last torn, and she passes over definitively into the eternal life of the Trinity. This is what is implied by her request to go out "early," that is, at the moment when the night is coming to an end and the dawn is already beginning to break forth over the earth. Experiencing such a profound and abiding intimacy with her Beloved, her only remaining desire is for God to "tear the veil of this sweet encounter," to use the words of John of the Cross. She yearns, in other words, simply to enter into an intimacy that is unmediated, hidden by no veil, in the total immersion of the whole of her being in the whole Being of her divine Beloved. Here will be the perfect kiss of mouth upon mouth, the perfect embrace without any obstruction coming between, or any fear of letting go! Here will be the final and definitive consummation!

This is how Saint Thomas Aquinas interpreted this passage of the Song, which was indeed the very last thing that he commented on at the end of his life. Is it not fitting that this great theologian, who wrote volume upon volume of words, would end his life by speaking about the simple longing of the bride to step beyond the limitations of words and ideas, beyond the shadows and imperfections of this life, and to be immersed forever, in the full light of vision and the perfect touch of consummation, in the unspeakable embrace of the Father, Son, and Holy Spirit?

And so she says, in a way that is quite restrained in comparison with all that has gone before: "There I will give you my love." She offers him her heart, the total gift of all that she is, the gentle and loving surrender of her inmost essence into the welcoming embrace of the One who loves her. And she glimpses what she longs for! Even if the full dawn has not yet come, love has drawn her to the point where she sees the light breaking through the threads of the veil, which has been stretched so thin that eternity itself is palpably touching time, and time is reaching out to kiss eternity!

The mandrakes give forth fragrance,
and over our doors are all choice fruits,
new as well as old,
which I have laid up for you, O my Beloved.
(Sg 7:13)

Already the fragrance of eternity fills her senses and inebriates her with joy. The choice fruits of her being, and indeed of her whole life, are gathered up within her heart as she approaches the moment of death. And as she at last breathes forth her final breath, all of her life, new as well as old, is surrendered to the Beloved who awaits her. Yes, she exhales this breath, the breath that had filled her bosom for so many years. She lets it loose in the final act of trust, the final act of love, the final donation of herself to another. And there he is, inhaling what is exhaled from her, his lips pressed intimately against her own.

EPILOGUE

LOVE IS STRONGER THAN DEATH

We have reached the conclusion of the Song, we have witnessed the final consummation in this life that anticipates, and passes over into, the definitive consummation of eternity. What more is there to say in addition to this? The Bridegroom has come and embraced his bride; he has drawn her into a deep and lasting intimacy with himself, enveloping her in his own peace and making her peaceful as she rests against his bosom at every moment, just as he rests in the bosom of the heavenly Father. And in experiencing this, the bride expresses her ardent longing that what she tastes so beautifully in this life may carry her over, beyond the shadows of night, into the fullness of eternal light in the heavenly Day. Indeed, she already begins to see this eternal light through faith, hope, and love, which have been purified and matured through the journey that she has walked. She is pressing up against the veil—stretched thin by the love that Bridegroom and bride have for one another—and it is only a matter of time until this veil is at last removed. Then the kiss of love that already occurs now, hidden by mortality, will occur in the full, unmediated contact of Lover and beloved in the consummation of eternal life.

What remains after this, then? Only an epilogue, which is itself just a glance back, gathering together all the strands of the drama into a single unified whole. Above all, there is a glance heavenward in gratitude for what has made this marriage possible—for what has restored fallen creation to integrity and has drawn it into true nuptial union with God himself: the Incarnation, Passion, and Resurrection of Jesus Christ. This is what we see so beautifully prophesied in the final verses of the Song of Songs. And we can look through these words, from our perspective in the fullness of time, to gain a deeper access into the beauty of the Paschal Mystery, into the throbbing heartbeat of our divine Beloved. Indeed, I have already referenced these verses a couple times at other places in these reflections, and so much of what I say here is just a confirmation of what I said then. It will not be necessary, therefore, to go into great detail. What I want to do, instead, as I bring these reflections to a close, is to gesture one last time to the beauty of the Crucified and Risen Christ, and to the intimate love of the Holy Trinity into whose eternal embrace he so lovingly draws us. Then I will be glad to fall silent, so that you may contemplate him directly, letting him speak in the depths of your heart in the intimate way that he alone can do.

The epilogue begins, as did the introduction, with the bride crying out with longing to the Bridegroom. This immediately puts us in contact with what is happening. We have witnessed the consummation of the drama; what we are witnessing now is a simple recapitulation, a gathering together of the story in a few words. This is the way that the Song began, and it is also the way that it ends, with a short beginning and a short conclusion, two bookends that hold between them a magnificent story that truly cannot be contained, but bursts forth in radiance, beauty, and power. The bride says:

O that you were a brother to me,
that nursed at my mother's breast!
If I met you outside, I would kiss you,
and none would despise me.
I would lead you and bring you
into the house of my mother,
and into the chamber of her that conceived me.
I would give you spiced wine to drink,
the juice of my pomegranates.
(Sg 8:1-2)

These words are an almost direct parallel to the words of the introductory stanza! Except that they go in the opposite direction! At the beginning of the Song, the bride called out for a kiss, and then found herself brought into the chambers of the King, inebriated with the wine of his love. And yet now, after calling out for a kiss, she expresses her desire to take the King himself into the chamber of her mother, into her own home, and there to give the wine of her own love as a gift for him to drink. Are these not really just two expressions of a single reality? For the Bridegroom to make his home within his bride is really for the bride to live within her Bridegroom. And yet this home within the Bridegroom's embrace is truly his home within the bride, for he does not only hold and shelter her from without, but he fills her with the fullness of his presence and his love. She is irradiated by his light; she is permeated by his presence; she is totally filled with the fullness of his Being!

But what strikes us about these words? In asking for a kiss, the bride says she wishes her Beloved were her brother, in order that she could kiss him without being despised by others. As I have said before, this is a request for the Incarnation of God. For how else could our lips touch the lips of God, how else could our body be joined to his Body, unless he had lips, unless he had a Body—unless, in other words, he were our Brother? Yes, he can only be our Spouse because he is first our Brother; and as our Brother he makes himself our Spouse, so that through nuptial intimacy with him we may be a sibling to him in the very bosom of the Father. In other words, he becomes our Brother in the flesh so that we may become his sibling in the Spirit.

Just as a woman, through marriage, becomes a part of her husband's family, a daughter-in-law of his parents, so, even more truly and deeply, the person who is espoused to Jesus Christ experiences what it means to be a daughter-in-grace or a son-in-grace of the heavenly Father! Here we can discern the beautiful meaning of this twofold "homemaking" that occurs through my adoption into the family of God and my intimacy with Jesus. First, I take him into my home, into the "chamber of my mother," united to him in the flesh that he has taken as his own. And yet as he unites himself to me here, he renews my nature from within, he transfigures my entire being through his perfect love. And thus I find myself lifted up in his embrace, passing through the limitations of mortality and into the very Home of the Blessed Trinity, there to abide, sheltered and loved, for all eternity!

Yes, this is the great gift that God has bestowed on me in Christ, and I can truly cry out as his bride:

His left hand is under my head,
and his right arm embraces me!
(Sg 8:3)

And the Bridegroom, for the last time, speaks those words of tenderness that shelter me in my rest against his Heart:

I adjure you, O daughters of Jerusalem,
not to stir my love, nor rouse her,
until she is pleased to awake.
(Sg 8:4)

He reverences my sleep, a sleep both of love and of frailty. He has cradled me, and will always cradle me, in the depth of my neediness and weakness throughout this life. He never grows weary, never grows impatient. Rather, he rejoices to hold me, to shelter me, at the heart of my desperate need for his love and his mercy. He gazes deep, with a look of tenderness that touches the very core of my heart and sees, reverences, and cherishes my unique beauty. Indeed, he sees the whole of me with this gaze of love, and rejoices that I am who I am. He rejoices that I am his, that I have been created to be his sibling and his spouse. And so he holds me, cradling my head in his hand with his arm wrapped around me.

But then what is this? I am awake! The chorus cries out for the last time:

Who is that coming up from the wilderness,
leaning upon her Beloved?

(Sg 8:5a)

Ah, yes, here we see clearly the meaning of the beginning of the third poem, in which the Bridegroom comes up from the wilderness like a column of fire and smoke. Here too is the commencement of the great marriage which is consummated at the end of the fifth poem. The Bridegroom is coming up from the wilderness because there he has redeemed his precious bride. He has taken her into his arms, and now he comes forth into the Promised Land of everlasting intimacy. He supports her in his arms as she willingly leans on him, knowing that he alone is her strength, her security, and her liberation...yes, that he alone is her peace, joy, and enduring happiness!

This is the true and final Exodus, in which God draws his bride definitively out of slavery and into the Home of his own indestructible Love. And how does he do it? How does he draw her up into lasting union? This is the question that he answers immediately, in response to the exclamation of the chorus. But he speaks not to them, but to his dearly beloved one, his spouse:

Under the apple tree I awakened you,
there where your mother was in travail with you,
there where she who bore you was in travail.

(Sg 8:5b)

Ah yes, it is through the Tree of the Cross—the true and lasting Tree of Life, under which the New Eve, the true mother of all the living, stands—that the Bridegroom has redeemed his bride. It is here, through the total gift of himself upon this Tree, that he definitively awakens his beloved for the last time. He pours himself as a gift into her, so that she may drink the fullness of the Trinity's own transforming life, the torrent of eternal joy, from his opened breast. He receives and shelters her, cradling her unceasingly within the space of his own opened Heart, where she is forever safe, forever seen, known, and loved.

It is through this awesome gift and this awesome acceptance, through this unspeakable intimacy effected between Bridegroom and bride—twitching the threads of unbreakable communion with fullness of perfect Love—that he brings his beloved all that she has sought. He awakens her from the slumber of sin; he awakens her from the slumber of shame; he awakens her from the sleep of darkness and incomprehension. And now, gazing upon him as he gazes upon her, she sees "the light of the knowledge of the glory of God shining in the face of Christ" (2 Cor 4:6), and is utterly transfigured by this vision!

How, then, does this greatest of all Songs end? With the Bridegroom and his bride both raising their voices together in unison, singing to one another of the indestructible power of Love:

Set me as a seal upon your heart,
as a seal upon your arm;
for love is stronger than death,
jealousy is relentless as the grave.
Its flashes are flashes of fire,
a flame of God himself.
Many waters cannot quench love,
neither can floods drown it.
(Sg 8:6-7)

And so the Song ends. The verses that follow are a later addition, which do not at all fit in with the rest of the Song, and so it is good for us to stop here. And what is the impression that this ending gives to us? Ah, how beautiful it is! The intimacy is profound, the intimacy is complete, even in the shadows of this life—for through the mystery of Christ's Passion and Resurrection, which has now completely taken up and transfigured the bride, love has been definitively victorious! The Lover and beloved are set as a seal, an indelible seal, upon the heart of one another. They live deep within the recesses of the one whom they love, in the inmost shelter of one another's heart, in an inexpressibly profound mutual indwelling.

And so they sing. And so they sing together of the victory of love. This love is stronger than any floods, in other words, than any of the assaults of the evil one, than any of the trials and tribulations of this world, than any of the forces that would seek to sever the bride from her Beloved. His love is stronger! The love of the Trinity has proven itself victorious, and the bride casts herself without reserve into this perfect love! How can we not see the ardent experience of Saint Paul present here? He wrote:

> What then shall we say to this? If God is for us, who is against us? He who did not spare his own Son but gave him up for us all, will he not also give us all things with him? Who shall bring any charge against God's elect? It is God who justifies; who is to condemn? Is it Christ Jesus, who died, yes, who was raised from the dead, who is at the right hand of God, who indeed intercedes for us? Who shall separate us from the love of Christ? Shall tribulation, or distress, or persecution, or famine, or nakedness, or peril, or sword? No, in all these things we are more than conquerors through him who loved us. For I am sure that neither death, nor life, nor angels, nor principalities, nor things present, nor things to come, nor powers, nor height, nor

depth, nor anything else in all creation, will be able to separate us from the love of God in Christ Jesus our Lord. (Rom 8:31-35, 37-39)

Yes, this love is stronger than death itself, since it has led the Son of the eternal Father even through death in order that he would conquer it by the inseparable union that he has with his Father. Nothing, absolutely nothing, could ever be able to tear the bond of intimacy between the Father and the Son. They are eternally one, living in one another in a perfect life of intimacy and joy, in a single embrace and kiss of the Holy Spirit. And when Christ entered into our world, when he descended into the very depths of our darkness, he did not depart from this intimacy of the Father's embrace, but rather brought this intimacy into our very loneliness and isolation, in order to burst it open from the inside! And so he has done. And so he does. Bearing me tenderly upon his Heart as a seal impressed by his ardent love, he passes across the estrangement caused by sin, across the boundary of death and the dissolution of the grave, and impresses himself as a seal upon my heart. Yes, he crosses over the distance with a jealousy purer and more passionate than the love of any husband, and he twitches the threads of indestructible and enduring intimacy between myself and him, weaving my heart together as one with his own Heart. He weaves my heart together as one with the very mystery of the Trinity, admitting me, already in this life, and perfectly forever in the next, into the eternal dance of mutual self-giving, and the endless bliss of intimacy, ever experienced by the Father, Son, and Holy Spirit.

Here I am in their midst, cradled gently in the arms of my heavenly Bridegroom and receiving ceaselessly the kiss in which he communicates himself entirely to me and welcomes me entirely into himself. Here we are, Lover and beloved, embracing one another, as we are cradled together in the single embrace of the Father of us both. And a single Spirit enshrouds us all together as one, vibrating through us and thrilling our hearts with delight, this single Spirit who is the Breath of Love passing eternally between the Father and the Son at the heart of this perfect Family of everlasting intimacy and joy.

END NOTES

1. Both quoted in Arminjon, 35-37. For the André Chouraqui quote: "Introduction au Poèmes des Poèmes," *La Bible* (Paris: Desclée de Brouwer, 1975), 27.

2. Bernard of Clairvaux, *On the Song of Songs I: Sermons 1-20*, trans. Kilian Walsh OCSO (Cistercian Publications, Inc.: Kalamazoo, MI, 1971), 1.IV.8 and VI.11; p. 5-7.

3. Bernard of Clairvaux, 1.IV.6; p. 4.

4. Ibid., 1.III.5; p. 3.

5. Ibid., 8.I.1-2, VI.6, II.3; p. 45-46, 50, 46.

6. Ibid., cf. 8.VI.7-VII.9; p. 50-52.

7. Arminjon, 72-73.

8. Ibid., 147-149.

9. Paul Claudel, *Paul Claudel interroge le Cantique des Cantiques* (Paris: NRF-Gallimard, 1948), 42. Quoted in Arminjon, 117.

10. Thérèse of Lisieux, *Story of a Soul*, 208.

11. Origen, *In Canticum Canticorum*, 162. Quoted in Arminjon, 156-157.

12. Teresa of Avila, *The Life of St.Teresa of Jesus, of the Order of Our Lady of Carmel*, trans. David Lewis, ed. Benedict Zimmerman. 3rd ed. enl. (London: T. Baker; New York: Benziger,1904), XXIX.16-18; 255-256.

13. John of the Cross, *The Living Flame of Love*, in *The Collected Works of St. John of the Cross*, trans. Kieran Kavanaugh, O.C.D. and Otilio Rodriguez, O.C.D. (ICS Publications: Washington, D.C., 1991), II.7-8; 660.

14. John of the Cross, *Spiritual Canticle*, in *The Collected Works*, 13.9; 523.

15. *The Way of Silent Love*, trans. An Anglican Solitary (The Carthusian Order in England: Gracewing Publishing, 2006), 85-86, footnote *.

16. Arminjon, 345.

17. Conrad Baars, *I Will Give Them a New Heart: Reflections on the Priesthood and the Renewal of the Church*, ed. Suzanne M. Baars, MA and Bonnie N. Shayne, MA (Alba House: New York, 2007), 46 and 56.

18. Ibid., 57, 67-68.

19. Karol Wojytla, *Love and Responsibility*, 207.

20. Dietrich von Hildebrand, *The Heart: An Analysis of Human and Divine Affectivity* (St. Augustine's Press, 2007), 69-71.

21. Benedict XVI, *Jesus of Nazareth Part Two: From the Entrance into Jerusalem to the Resurrection* (Ignatius Press: San Francisco, 2011), 244, 247.

22. "Eternity includes time because it is the fifth dimension. A line includes points; a surface includes lines; a solid body includes surfaces; and motion through time includes solid bodies moving. As the fourth dimension includes the third, the fifth includes the fourth. ... The square walls of a house are rather boring when flat and detached from the house. But when the two-dimensional walls are part of the three-dimensional house, they come alive. And the three-dimensional house itself comes alive as part of

someone's four-dimensional lifetime. Our four-dimensional lifetimes are the walls of our five-dimensional heavenly house."

Peter Kreeft, *Heaven: the Heart's Deepest Longing* (Ignatius Press: San Francisco, 1989), 88.

23. Benedict XVI, 273-274.

24. David L. Schindler, "The Embodied Person as Gift and the Cultural Task of America" in *Ordering Love: Liberal Societies and the Memory of God* (Wm B. Eerdmans Publishing Co.: Grand Rapids, Michigan, 2011), 246-249.

25. Benedict XVI, *Caritas in Veritate* (2009), n. 54. Quoted in Schindler, "The Embodied Person," 248, footnote 10.

26. David L. Schindler, "Truth and Freedom," Communio: International Catholic Review 23, no. 1 (Spring 1996: 16-35, at 27. Quoted in "The Embodied Persons," 249, footnote 11.

27. Alexander Schmemann, *For the Life of the World* (Crestwood, NY: St. Vladimir's Seminary Press, 1998 [1963]), 121.

28. Arminjon, 299.

29. André Chouraqui, *Le Cantique des Cantiques*, 71. Quotes in Arminjon, 301-302.

30. From *Catechesis* 3, 13-19: SC 50, 174-177. In the Liturgy of the Hours: Volume II (Catholic Book Publishing Corp: New York, 1976), 474-475.

Made in the USA
Monee, IL
22 April 2023